# COMPREHENSIVE CURRICULUM
## OF BASIC SKILLS

## GRADE 2

Edited by
**Kathy Whisler, Dawn Downs Purney, Judy Coy**

AMERICAN EDUCATION PUBLISHING®

## READING

## READING COMPREHENSION

## ENGLISH

## SPELLING

# READING

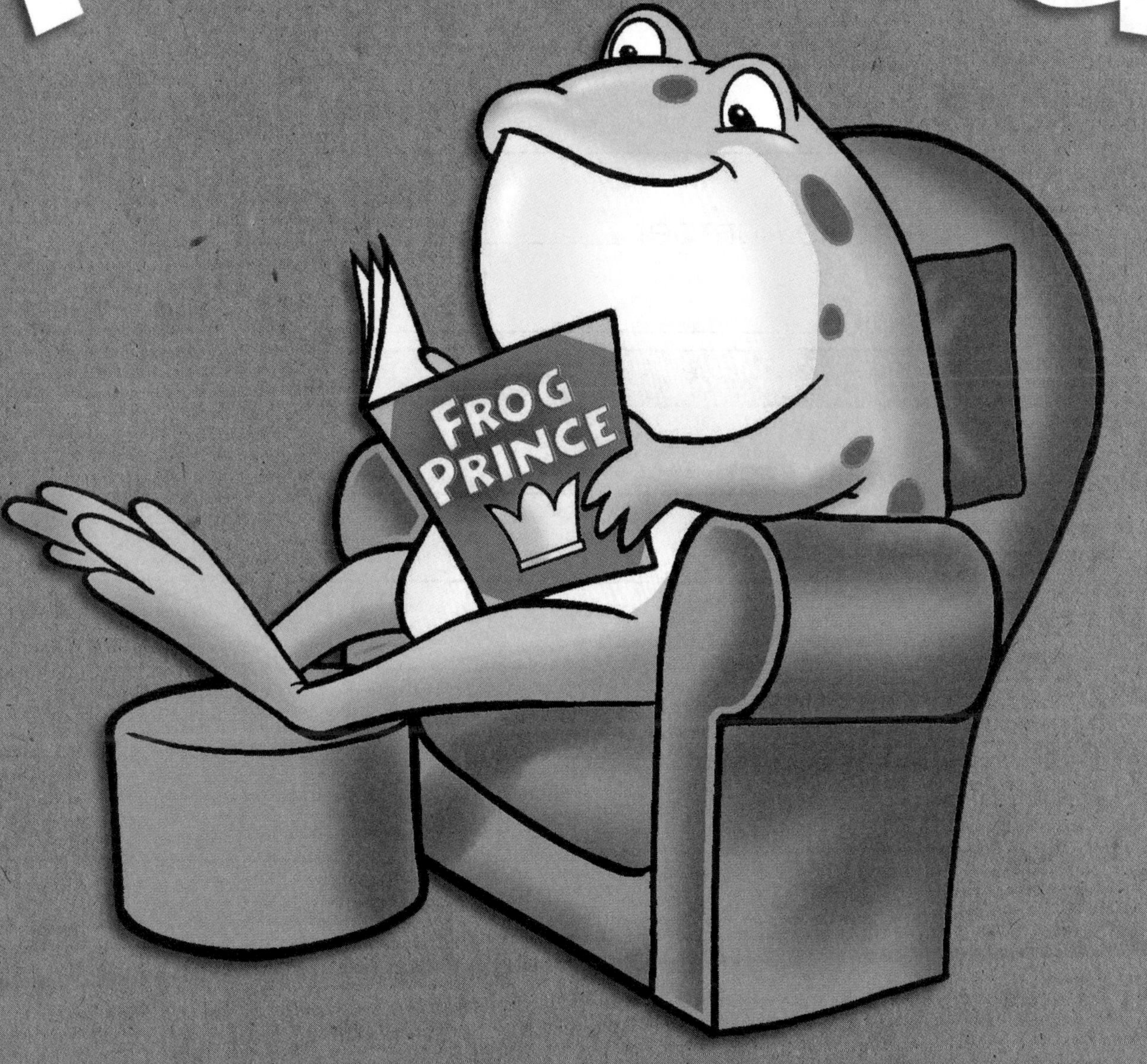

# All About Me!

**Directions:** Fill in the blanks to tell all about you!

Name _____

          (First)                  (Last)

Address _____

City _____ State _____

Phone number _____

Age _____

Places I have visited: _____

_____

_____

_____

My favorite vacation: _____

_____

_____

_____

Name: _____

# Beginning Consonants: b, c, d, f, g, h, j

**Directions:** Fill in the beginning consonant for each word.

**Example:** __c__ at

_____ ox

_____ acket

_____ oat

_____ ouse

_____ og

_____ ire

Name: _____

# Beginning Consonants: k, l, m, n, p, q, r

**Directions:** Write the letter that makes the beginning sound for each picture.

_____     _____     _____     _____

_____     _____     _____     _____

_____     _____     _____     _____

_____     _____     _____     _____

# Beginning Consonants: k, l, m, n, p, q, r

**Directions:** Fill in the beginning consonant for each word.

**Example:** __r__ ose

____ oney

____ uilt

____ ion

____ an

____ ey

____ ose

Name: _____

# Beginning Consonants: s, t, v, w, x, y, z

**Directions:** Write the letter under each picture that makes the beginning sound.

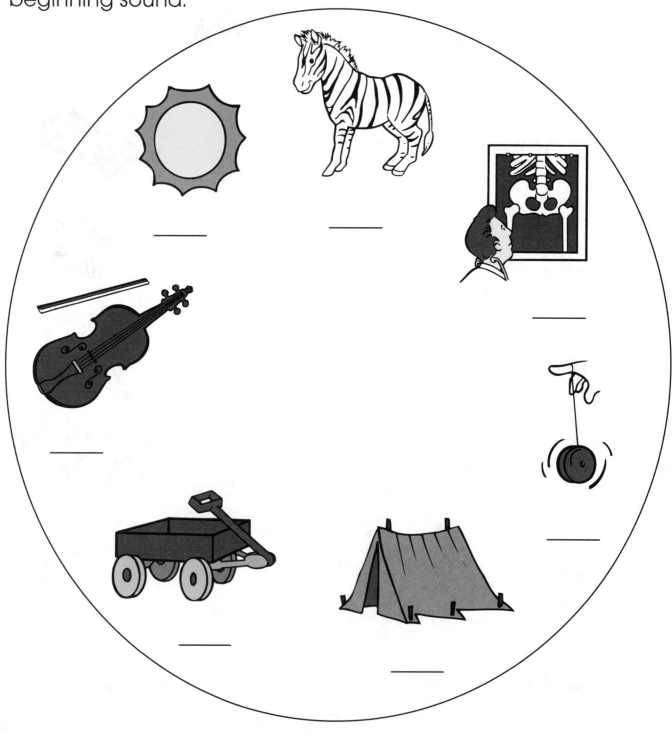

Name: _____

# Beginning Consonants: s, t, v, w, x, y, z

**Directions:** Fill in the beginning consonant for each word.

Example: __s__ ock

____ ipper

____ able

____ ray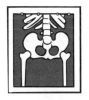

____ ase

____ olk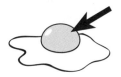

____ and

Name: _____

# Ending Consonants: b, d, f, g

**Directions:** Fill in the ending consonant for each word.

ma _____

cu _____

roo _____

do _____

be _____

bi _____

Name: _____

# Ending Consonants: k, l, m, n, p, r

**Directions:** Fill in the ending consonant for each word.

nai ____

ca ____

gu ____

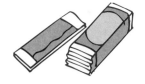

ca ____

truc ____

ca ____

pai ____

**Grade 2 - Comprehensive Curriculum**

Name: _____

# Ending Consonants: s, t, x

**Directions:** Fill in the ending consonant for each word.

ca ____

bo ____

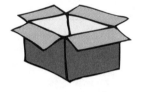

bu ____

fo ____

boa ____

ma ____

# Consonant Blends

**Consonant blends** are two or three consonant letters in a word whose sounds combine, or blend. **Examples: br, fr, gr, pr, tr**

**Directions:** Look at each picture. Say its name. Write the blend you hear at the beginning of each word.

_____     _____     _____

_____     _____     _____

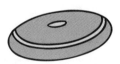          

_____     _____     _____

_____     _____     _____

**Grade 2 - Comprehensive Curriculum**

# Blends: fl, br, pl, sk, sn

**Blends** are two consonants put together to form a single sound.

**Directions:** Look at the pictures and say their names. Write the letters for the beginning sound in each word.

# Blends: bl, sl, cr, cl

**Directions:** Look at the pictures and say their names. Write the letters for the beginning sound in each word.

_____own

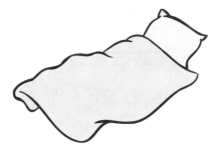

_____anket

_____ayon

_____ock

_____ide

_____oud

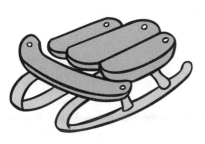

_____ed

_____ab

_____ocodile

# Consonant Blends

**Directions:** Write a word from the word box to answer each riddle.

| | | | | |
|---|---|---|---|---|
| clock | glass | blow | climb | slipper |
| sleep | gloves | clap | blocks | flashlight |

1. You need me when the lights go out.
   **What am I?** _____

2. People use me to tell the time.
   **What am I?** _____

3. You put me on your hands in the winter to keep them warm. **What am I?** _____

4. Cinderella lost one like me at midnight.
   **What am I?** _____

5. This is what you do with your hands when you are pleased. **What is it?** _____

6. You can do this with a whistle or with bubble gum. **What is it?** _____

7. These are what you might use to build a castle when you are playing.
   **What are they?** _____

8. You do this to get to the top of a hill.
   **What is it?** _____

9. This is what you use to drink water or milk.
   **What is it?** _____

10. You do this at night with your eyes closed.
    **What is it?** _____

# Consonant Teams

**Directions:** Read the words in the box. Write a word from the word box to finish each sentence. Circle the consonant team in each word. **Hint:** There are three letters in each team!

| | | | | |
|---|---|---|---|---|
| splash | screen | spray | street | scream |
| screw | shrub | split | strong | string |

1. Another word for a bush is a _____ .

2. I tied a _____ to my tooth to help pull it out.

3. I have many friends who live on my _____ .

4. We always _____ when we ride the roller coaster.

5. A _____ helps keep bugs out of the house.

6. It is fun to _____ in the water.

7. My father uses an ax to _____ the firewood.

8. We will need a _____ to fix the chair.

9. You must be very _____ to lift this heavy box.

10. The firemen _____ the fire with water.

Name: _____

# Consonant Teams

**Consonant teams** are two or three consonant letters that have a single sound. **Examples: sh** and **tch**

**Directions:** Write each word from the word box next to its picture. Underline the consonant team in each word. Circle the consonant team in each word in the box.

| | | | |
|---|---|---|---|
| bench | match | shoe | thimble |
| shell | brush | peach | watch |
| whale | teeth | chair | wheel |

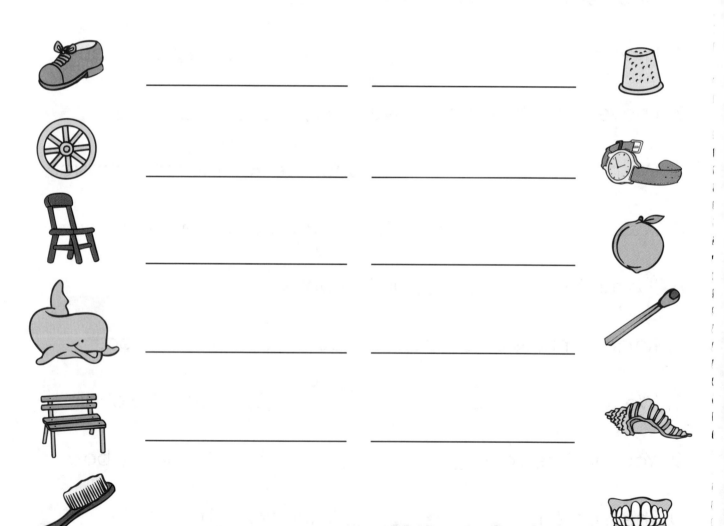

Name: _____

# Letter Teams: sh, ch, wh, th

**Directions:** Look at the first picture in each row. Circle the pictures that have the same sound.

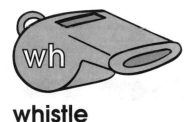

**whistle**

**shoe**

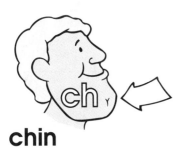

**chin**

**thumb**

Name: _____

# Letter Teams: sh, ch, wh, th

**Directions:** Look at the pictures and say the words. Write the first two letters of the word on the space below each picture.

_____

_____

_____

_____

_____

_____

_____

_____

_____

Name: _____

# Consonant Teams

**Directions:** Circle the consonant teams in each word in the word box. Write a word from the word box to finish each sentence. Circle the consonant teams in your words.

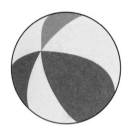

| trash | splash | chain |
|-------|---------|-------|
| shut | chicken | catch |
| ship | when | patch |
|  | which |  |

1. My _____ won't lay eggs.

2. I put a _____ on my bicycle so nobody can take it.

3. We watched the big _____ dock and let off its passengers.

4. It is my job to take out the _____ .

5. I have to wear a _____ over my eye until it is better.

6. The baby likes to _____ in the bathtub.

7. Can you _____ the ball with one hand?

8. Please _____ the windows before it rains.

9. _____ are we going to leave for school?

10. I don't know _____ of these books is mine.

Name: _____

# Consonant Teams

**Directions:** Look at the words in the word box. Write all of the words that end with the **ng** sound in the column under the picture of the **ring**. Write all of the words that end with the **nk** sound under the picture of the **sink**. Finish the sentences with words from the word box.

| strong | rank | bring | bank | honk | hang | thank |
| long | hunk | song | stung | bunk | sang | junk |

_____          _____

_____          _____

_____          _____

_____          _____

_____          _____

_____          _____

1. _____ your horn when you get to my house.

2. He was _____ by a bumblebee.

3. We are going to put our money in a _____.

4. I want to _____ you for the birthday present.

5. My brother and I sleep in _____ beds.

Name: _____

# Silent Letters

Some words have letters you can't hear at all, such as the **gh** in **night**, the **w** in **wrong**, the **l** in **walk**, the **k** in **knee**, the **b** in **climb** and the **t** in **listen**.

**Directions:** Look at the words in the word box. Write the word under its picture. Underline the silent letters.

| knife | light | calf | wrench | lamb | eight |
|-------|-------|------|--------|------|-------|
| wrist | whistle | comb | thumb | knob | knee |

_____   _____   _____   _____

_____   _____   _____   _____

_____   _____   _____   _____

Grade 2 - Comprehensive Curriculum

# Review

**Directions:** Read the story. Circle the consonant teams (two or three letters) and silent letters in the underlined words. Be sure to check for more than one team in a word! One has been done for you.

One day last (Spring) my family went on a picnic. My father picked out a <u>pretty</u> <u>spot</u> next to a <u>stream.</u> <u>While</u> my <u>brother</u> and I <u>climbed</u> a <u>tree</u>, my mother <u>spread</u> out a <u>sheet</u> and <u>placed</u> the food on it. But before we could eat, a <u>skunk</u> <u>walked</u> out of the woods! Mother <u>screamed</u> and <u>scared</u> the skunk. It <u>sprayed</u> us with a terrible <u>smell!</u> Now, we <u>think</u> it is a funny <u>story</u>. But <u>that</u> day, we ran!

**Directions:** Write the words with three-letter blends on the lines.

_____   _____   _____

_____   _____

Name: _____

# Hard and Soft c

When **c** is followed by **e**, **i** or **y**, it usually has a **soft** sound. The **soft** c sounds like **s**. For example, **c**ircle and fen**c**e. When **c** is followed by **a** or **u**, it usually has a **hard** sound. The **hard c** sounds like **k**.

**Example:** **c**up and **c**art

**Directions:** Read the words in the word box. Write the words in the correct lists. One word will be in both. Write a word from the word box to finish each sentence.

| Words with soft c | Words with hard c | | |
|---|---|---|---|
| | | pencil | cookie |
| _pencil_ | _____ | dance | cent |
| _____ | _____ | popcorn | circus |
| _____ | _____ | lucky | mice |
| _____ | _____ | tractor | card |
| _____ | _____ | | |

1. Another word for a penny is a _____.

2. A cat likes to chase _____.

3. You will see animals and clowns at the _____.

4. Will you please sharpen my _____?

# Hard and Soft g

When **g** is followed by **e**, **i** or **y**, It usually has a **soft** sound. The **soft g** sounds like **j**. **Example:** chan**g**e and **g**entle. The **hard g** sounds like the **g** in **g**irl or **g**ate.

**Directions:** Read the words in the word box. Write the words in the correct lists. Write a word from the box to finish each sentence.

| | | | | |
|---|---|---|---|---|
| engine | glove | cage | magic | frog |
| giant | flag | large | glass | goose |

**Words with soft g**

_engine_

_____

_____

_____

_____

**Words with hard g**

_____

_____

_____

_____

_____

1. Our bird lives in a _____.

2. Pulling a rabbit from a hat is a good _____ trick.

3. A car needs an _____ to run.

4. A _____ is a huge person.

5. An elephant is a very _____ animal.

Name: _____

# Hard and Soft c and g

**Directions:** Look at the **c** and **g** words at the bottom of the page. Cut them out and glue them in the correct box below.

|  soft sound |  hard sound |
|---|---|
|  |  |

cut ✂ - - - - - - - - - - - - - - - - - - - - - - - - - - - - - - - - - - - -

| | | | |
|---|---|---|---|
| jug | gem | giant | crayon |
| grass | goat | grow | age |
| juice | face | engine | cart |

Page is blank for cutting exercise on previous page.

Name: _____

# Short Vowels

**Vowels** can make **short** or **long** sounds. The **short a** sounds like the **a** in cat. The short **e** is like the **e** in leg. The short **i** sounds like the **i** in pig. The short **o** sounds like the **o** in box. The short **u** sounds like the **u** in cup.

**Directions:** Look at each picture. Write the missing short vowel letter.

p__p

n__t

s ___ ck

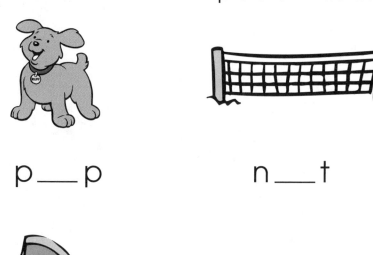

__ x

l__ps

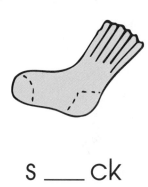

h__t

f__x

t__nt

p__n

Name: _____

# Short Vowels

Vowels can make **short** or **long** sounds. The short **a** sounds like the **a** in **cat**. The short **e** is like the **e** in **leg**. The short **i** sounds like the **i** in **pig**. The short **o** sounds like the **o** in **box**. The short **u** is like the **u** in **cup**.

**Directions:** Look at the pictures. Their names all have short vowel sounds. But the vowels are missing! Fill in the missing vowels in each word.

# a     e     i     o     u

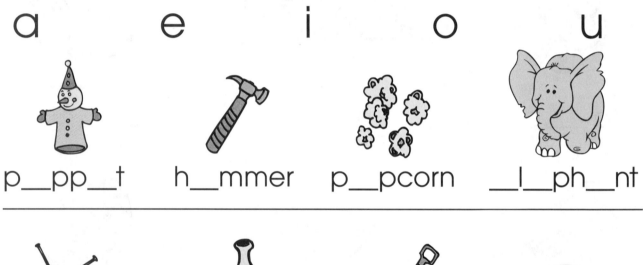

p__pp__t     h__mmer     p__pcorn     __l__ph__nt

t__l__v__sion     b__ttle     sh__v__l     th__mble

 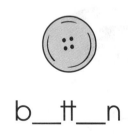  

c__ndle     b__tt__n     p__nny     l__dder

# Short Vowels

**Directions:** Cut out the giant vowel letters. Draw pictures, write words or cut pictures from magazines with the short vowel sound and put them on both sides of the letters. Then hang the letters with string!

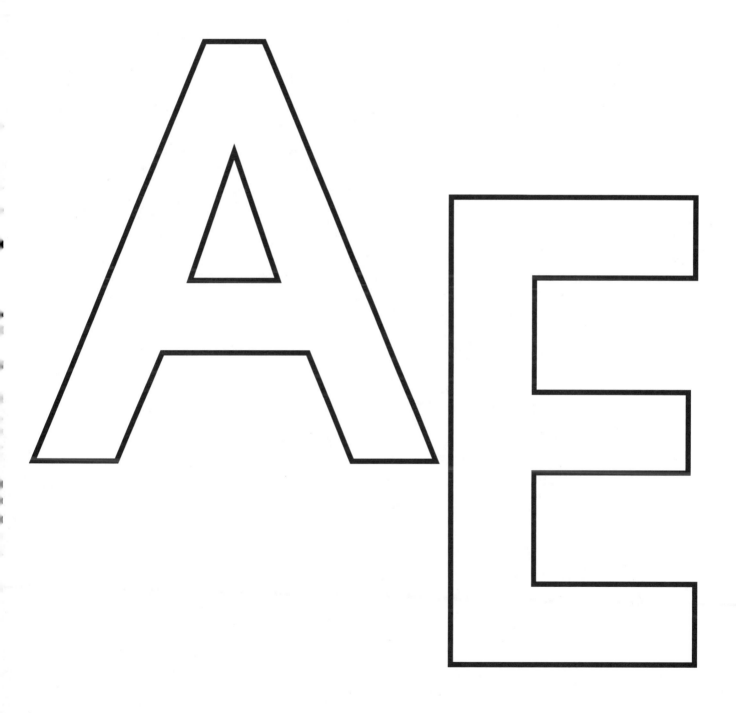

Page is blank for cutting exercise on previous page.

Name: _____

## Short Vowels

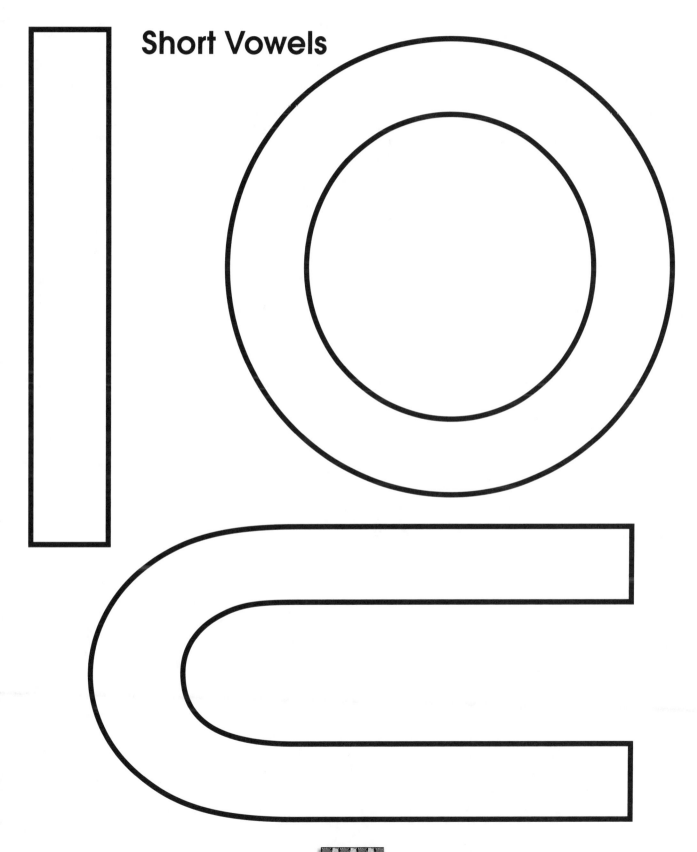

Page is blank for cutting exercise on previous page.

# Super Silent e

Long vowel sounds have the same sound as their names. When a **Super Silent e** appears at the end of a word, you can't hear it, but it makes the other vowel have a long sound. For example: **tub** has a **short** vowel sound, and **tube** has a **long** vowel sound.

**Directions:** Look at the following pictures. Decide if the word has a short or long vowel sound. Circle the correct word. Watch for the **Super Silent e**!

can   cane        tub   tube        rob   robe        rat   rate

pin   pine        cap   cape        not   note        pan   pane

slid   slide        dim   dime        tap   tape        cub   cube

Name: _____

# Long Vowels

Long vowel sounds have the same sound as their names. When a **Super Silent e** comes at the end of a word, you can't hear it, but it changes the short vowel sound to a long vowel sound.

**Example:** rope, skate, bee, pie, cute

**Directions:** Say the name of the pictures. Listen for the long vowel sounds. Write the missing long vowel sound under each picture.

c __ ke

h __ ke

n __ se

__ pe

c __ be

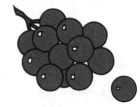

gr __ pe

r __ ke

b __ ne

k __ te

Name: _____

# Review

**Directions:** Read the words in each box. Cross out the word that does not belong.

| long vowels  | short vowels  |
|---|---|
| cube | man |
| cup | pet |
| rake | fix |
| me | ice |

| long vowels  | short vowels  |
|---|---|
| soap | cat |
| seed | pin |
| read | rain |
| mat | frog |

**Directions:** Write **short** or **long** to label the words in each box.

| _____ vowels  | _____ vowels  |
|---|---|
| hose | frog |
| take | hot |
| bead | sled |
| cube | lap |
| eat | block |
| see | sit |

Name: _____

# R-Controlled Vowels

When a vowel is followed by the letter **r**, it has a different sound.

**Example: he** and **her**

**Directions:** Write a word from the word box to finish each sentence. Notice the sound of the vowel followed by an **r**.

| park | chair | horse | bark | bird |
| hurt | girl | hair | store | ears |

1. A dog likes to _____.

2. You buy food at a _____.

3. Children like to play at the _____.

4. An animal you can ride is a _____.

5. You hear with your _____.

6. A robin is a kind of _____.

7. If you fall down, you might get _____.

8. The opposite of a boy is a _____.

9. You comb and brush your _____.

10. You sit down on a _____.

Name: _____

# R-Controlled Words

**R-controlled vowel words** are words in which the **r** that comes after the vowel changes the sound of the vowel. **Examples:** bird, star, burn

**Directions:** Write the correct word in the sentences below.

| | |
|---|---|
| horse | purple |
| jar | bird |
| dirt | turtle |

1. Jelly comes in one of these. _____

2. This creature has feathers and can fly. _____

3. This animal lives in a shell. _____

4. This animal can pull wagons. _____

5. If you mix water and this,
   you will have mud. _____

6. This color starts with the letter **p**. _____

Name: _____

# R-Controlled Vowels

**Directions:** Answer the riddles below. You will need to complete the words with the correct vowel followed by **r**.

1. I am something you may use to eat.
   What am I?

   f _____ k

2. My word names the opposite of tall.
   What am I?

   sh _____ t

3. I can be seen high in the sky. I twinkle.
   What am I?

   st _____

4. I am a kind of clothing a girl might wear.
   What am I?

   sk _____ t

5. My word tells what a group of cows is
   called. What am I?

   h _____ d

6. I am part of your body. What am I?

   _____ m

# Double Vowel Words

Usually when two vowels appear together, the first one says its name and the second one is silent.

**Example: b<u>e</u>an**

**Directions:** Unscramble the double vowel words below. Write the correct word on the line.

 ocat _____

 etar _____

 mtea _____

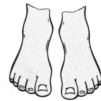 eetf _____

 teas _____

 otab _____

 ogat _____

 spea _____

 atli _____

 apil _____

Name: _____

# Vowel Teams

The vowel teams **ou** and **ow** can have the same sound. You can hear it in the words **clown** and **cloud**. The vowel teams **au** and **aw** have the same sound. You hear it in the words **because** and **law**.

**Directions:** Look at the pictures. Write the correct vowel team to complete the words. The first one is done for you. You may need to use a dictionary to help you with the correct spelling.

<u>au</u>to

cl_____n

h_____se

fl_____er

s_____

_____l

p_____der

m_____th

j_____

p_____

m_____se

cl_____d

Name: _____

# Vowel Teams

The vowel team **ea** can have a short **e** sound like in **head**, or a long **e** sound like in **bead**. An **ea** followed by an **r** makes a sound like the one in **ear** or like the one in **heard**.

**Directions:** Read the story. Listen for the sound **ea** makes in the bold words.

Have you ever **read** a book or **heard** a story about a **bear**? You might have **learned** that bears sleep through the winter. Some bears may sleep the whole **season**. Sometimes they look almost **dead**! But they are very much alive. As the cold winter passes and the spring **weather** comes **near**, they wake up. After such a nice rest, they must be **ready** to **eat** a **really** big **meal**!

| words with long **ea** | words with short **ea** | **ea** followed by **r** |
|---|---|---|
| _____ | _____ | _____ |
| _____ | _____ | _____ |
| _____ | _____ | _____ |
| _____ | _____ | _____ |

Name: _____

# Vowel Teams

The vowel team **ie** makes the long **e** sound like in **believe**. The team **ei** also makes the long **e** sound like in **either**. But **ei** can also make a long **a** sound like in **eight**.

**Directions:** Circle the **ei** words with the long **a** sound.

| | |
|---|---|
| neighbor | veil |
| receive | reindeer |
| reign | ceiling |

---

The teams **eigh** and **ey** also make the long **a** sound.

**Directions:** Finish the sentences with words from the word box.

| chief | sleigh | obey | weigh | thief | field | ceiling |
|---|---|---|---|---|---|---|

1. Eight reindeer pull Santa's _____ .

2. Rules are for us to _____ .

3. The bird got out of its cage and flew up to the _____ .

4. The leader of an Indian tribe is the _____ .

5. How much do you _____ ?

6. They caught the _____ who took my bike.

7. Corn grows in a _____ .

# Vowel Teams: oi, oy, ou, ow

**Directions:** Look at the first picture in each row. Circle the pictures that have the same sound.

**oil**

**toy**

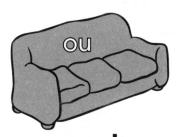   

**couch**

**howl**

Name: _____

# Vowel Teams: ai, ee

**Directions:** Write in the vowel team **ai** or **ee** to complete each word.

r _\_ \_\_ n

f \_\_ \_\_ d

s \_\_ \_\_ d

p \_\_ \_\_ l

s \_\_ \_\_ l

cr\_\_ \_\_ k

Name: _____

# Review

**Directions:** Read the story. Fill in the blanks with words from the word box.

| cookies | Joe | bowl | tooth | flour | eight |
|---------|-----|------|-------|-------|-------|
| spoon | eats | enjoys | round | boy | either |

Do you like to cook? I know a _____ named

_____ who loves to cook. When Joe has a sweet

_____, he makes _____. He puts

_____ and sugar in a _____ and

stirs it with a _____. Then he adds the butter and

eggs. He makes cookies that are _____ or other

shapes. He likes them _____ way. Now is the part he

_____ the most: Joe _____

the cookies. He might eat seven or _____ at a time!

**Grade 2 - Comprehensive Curriculum**

Name: _____

# Y as a Vowel

When **y** comes at the end of a word, it is a vowel. When **y** is the only vowel at the end of a one-syllable word, it has the sound of a long **i** (like in **my**). When **y** is the only vowel at the end of a word with more than one syllable, it has the sound of a long **e** (like in **baby**).

**Directions:** Look at the words in the word box. If the word has the sound of a long **i**, write it under the word **my**. If the word has the sound of a long **e**, write it under the word **baby**. Write the word from the word box that answers each riddle.

| happy | penny | fry | try | sleepy | dry |
|-------|-------|-----|-----|--------|-----|
| bunny | why | windy | sky | party | fly |

**my**                                    **baby**

_____                      _____

_____                      _____

_____                      _____

_____                      _____

_____                      _____

_____                      _____

1. It takes five of these to make a nickel.          _____

2. This is what you call a baby rabbit.              _____

3. It is often blue and you can see it if you look up. _____

4. You might have one of these on your birthday.     _____

5. It is the opposite of wet.                        _____

6. You might use this word to ask a question.        _____

Name: _____

# Y as a Vowel

**Directions:** Read the rhyming story. Choose the words from the box to fill in the blanks.

| Larry | Mary |
|-------|------|
| money | funny |
| honey | bunny |

_____ and _____ are friends. Larry is

selling _____ . Mary needs _____ to

buy the honey. "I want to feed it to my _____ ," said

Mary. Larry laughed and said, "That is _____ . Everyone

knows that bunnies do not eat honey."

# Y as a Vowel

**Directions:** Read the story. Choose the words from the box to fill in the blanks.

| try | my | Why | cry | shy | fly |
|-----|-----|-----|-----|-----|-----|

Sam is very _____. Ann asks, "Would you like to

_____ my kite?" Sam starts to _____ .

Ann asks, "_____ are you crying?"

Sam says, "I am afraid to _____ ."

"Oh, _____ ! You are a good kite flyer," cries Ann.

Name: _____

# School Words

| | | |
|---|---|---|
| pencil | teacher | crayons |
| recess | lunchbox | play |
| fun | math | |

**Directions:** Fill in the blanks with a word from the word box.

1. I need to sharpen my _____.

2. I like to _____ at recess.

3. School is _____!

4. My _____ helps me learn.

5. I need to color the picture with _____.

6. I play kickball at _____.

7. My sandwich is in my _____.

8. In _____ I can add and subtract.

Grade 2 - Comprehensive Curriculum

Name: _____

# Days of the Week

**Directions:** Write the day of the week that answers each question.

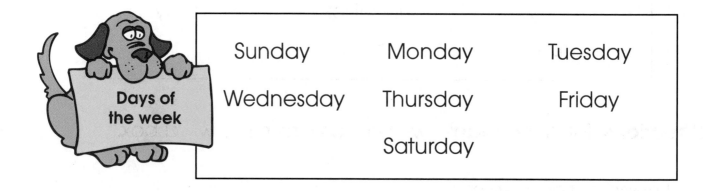

| Sunday | Monday | Tuesday |
| Wednesday | Thursday | Friday |
| | Saturday | |

1. What is the first day of the week?

   _____

2. What is the last day of the week?

   _____

3. What day comes after Tuesday?

   _____

4. What day comes between Wednesday and Friday?

   _____

5. What is the third day of the week?

   _____

6. What day comes before Saturday?

   _____

7. What day comes after Sunday?

   _____

Name: _____

# Compound Words

**Compound words** are formed by putting together two smaller words.

**Directions:** Help the cook brew her stew. Mix words from the first column with words from the second column to make new words. Write your new words on the lines at the bottom.

| | |
|---|---|
| grand | brows |
| snow | light |
| eye | stairs |
| down | string |
| rose | book |
| shoe | mother |
| note | ball |
| moon | bud |

1. _____

2. _____

3. _____

4. _____

5. _____

6. _____

7. _____

8. _____

# Compound Words

**Compound words** are two words that are put together to make one new word.

**Directions:** Read the sentences. Fill in the blank with a compound word from the box.

| raincoat | bedroom | lunchbox | hallway | sandbox |

1. A box with sand is a

_____.

2. The way through a hall is a

_____.

3. A box for lunch is a

_____.

4. A coat for the rain is a

_____.

5. A room with a bed is a

_____.

# Compound Words

**Directions:** Cut out the words below. Glue them together in the box to make compound words.

Can you think of any more compound words?

| sun | air | mail | ball |
|-----|-----|------|------|
| box | room | water | guard |
| foot | living | class | flower |
| plane | room | melon | body |

Page is blank for cutting exercise on previous page.

Name: _____

# Compound Words

**Directions:** Draw a line under the compound word in each sentence. On the line, write the two words that make up the compound word.

1. A firetruck came to help put out the fire.

_____

2. I will be nine years old on my next birthday.

_____

3. We built a treehouse at the back.

_____

4. Dad put a scarecrow in his garden.

_____

5. It is fun to make footprints in the snow.

_____

6. I like to read the comics in the newspaper.

_____

7. Cowboys ride horses and use lassos.

_____

# Contractions

**Contractions** are a short way to write two words, such as **isn't**, **I've** and **weren't**. **Example: it is = it's**

**Directions:** Draw a line from each word pair to its contraction.

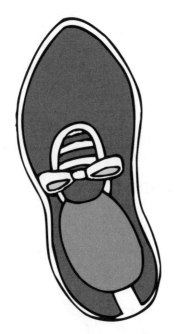 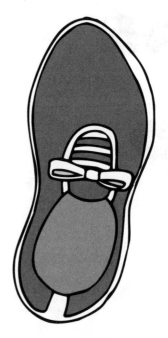

| | |
|---|---|
| I am | she's |
| it is | they're |
| you are | we're |
| we are | he's |
| they are | I'm |
| she is | it's |
| he is | you're |

Name: _____

# Contractions

**Directions:** Circle the contraction that would replace the underlined words.

**Example: were not = weren't**

1. The boy ____was not____ sad.

           wasn't     weren't

2. We _____were not_____ working.

     wasn't       weren't

3. Jen and Caleb ____have not____ eaten lunch yet.

           haven't     hasn't

4. The mouse ____has not____ been here.

          haven't     hasn't

Name: _____

# Contractions

**Directions:** Match the words with their contractions.

would not          I've

was not            he'll

he will            wouldn't

could not          wasn't

I have             couldn't

**Directions:** Make the words at the end of each line into contractions to complete the sentences.

1. He _____ know the answer.          **did not**

2. _____ a long way home.          **It is**

3. _____ my house.          **Here is**

4. _____ not going to school today.          **We are**

5. _____ take the bus home tomorrow.          **They will**

Name: _____

# Contractions

**Directions:** Cut out the two words and put them together to show what two words make the contraction. Glue them over the contraction.

cut ✂ - - - - - - - - - - - - - - - - - - - - - - - - - - - - - - - - - - - - - - - - - - - - - - - - - - - - - - - - - - - - - -

**Grade 2 - Comprehensive Curriculum**

Page is blank for cutting exercise on previous page.

Name: _____

# Syllables

Words are made up of parts called **syllables**. Each syllable has a vowel sound. One way to count syllables is to clap as you say the word.

**Example:** cat          1 clap          1 syllable

table          2 claps          2 syllables

butterfly          3 claps          3 syllables

**Directions:** "Clap out" the words below. Write how many syllables each word has.

movie _____          dog _____

piano _____          basket _____

tree _____          swimmer _____

bicycle _____          rainbow _____

sun _____          paper _____

cabinet _____          picture _____

football _____          run _____

television _____          enter _____

Name: _____

# Syllables

Dividing a word into syllables can help you read a new word. You also might divide syllables when you are writing if you run out of space on a line.
Many words contain two consonants that are next to each other. A word can usually be divided between the consonants.

**Directions:** Divide each word into two syllables. The first one is done for you.

kitten     _____ kit _____ ten _____

lumber     _____

batter     _____

winter     _____

funny     _____

harder     _____

dirty     _____

sister     _____

little     _____

dinner     _____

Name: _____

# Syllables

One way to help you read a word you don't know is to divide it into parts called **syllables**. Every syllable has a vowel sound.

**Directions:** Say the words. Write the number of syllables. The first one is done for you.

straw • ber • ry

bird _____1_____          rabbit _____

apple _____          elephant _____

balloon _____          family _____

basketball _____          fence _____

breakfast _____          ladder _____

block _____          open _____

candy _____          puddle _____

popcorn _____          Saturday _____

yellow _____          wind _____

understand _____          butterfly _____

Name: _____

# Syllables

When a double consonant is used in the middle of a word, the word can usually be divided between the consonants.

**Directions:** Look at the words in the word box. Divide each word into two syllables. Leave space between each syllable. One is done for you.

| butter | puppy | kitten | yellow |
| dinner | chatter | ladder | happy |
| pillow | letter | mitten | summer |

**but   ter**

_____    _____    _____

_____    _____    _____

_____    _____    _____

Many words are divided between two consonants that are not alike.

**Directions:** Look at the words in the word box. Divide each word into two syllables. One is done for you.

| window | doctor | number | carpet |
| mister | winter | pencil | candle |
| barber | sister | picture | under |

**win   dow**

_____    _____    _____

_____    _____    _____

_____    _____    _____

# Syllables

**Directions:** Write 1 or 2 on the line to tell how many syllables are in each word. If the word has 2 syllables, draw a line between the syllables. **Example: sup|per**

dog _____

bedroom _____

slipper _____

tree _____

batter _____

chair _____

fish _____

master _____

timber _____

cat _____

street _____

chalk _____

blanket _____

marker _____

brush _____

rabbit _____

Name: _____

# Haiku

A **haiku** is an Oriental form of poetry. Most haiku are about nature.

first line - 5 syllables
second line - 7 syllables
third line - 5 syllables

**Example:**     The squirrel is brown.
He lives in a great big tree.
He eats nuts all day.

**Directions:** Write your own haiku. Draw a picture to go with it.

_____

_____

_____

Name: _____

# Suffixes

A **suffix** is a syllable that is added at the end of a word to change its meaning.

**Directions:** Add the suffixes to the root words to make new words. Use your new words to complete the sentences.

help + ful = _____

care + less = _____

build + er = _____

talk + ed = _____

love + ly = _____

loud + er = _____

1. My mother _____ to my teacher about my homework.

2. The radio was _____ than the television.

3. Sally is always _____ to her mother.

4. A _____ put a new garage on our house.

5. The flowers are _____ .

6. It is _____ to cross the street without looking both ways.

**Grade 2 - Comprehensive Curriculum**

# Suffixes

Adding **ing** to a word means that it is happening now. Adding **ed** to a word means it happened in the past.

**Directions:** Look at the words in the word box. Underline the root word in each one. Write a word to complete each sentence.

| | | | | |
|---|---|---|---|---|
| snowing | wished | played | looking | crying |
| talking | walked | eating | going | doing |

1. We like to play. We _____ yesterday.

2. Is that snow? Yes, it is _____.

3. Do you want to go with me? No, I am _____ with my friend.

4. The baby will cry if we leave. The baby is _____.

5. We will walk home from school. We _____ to school this morning.

6. Did you wish for a new bike? Yes, I _____ for one.

7. Who is going to do it while we are away? I am _____ it.

8. Did you talk to your friend? Yes, we are _____ now.

9. Will you look at my book? I am _____ at it now.

10. I like to eat pizza. We are _____ it today.

Name: _____

# Suffixes

**Directions:** Write a word from the word box next to its root word.

| | | |
|---|---|---|
| coming | running | sitting |
| lived | rained | swimming |
| visited | carried | racing |
| hurried | | |

run _____          come _____

live _____          carry _____

hurry _____          race _____

swim _____          rain _____

visit _____          sit _____

---

**Directions:** Write a word from the word box to finish each sentence.

1. I _____ my grandmother during vacation.

2. Mary went _____ at the lake with her cousin.

3. Jim _____ the heavy package for his mother.

4. It _____ and stormed all weekend.

5. Cars go very fast when they are _____ .

Name: _____

# Suffixes

**Directions:** Read the story. Underline the words that end with **est**, **ed** or **ing**. On the lines below, write the root words for each word you underlined.

    The funniest book I ever read was about a girl named Nan. Nan did everything backward. She even spelled her name backward. Nan slept in the day and played at night. She dried her hair before washing it. She turned on the light after she finished her book—which she read from the back to the front! When it rained, Nan waited until she was inside before opening her umbrella. She even walked backward. The silliest part: The only thing Nan did forward was back up!

1. _____   6. _____   11. _____

2. _____   7. _____   12. _____

3. _____   8. _____   13. _____

4. _____   9. _____

5. _____   10. _____

Name: _____

# Prefixes: The Three R's

**Prefixes** are syllables added to the beginning of words that change their meaning. The prefix **re** means "again."

**Directions:** Read the story. Then follow the instructions.

Kim wants to find ways she can save the Earth. She studies the "three R's"—reduce, reuse and recycle. Reduce means to make less. Both reuse and recycle mean to use again.

Add **re** to the beginning of each word below. Use the new words to complete the sentences.

_____ build          _____ fill

_____ read          _____ tell

_____ write          _____ run

1. The race was a tie, so Dawn and Kathy had to _____ it.

2. The block wall fell down, so Simon had to _____ it.

3. The water bottle was empty, so Luna had to _____ it.

4. Javier wrote a good story, but he wanted to _____ it to make it better.

5. The teacher told a story, and students had to _____ it.

6. Toni didn't understand the directions, so she had to

_____ them.

# Prefixes

**Directions:** Read the story. Change Unlucky Sam to Lucky Sam by taking the **un** prefix off of the **bold** words.

## Unlucky Sam

Sam was **unhappy** about a lot of things in his life. His parents were **uncaring**. His teacher was **unfair**. His big sister was **unkind**. His neighbors were **unfriendly**. He was **unhealthy**, too! How could one boy be as **unlucky** as Sam?

## Lucky Sam

Sam was _____ about a lot of things in his life. His parents were _____ . His teacher was _____ . His big sister was _____ . His neighbors were _____ . He was _____, too! How could one boy be as _____ as Sam?

# Prefixes

**Directions:** Change the meaning of the sentences by adding the prefixes to the **bold** words.

The boy was **lucky** because he guessed the answer **correctly**.

The boy was (un) _____ because he guessed the

answer (in) _____ .

When Mary **behaved**, she felt **happy**.

When Mary (mis) _____ ,

she felt (un) _____ .

Mike wore his jacket **buttoned** because the dance was **formal**.

Mike wore his jacket (un) _____ because the dance

was (in) _____ .

Tim **understood** because he was **familiar** with the book.

Tim (mis) _____ because he was

(un) _____ with the  book.

# Prefixes

**Directions:** Read the story. Change the story by removing the prefix **re** from the **bold** words. Write the new words in the new story.

**Repete** is a **rewriter** who has to **redo** every story. He has to **rethink** up the ideas. He has to **rewrite** the sentences. He has to **redraw** the pictures. He even has to **retype** the pages. Who will **repay** **Repete** for all the work he **redoes**?

_____ is a _____ who has to

_____ every story. He has to _____

up the ideas. He has to _____ the sentences.

He has to _____ the pictures.

He even has to _____ the pages.

Who will _____ _____ for all the

work he _____?

Name: _____

# Review

**Directions:** Read each sentence. Look at the words in **bold**. Circle the prefix and write the root word on the line.

1. The **preview** of the movie was funny.                   _____

2. We always drink **nonfat** milk.                          _____

3. We will have to **reschedule** the trip.                  _____

4. Are you tired of **reruns** on television?                _____

5. I have **outgrown** my new shoes already.                 _____

6. You must have **misplaced** the papers.                   _____

7. Police **enforce** the laws of the city.                  _____

8. I **disliked** that book.                                 _____

9. The boy **distrusted** the big dog.                       _____

10. Try to **enjoy** yourself at the party.                  _____

11. Please try to keep the cat **inside** the house.         _____

12. That song is total **nonsense**!                         _____

13. We will **replace** any parts that we lost.              _____

14. Can you help me **unzip** this jacket?                   _____

15. Let's **rework** today's arithmetic problems.            _____

Name: _____

# Parts of a Book

A book has many parts. The title is the name of the book. The author is the person who wrote the words. The illustrator is the person who drew the pictures. The table of contents is located at the beginning to list what is in the book. The glossary is a little dictionary in the back to help you with unfamiliar words. Books are often divided into smaller sections of information called chapters.

**Directions:** Look at one of your books. Write the parts you see below.

The title of my book is      _____

The author is      _____

The illustrator is      _____

My book has a table of contents.                    Yes or No

My book has a glossary.                    Yes or No

My book is divided into chapters.                    Yes or No

# READING COMPREHENSION

**Directions**
1. Take boat out of box.
2. Add sail.
3. Tighten with wrench.
4. Have fun!

Name: _____

# Recalling Details: Nikki's Pets

**Directions:** Road about Nikki's pets, Then answer the questions.

Nikki has two cats, Tiger and Sniffer, and two dogs, Spot and Wiggles. Tiger is an orange striped cat who likes to sleep under a big tree and pretend she is a real tiger. Sniffer is a gray cat who likes to sniff the flowers in Nikki's garden. Spot is a Dalmatian with many black spots. Wiggles is a big furry brown dog who wiggles all over when he is happy.

1. Which dog is brown and furry? _____

2. What color is Tiger? _____

3. What kind of dog is Spot? _____

4. Which cat likes to sniff flowers? _____

5. Where does Tiger like to sleep? _____

6. Who wiggles all over when he is happy? _____

Nikki's Garden

Name: _____

# Recalling Details: Pet Pests

**Directions:** Read the story. Then answer the questions.

Sometimes Marvin and Mugsy scratch and itch. Marcy knows that fleas or ticks are insect pests to her pets. Their bites are painful. Fleas suck the blood of animals. They don't have wings, but they can jump. Ticks are very flat, suck blood and are related to spiders. They like to hide in dogs' ears. That is why Marcy checks Marvin and Mugsy every week for fleas and ticks.

1. What is a pest? _____

_____

2. List three facts about fleas.

   1) _____

   2) _____

   3) _____

3. List three facts about ticks.

   1) _____

   2) _____

   3) _____

Name: _____

# Reading for Details

**Directions:** Read the story about baby animals. Answer the questions with words from the story.

Baby cats are called kittens. They love to play and drink lots of milk. A baby dog is a puppy. Puppies chew on old shoes. They run and bark. A lamb is a baby sheep. Lambs eat grass. A baby duck is called a duckling. Ducklings swim with their wide, webbed feet. Foals are baby horses. A foal can walk the day it is born! A baby goat is a kid. Some people call children kids, too!

1. A baby cat is called a _____.

2. A baby dog is a _____.

3. A _____ is a baby sheep.

4. _____ swim with their webbed feet.

5. A _____ can walk the day it is born.

6. A baby goat is a _____.

# Reading for Details

**Directions:** Read the story about bike safety. Answer the questions below the story.

Mike has a red bike. He likes his bike. Mike wears a helmet. Mike wears knee pads and elbow pads. They keep him safe. Mike stops at signs. Mike looks both ways. Mike is safe on his bike.

1. What color is Mike's bike? _____

2. Which sentence in the story tells why Mike wears pads and a helmet? Write it here.

   _____

3. What else does Mike do to keep safe?

   He _____ at signs and _____ both ways.

# Reading for Details

**Directions:** Read the story about different kinds of transportation. Answer the questions with words from the story.

People use many kinds of transportation. Boats float on the water. Some people fish in a boat. Airplanes fly in the sky. Flying in a plane is a fast way to get somewhere. Trains run on a track. The first car is the engine. The last car is the caboose. Some people even sleep in beds on a train! A car has four wheels. Most people have a car. A car rides on roads. A bus can hold many people. A bus rides on roads. Most children ride a bus to school.

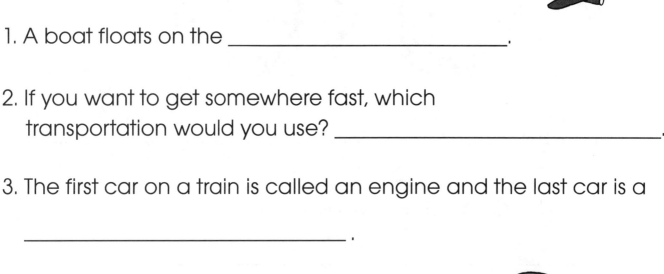

1. A boat floats on the _____.

2. If you want to get somewhere fast, which transportation would you use? _____.

3. The first car on a train is called an engine and the last car is a

   _____ .

4. _____ ride on a bus.

5. A _____ has four wheels.

# Following Directions

**Directions:** Read the story. Answer the questions. Try the recipe.

## Cows Give Us Milk

Cows live on a farm. The farmer milks the cow to get milk. Many things are made from milk. We make ice cream, sour cream, cottage cheese and butter from milk. Butter is fun to make! You can learn to make your own butter. First, you need cream. Put the cream in a jar and shake it. Then you need to pour off the liquid. Next, you put the butter in a bowl. Add a little salt and stir! Finally, spread it on crackers and eat!

1. What animal gives us milk?_____

2. What 4 things are made from milk?

_____  _____  _____  _____

3. What did the story teach you to make?_____

4. Put the steps in order. Place 1, 2, 3, 4 by the sentence.

_____ Spread the butter on crackers and eat!

_____ Shake cream in a jar.

_____ Start with cream.

_____ Add salt to the butter.

# Following Directions: Parrot Art

**Directions:** Draw the missing parts on each parrot.

1. Draw the parrot's eye.

2. Draw the parrot's tail.

3. Draw the parrot's beak.

4. Draw the parrot's wings.

# Following Directions: How to Treat a Ladybug

**Directions:** Read about how to treat ladybugs. Then follow the instructions.

Ladybugs are shy. If you see a ladybug, sit very still. Hold out your arm. Maybe the ladybug will fly to you. If it does, talk softly. Do not touch it. It will fly away when it is ready.

1. Complete the directions on how to treat a ladybug.

   a. Sit very still.

   b. _____

   c. Talk softly.

   d. _____

2. Ladybugs are red. They have black spots. Color the ladybug.

Name: _____

# Following Directions: Insect Art

**Directions:** Read about Insects. Then follow the instructions.

All insects have these body parts:

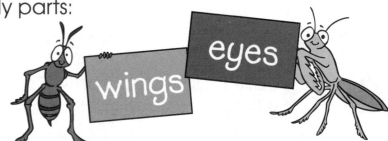

*Head* at the front

*Thorax* in the middle

*Abdomen* at the back

Six *legs*—three on each side of the thorax

Two *eyes* on the head

Two *antennae* attached to the head

Some insects also have *wings*.

Draw your favorite insect. Include all the body parts listed above.

# Sequencing: Packing Bags

**Directions:** Read about packing bags. Then number the objects in the order they should be packed.

Cans are heavy. Put them in first. Then put in boxes. Now, put in the apple. Put the bread in last.

# Sequencing: 1, 2, 3, 4!

**Directions:** Write numbers by each sentence to show the order of the story.

The pool is empty. _____    Ben plays in the pool. _____

Ben gets out. _____    Ben fills the pool. _____

# Sequencing/Predicting: A Game for Cats

**Directions:** Read about what cats like. Then follow the instructions.

Cats like to play with paper bags. Pull a paper bag open. Take everything out. Now, lay it on its side.

1. Write 1, 2 and 3 to put the pictures in order.

2. In box 4, draw what you think the cat will do.

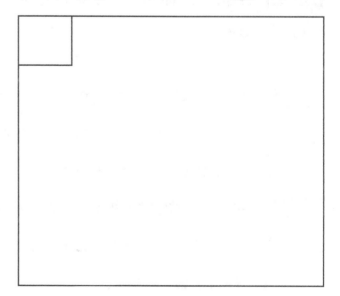

Name _____

# Sequencing: Story Events

Spencer likes to make new friends. Today, he made friends with the dog in the picture.

**Directions:** Number the sentences in order to find out what Spencer did today.

\_\_\_\_ Spencer kissed his mother good-bye.

\_\_\_\_ Spencer saw the new dog next door.

\_\_\_\_ Spencer went outside.

\_\_\_\_ Spencer said hello.

\_\_\_\_ Spencer got dressed and ate breakfast.

\_\_\_\_ Spencer woke up.

Name: _____

# Sequencing: Yo-Yo Trick

**Directions:** Read about the yo-yo trick.

Wind up the yo-yo string. Hold the yo-yo in your hand. Now, hold your palm up. Throw the yo-yo downward on the string. Hold your palm down. Now, swing the yo-yo forward. Make it "walk." This yo-yo trick is called "walk the dog."

**Directions:** Number the directions in order.

_____ Swing the yo-yo forward and make it "walk."

_____ Hold your palm up and drop the yo-yo.

_____ Turn your palm down as the yo-yo reaches the ground.

# Sequencing: Make a Hat

Mrs. Posey made a new hat, but she forgot how she did it. When she tried to tell her friend, she got all mixed up.

**Directions:** Read Mrs. Posey's story. Write her story on the lines in the order you think it happened. Then color the picture.

I glued flowers on it. Then I bought this straw hat. Now, I am wearing my hat. Then I added ribbon around the flowers. I tried on many hats at the store.

The real story:

_____

_____

_____

_____

_____

_____

_____

Name: _____

# Sequencing: Follow a Recipe

Here is a recipe for chocolate peanut butter cookies. When you use a recipe, you must follow the directions carefully. The sentences below are not in the correct order.

**Directions:** Write number 1 to show what you would do first. Then number each step to show the correct sequence.

_____ Melt the chocolate almond bark in a microsafe bowl.

_____ Eat!

_____ While the chocolate is melting, spread peanut butter on a cracker and place another cracker on top.

_____ Let the melted candy drip off the cracker into the bowl before you place it on wax paper.

_____ Let it cool!

_____ Carefully use a fork or spoon to dip the crackers into the melted chocolate.

Try the recipe with an adult.

Do you like to cook? _____

# Sequencing: Follow a Recipe

Alana and Marcus are hungry for a snack. They want to make nacho chips and cheese. The steps they need to follow are all mixed up.

**Directions:** Read the steps. Number them in 1, 2, 3 order. Then color the picture.

_____ Bake the chips in the oven for 2 minutes.

_____ Get a cookie sheet to bake on.

_____ Get out the nacho chips and cheese.

_____ Eat the nachos and chips.

_____ Put the chips on the cookie sheet.

_____ Put grated cheese on the chips.

Name: _____

# Sequencing: Making a Snowman

**Directions:** Read about how to make a snowman. Then follow the instructions.

It is fun to make a snowman. First, find things for the snowman's eyes and nose. Dress warmly. Then go outdoors. Roll a big snowball. Then roll another to put on top of it. Now, roll a small snowball for the head. Put on the snowman's face.

1. Number the pictures in order.

2. Write two things to do before going outdoors.

1) _____

2) _____

**Grade 2 - Comprehensive Curriculum**

# Sequencing: Baking a Cake

**Directions:** Read about baking a cake. Then write the missing steps.

Dylan, Dana and Dad are baking a cake. Dad turns on the oven. Dana opens the cake mix. Dylan adds the eggs. Dad pours in the water. Dana stirs the batter. Dylan pours the batter into a cake pan. Dad puts it in the oven.

1. Turn on the oven.

2. _____

3. Add the eggs.

4. _____

5. Stir the batter.

6. _____

7. _____

Name: _____

# Sequencing: Story Events

Mari was sick yesterday.

**Directions:** Number the events in 1, 2, 3 order to tell the story about Mari.

_____ She went to the doctor's office.

_____ Mari felt much better.

_____ Mari felt very hot and tired.

_____ Mari's mother went to the drugstore.

_____ The doctor wrote down something.

_____ The doctor looked in Mari's ears.

_____ Mari took a pill.

_____ The doctor gave Mari's mother the piece of paper.

_____ Mari drank some water with her pill.

**Grade 2 - Comprehensive Curriculum**

Name: _____

# Sequencing: Making a Card

**Directions:** Read about how to make a card. Then follow the instructions.

You will need scissors, glue and colored paper. First, look at all your old cards. Then, cut out what you like. Now, fold the colored paper in half. Glue the cut-outs to the front of your card. Write your name inside.

1. Write the steps in order for making a card.

   1) Look at all your old cards.

   2) _____

   3) _____

   4) _____

2. Write your name inside.

3. Draw a picture of a new card you could make.

# Sequencing: Making Clay

**Directions:** Read about making clay. Then follow the instructions.

It is fun to work with clay. Here is what you need to make it:

1 cup salt

2 cups flour

3/4 cup water

Mix the salt and flour. Then add the water. DO NOT eat the clay. It tastes bad. Use your hands to mix and mix. Now, roll it out. What can you make with your clay?

1. Circle the main idea:

   Do not eat clay.

   Mix salt, flour and water to make clay.

2. Write the steps for making clay.

   a. _____

   b. _____

   c. Mix the clay.

   d. _____

3. Write why you should not eat clay. _____

   _____

# Sequencing: Play a Game

Children all around the world like to play games. Think about your favorite game. Maybe you could teach your friends to play it.

**Directions:** Write, in order, how to play your game.

_____

_____

_____

_____

_____

_____

_____

**Directions:** Draw a picture of you playing your favorite game.

# Sequencing: A Visit to the Zoo

**Directions:** Read the story. Then follow the instructions.

One Saturday morning in May, Gloria and Anna went to the zoo. First, they bought tickets to get into the zoo. Second, they visited the Gorilla Garden and had fun watching the gorillas stare at them. Then they went to Tiger Town and watched the tigers as they slept in the sunshine. Fourth, they went to Hippo Haven and laughed at the hippos cooling off in their pool. Next, they visited Snake Station and learned about poisonous and nonpoisonous snakes. It was noon, and they were hungry, so they ate lunch at the Parrot Patio.

Write **first**, **second**, **third**, **fourth**, **fifth** and **sixth** to put the events in order.

_____ They went to Hippo Haven.

_____ Gloria and Anna bought zoo tickets.

_____ They watched the tigers sleep.

_____ They ate lunch at Parrot Patio.

_____ The gorillas stared at them.

_____ They learned about poisonous and nonpoisonous snakes.

# Sequencing: Why Does It Rain?

**Directions:** Read about rain. Then follow the instructions.

Clouds are made up of little drops of ice and water. They push and bang into each other. Then they join together to make bigger drops and begin to fall. More raindrops cling to them. They become heavy and fall quickly to the ground.

Write **first**, **second**, **third**, **fourth** and **fifth** to put the events in order.

_____ More raindrops cling to them.

_____ Clouds are made up of little drops of ice and water.

_____ They join together and make bigger drops that begin to fall.

_____ The drops of ice and water bang into each other.

_____ The drops become heavy and fall quickly to the ground.

# Sequencing: Make a Pencil Holder

**Directions:** Read how to make a pencil holder. Then follow the instructions.

You can use "junk" to make a pencil holder! First, you need a clean can with one end removed. Make sure there are no sharp edges. Then you need glue, scissors and paper. Find colorful paper such as wrapping paper, wallpaper or construction paper. Cut the paper to fit the can. Glue the paper around the can. Decorate your can with glitter, buttons and stickers. Then put your pencils inside!

1. Write **first**, **second**, **third**, **fourth**, **fifth**, **sixth** and **seventh** to put the steps in order.

_____ Make sure there are no sharp edges.

_____ Get glue, scissors and paper.

_____ Cut the paper to fit the can.

_____ Put your pencils in the can!

_____ Glue colorful paper to the can.

_____ Remove one end of a clean can.

_____ Decorate the can with glitter and stickers.

**Grade 2 - Comprehensive Curriculum**

# Tracking: Where Does She Go?

Every morning when Lisa wakes up, she goes somewhere. Find out where she goes.

**Directions:**
Read the sentences. Follow the instructions.

1. On Monday, Lisa needs bread. Use a red crayon to mark her path from her house to that building. Where does she go? _____

2. On Tuesday, Lisa wants to read books. Use a green crayon to mark her path. Where does she go? _____

3. On Wednesday, Lisa wants to swing. Use a yellow crayon to mark her path. Where does she go? _____

4. On Thursday, Lisa wants to buy stamps. Use a black crayon to mark her path. Where does she go? _____

5. On Friday, Lisa wants to get money. Use a purple crayon to mark her path. Where does she go? _____

# Tracking: Sequencing

**Directions:** Look at the paths you drew for Lisa on page 108. Number, in order, the places that Lisa went each day. Draw a line to connect the place with the day of the week.

| | | |
|---|---|---|
| _____ Bank | | Monday |
| _____ Park | | Tuesday |
| _____ Library | | Wednesday |
| _____ Bakery | | Thursday |
| _____ Post Office | | Friday |

**Grade 2 - Comprehensive Curriculum**

# Tracking: With a Map

Greg and Tess walk to and from school together each day. After school, they stop at the park to play. Then they go home.

**Directions:** Read the sentences. Draw Greg's path in red and Tess's path in blue.

Greg starts at his home.
He walks to school.
When he leaves school, he stops at the park.
Then he goes home.
Tess goes the same places that Greg goes.
Some of their paths will be the same.

# Tracking: With a Map

**Directions:** Study the map of the United States. Follow the instructions.

1. Draw a star on the state where you live.
2. Draw a line from your state to the Atlantic Ocean.
3. Draw a triangle in the Gulf of Mexico.
4. Draw a circle in the Pacific Ocean.
5. Color each state that borders your state a different color.

**Grade 2 - Comprehensive Curriculum**

# Tracking: Alternate Paths

Look at Spotty Dog's home. Look at the paths he takes to the oven and the back door. The numbers by each path show how many steps Spotty must take to get there.

**Directions:** Follow the instructions.

1. Spotty Dog's cookies are done. Trace Spotty's path from his chair to the oven.

2. How many steps does Spotty take?

3. While Spotty is looking in his oven, he hears a noise in the backyard. Trace Spotty's path to the door.

4. How many steps has Spotty taken in all?

5. Spotty goes back to his chair. How many steps must he take?

6. How many steps has he taken in all?

7. Spotty's path has made a shape. What shape is it?

Name: _____

# Same/Different: Objects

**Directions:** Look at the pictures. Draw an **X** on the picture in each row that is different.

**Grade 2 - Comprehensive Curriculum**

# Same/Different: Stuffed Animals

Kate and Oralia like to collect and trade stuffed animals.

**Directions:** Draw two stuffed animals that are alike and two that are different.

## Alike

## Different

# Same/Different: Shell Homes

**Directions:** Read about shells. Then answer the questions.

Shells are the homes of some animals. Snails live in shells on the land. Clams live in shells in the water. Clam shells open. Snail shells stay closed. Both shells keep the animals safe.

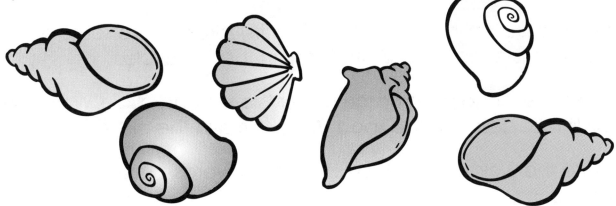

1. (Circle the correct answer.) Snails live in shells on the

   water.          land.


2. (Circle the correct answer.)
   Clam shells are different from snail shells because

   they open.

   they stay closed.


3. Write one way all shells are the same. _____

   _____

# Same/Different: Venn Diagram

A **Venn diagram** is a diagram that shows how two things are the same and different.

**Directions:** Choose two outdoor sports. Then follow the instructions to complete the Venn diagram.

1. Write the first sport name under the first circle. Write some words that describe the sport. Write them in the first circle.

2. Write the second sport name under the second circle. Write some words that describe the sport. Write them in the circle.

3. Where the 2 circles overlap, write some words that describe both sports.

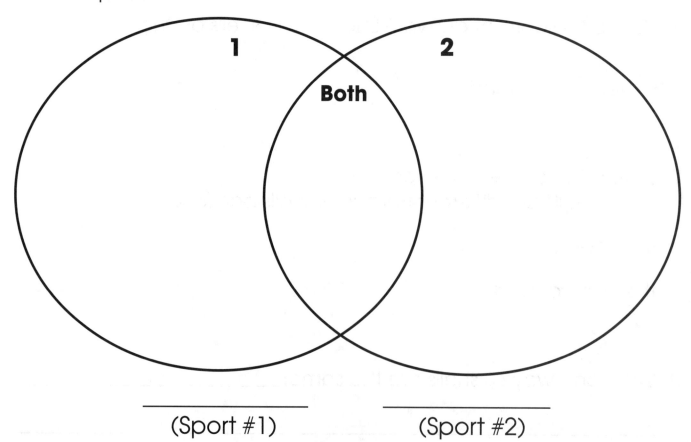

(Sport #1)          (Sport #2)

# Same/Different: Dina and Dina

**Directions:** Read the story. Then complete the Venn diagram, telling how Dina, the duck, is the same or different than Dina, the girl.

One day in the library, Dina found a story about a duck named Dina!

My name is Dina. I am a duck, and I like to swim. When I am not swimming, I walk on land or fly. I have two feet and two eyes. My feathers keep me warm. Ducks can be different colors. I am gray, brown and black. I really like being a duck. It is fun.

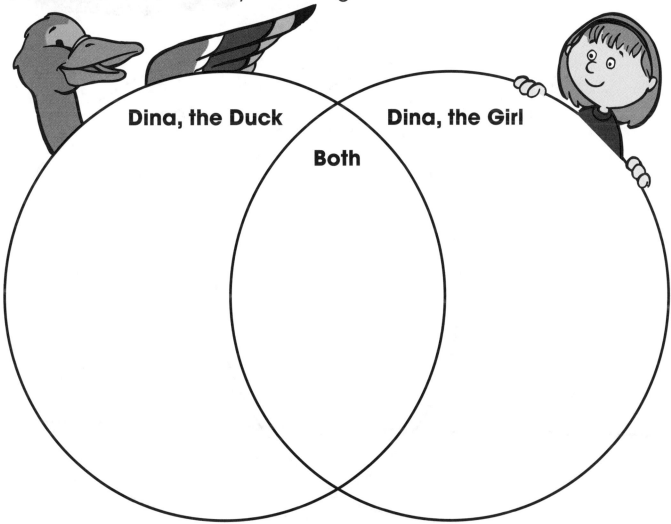

**Dina, the Duck**

**Dina, the Girl**

**Both**

# Same/Different: Ann and Lee Have Fun

**Directions:** Read about Ann and Lee. Then write how they are the same and different in the Venn diagram.

Ann and Lee like to play ball. They like to jump rope. Lee likes to play a card game called "Old Maid." Ann likes to play a card game called "Go Fish." What do you do to have fun?

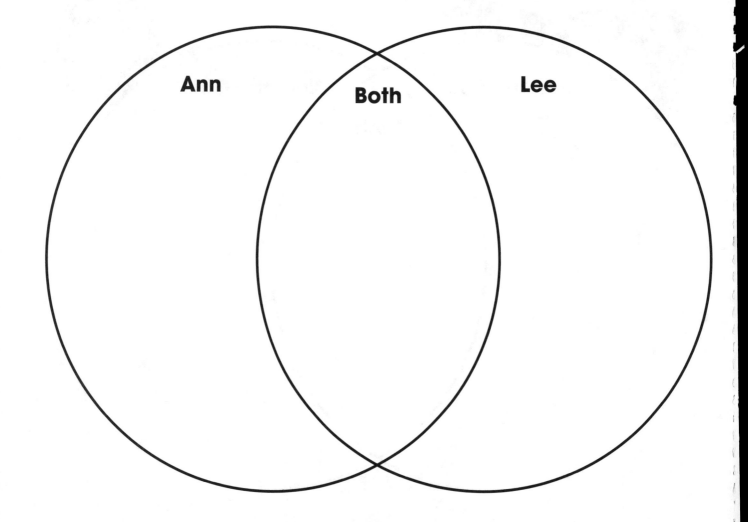

**Ann**        **Both**        **Lee**

# Same/Different: Cats and Tigers

**Directions:** Read about cats and tigers. Then complete the Venn diagram, telling how they are the same and different.

Tigers are a kind of cat. Pet cats and tigers both have fur. Pet cats are small and tame. Tigers are large and wild.

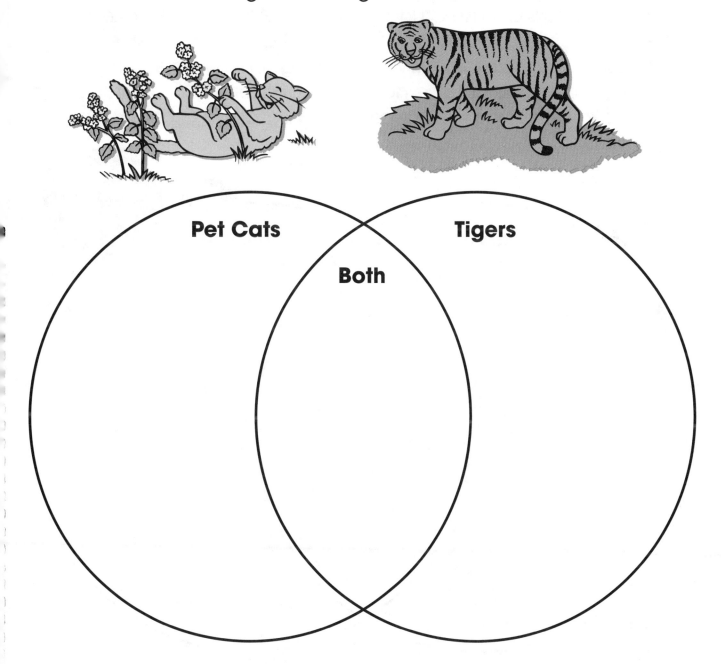

Name: _____

# Same/Different: Marvin and Mugsy

**Directions:** Read about Marvin and Mugsy. Then complete the Venn diagram, telling how they are the same and different.

    Marcy has two dogs, Marvin and Mugsy. Marvin is a black-and-white spotted Dalmatian. Marvin likes to run after balls in the backyard. His favorite food is Canine Crunchy Crunch. Marcy likes to take Marvin for walks, because dogs need exercise. Marvin loves to sleep in his doghouse. Mugsy is a big furry brown dog, who wiggles when she is happy. Since she is big, she needs lots of exercise. So Marcy takes her for walks in the park. Her favorite food is Canine Crunchy Crunch. Mugsy likes to sleep on Marcy's bed.

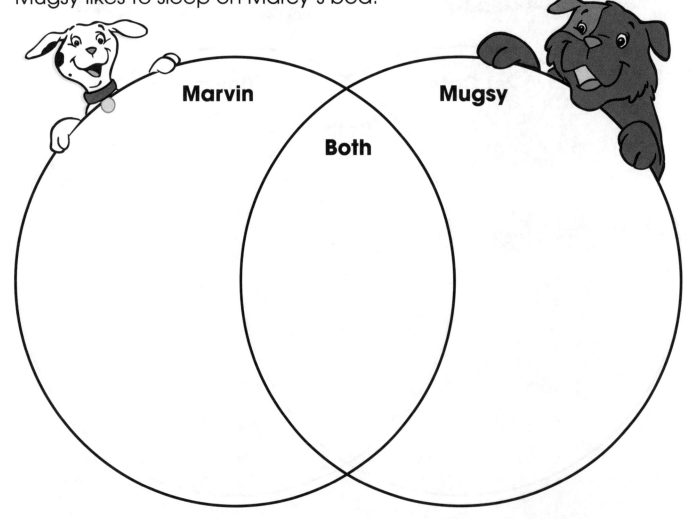

Marvin

Mugsy

Both

Name: _____

# Same/Different: Bluebirds and Parrots

**Directions:** Read about parrots and bluebirds. Then complete the Venn diagram, telling how they are the same and different.

Bluebirds and parrots are both birds. Bluebirds and parrots can fly. They both have beaks. Parrots can live inside a cage. Bluebirds must live outdoors.

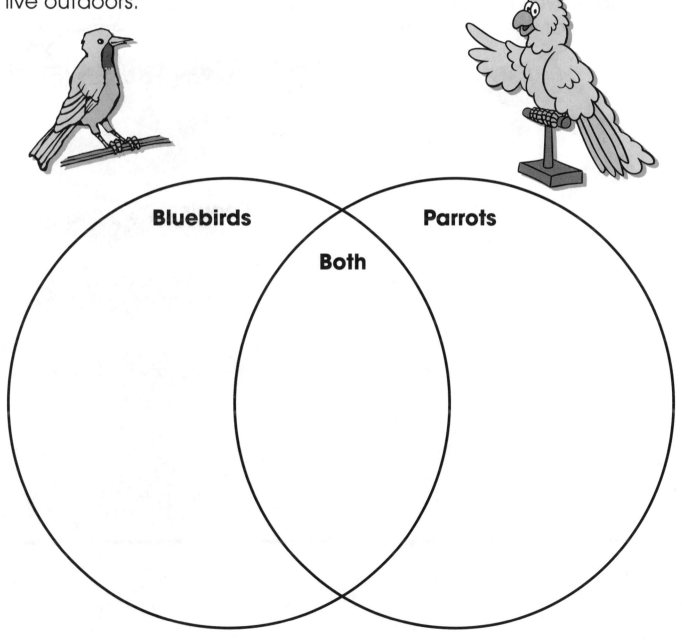

**Bluebirds**

**Parrots**

**Both**

**Grade 2 - Comprehensive Curriculum**

Name: _____

# Same/Different: Sleeping Whales

**Directions:** Read more about whales. Then complete the Venn diagram, telling how whales and people are the same and different.

Whales do not sleep like we do. They take many short naps. Like us, whales breathe air. Whales live in very cold water, but they have fat that keeps them warm.

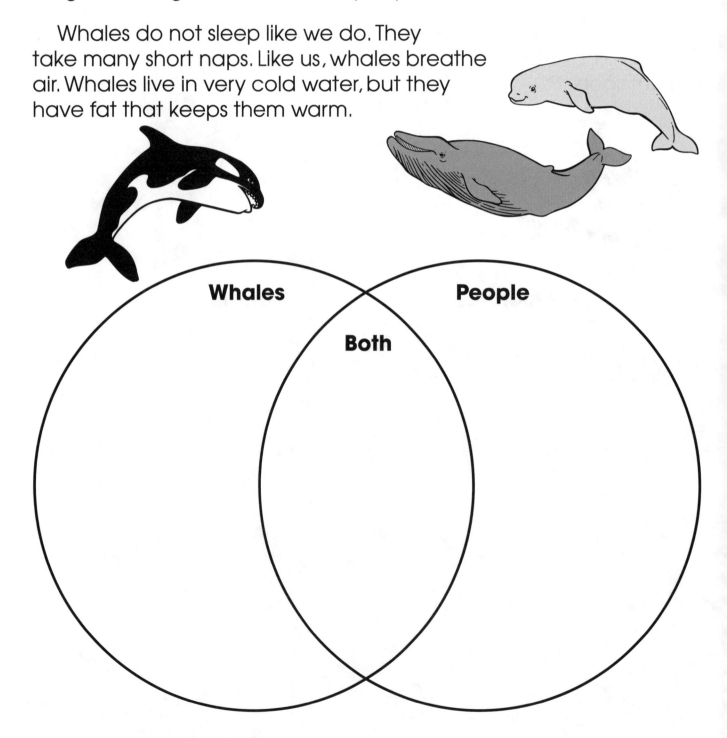

**Whales**          **People**

**Both**

# Similes

A **simile** is a figure of speech that compares two different things. The words **like** or **as** are used in similes.

**Directions:** Draw a line to the picture that goes with each set of words.

as hard as a

as hungry as a

as quiet as a

as soft as a

as easy as

as light as a

as tiny as an

# Classifying: A Rainy Day

**Directions:** Read the story. Then circle the objects Jonathan needs to stay dry.

It is raining. Jonathan wants to play outdoors. What should he wear to stay dry? What should he carry to stay dry?

# Classifying: Outdoor/Indoor Games

**Classifying** is putting things that are alike into groups.

**Directions:** Read about games. Draw an **X** on the games you can play indoors. Circle the objects used for outdoor games.

Some games are outdoor games. Some games are indoor games. Outdoor games are active. Indoor games are quiet.

Which do you like best? _____

# Classifying: Art Tools

**Directions:** Read about art tools. Then color only the art tools.

Andrea uses different art tools to help her design her masterpieces. To cut, she needs scissors. To draw, she needs a pencil. To color, she needs crayons. To paint, she needs a brush.

Write which tools are needed to:

draw                     color                      cut

_____    _____    _____

# Classifying

**Classifying** is putting similar things into groups.

**Directions:** Write each word from the word box on the correct line.

| baby | donkey | whale | family | fox |
|------|--------|-------|--------|-----|
| uncle | goose | grandfather | kangaroo | policeman |

people                                    animals

_____

_____

_____

_____

_____

_____

_____

_____

_____

Name: _____

# Classifying

**Directions:** Read the sentences. Write the words from the word box where they belong.

| bush | rocket | cake | thunder | bicycle | Danger |
|------|--------|------|---------|---------|--------|
| airplane | wind | candy | rain | car | grass |
| Stop | truck | Poison | flower | pie | bird |

1. These things taste sweet.

_____    _____    _____

2. These things come when it storms.

_____    _____    _____

3. These things have wheels.

_____    _____    _____

4. These are words you see on signs.

_____    _____    _____

5. These things can fly.

_____    _____    _____

6. These things grow in the ground.

_____    _____    _____

Name: _____

# Classifying: Animals

**Directions:** Use a red crayon to circle the names of three animals that would make good pets. Use a blue crayon to circle the names of three wild animals. Use an orange crayon to circle the two animals that live on a farm.

| BEAR | CAT | LION | SHEEP | BIRD | DOG | COW | TIGER |
|------|-----|------|-------|------|-----|-----|-------|

A M E O W W N L I O N

B M D O G G X I I S O

A B E A R R V L M H R

R M R M O O U S E E K

K C A B B I R D S E M

I O T T I G E R M P Q

B W N O W W R Q N E N

D N C P H H I D U D N

F K C A T T R O A R M

# Classifying

**Directions:** The words in each box form a group. Choose the word from the word box that describes each group and write it on the line.

| clothes | family | noises | colors | flowers |
|---|---|---|---|---|
| fruits | animals | coins | toys | |

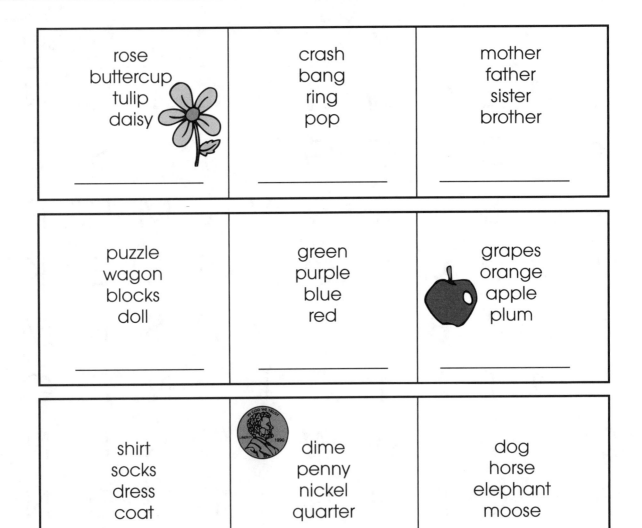

rose
buttercup
tulip
daisy

_____

crash
bang
ring
pop

_____

mother
father
sister
brother

_____

puzzle
wagon
blocks
doll

_____

green
purple
blue
red

_____

grapes
orange
apple
plum

_____

shirt
socks
dress
coat

_____

dime
penny
nickel
quarter

_____

dog
horse
elephant
moose

_____

# Classifying

**Living** things need air, food and water to live. **Non-living** things are not alive.

**Directions:** Cut out the words on the bottom. Glue each word in the correct column.

| Living | Non-living |
|--------|------------|
|        |            |

cut ✂ - - - - - - - - - - - - - - - - - - - - - - - - - - - - - - - - - - - - - -

| flower | book | boy | dog |
|--------|------|-----|-----|
| chair | bread | tree | camera |
| car | horse | ant | shoe |

Page is blank for cutting exercise on previous page.

# Classifying: Foods

Darcy likes fruit and things made from fruit. She also likes bread.

**Directions:** Circle the things on the menu that Darcy will eat.

## MENU

apple pie                corn
peas                     rolls
beans                    banana bread
oranges                  grape drink
chicken

# Classifying: Words

Dapper Dog is going camping.

**Directions:** Draw an **X** on the word in each row that does not belong in that group.

| 1. | flashlight | candle | radio | fire |
| 2. | shirt | pants | coat | bat |
| 3. | cow | car | bus | train |
| 4. | beans | hot dog | ball | bread |
| 5. | gloves | hat | book | boots |
| 6. | fork | butter | cup | plate |
| 7. | book | ball | bat | milk |
| 8. | dogs | bees | flies | ants |

# Classifying: Leaves

**Directions:** Look at each leaf and read its name. Write the name of each leaf on the line. Then color the leaves.

white oak         silver maple         poison ivy         ash

_____         _____

_____         _____

# Classifying: Leaves

This tricky tree has four different kinds of leaves: ash, poison ivy, silver maple and white oak.

**Directions:** Follow the instructions. Then answer the questions.

1. Underline the white oak leaves.    How many are there? _____

2. Circle the ash leaves.    How many are there? _____

3. Draw an **X** on the poison ivy leaves.    How many are there? _____

4. Draw a box around the silver  maple leaves.   How many are there? _____

Name: _____

# Classifying: Watch Out for Poison Ivy!

Poison ivy is not safe. If you touch it, it can make your skin red and itchy. It can hurt. It grows on the ground. It has three leaves. It can be green or red. Watch out, Jay! There is poison ivy in these woods.

**Directions:** Color the poison ivy leaves red. Then color the "safe" leaves other colors.

**Grade 2 - Comprehensive Curriculum**

# Classifying: Leaves

**Directions:** Gather some leaves. Put your leaves into groups by type. Then answer the questions.

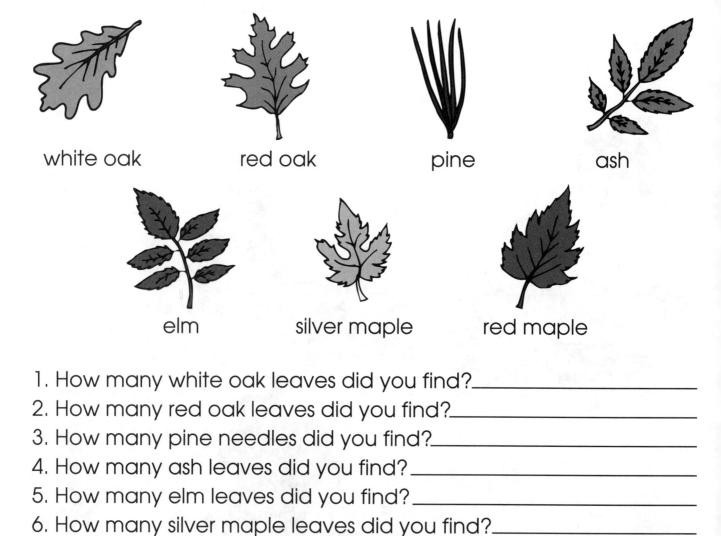

white oak          red oak          pine          ash

elm          silver maple          red maple

1. How many white oak leaves did you find?_____

2. How many red oak leaves did you find?_____

3. How many pine needles did you find?_____

4. How many ash leaves did you find?_____

5. How many elm leaves did you find?_____

6. How many silver maple leaves did you find?_____

7. How many red maple leaves did you find?_____

8. What other kinds of leaves did you find? Use a book to help you name them. Write their names on the lines. _____

_____

_____

_____

# Classifying: Animal Habitats

**Directions:** Read the story. Then write each animal's name under **Water** or **Land** to tell where it lives.

Animals live in different habitats. A habitat is the place of an animal's natural home. Many animals live on land and others live in water. Most animals that live in water breathe with gills. Animals that live on land breathe with lungs.

| fish | shrimp | giraffe | dog |
|------|--------|---------|-----|
| cat | eel | whale | horse |
| bear | deer | shark | jellyfish |

**WATER**

1. _____      4. _____

2. _____      5. _____

3. _____      6. _____

**LAND**

1. _____      4. _____

2. _____      5. _____

3. _____      6. _____

Name: _____

# Review

**Directions:** Compare the leaves on the left to the pictures of the other leaves. Write the missing names under the leaves.

_____     red oak          poison ivy          ash

_____     silver maple          elm          white oak

**Directions:** Color the pictures that are fruits.

apple          carrot          peach          corn

**Directions:** Draw an **X** on the word in each group that does not belong.

night          black          dark          sun

rose          ash          oak          elm

muffin          banana          rolls          bread

Name: _____

# Comprehension: Ladybugs

**Directions:** Read about ladybugs. Then answer the questions.

   Have you ever seen a ladybug? Ladybugs are red. They have black spots. They have six legs. Ladybugs are pretty!

1. What color are ladybugs? _____

2. What color are their spots? _____

3. How many legs do ladybugs have? _____

# Comprehension: Playful Cats

**Directions:** Read about cats. Then follow the instructions.

Cats make good pets. They like to play. They like to jump. They like to run. Do you?

1. (Circle the correct answer.)
   Cats make good

   pets.

   friends.

2. Write three things cats like to do:

   1) _____

   2) _____

   3) _____

3. Think of a good name for a cat. Write it on the cat's tag.

Name: _____

# Comprehension: Types of Tops

The **main idea** is the most important point or idea in a story.

**Directions:** Read about tops. Then answer the questions.

Tops come in all sizes. Some tops are made of wood. Some tops are made of tin. All tops do the same thing. They spin! Do you have a top?

1. Circle the main idea:

   There are many kinds of tops.

   Some tops are made of wood.

2. What are some tops made of? _____

3. What do all tops do? _____

**Grade 2 - Comprehensive Curriculum**

# Comprehension: Playing Store

**Directions:** Read about playing store. Then answer the questions.

Tyson and his friends like to play store. They use boxes and cans. They line them up. Then they put them in bags.

1. Circle the main idea:

   Tyson and his friends use boxes, cans and bags to play store.

   You need bags to play store.

2. (Circle your answer.) Who likes to play store?

   all kids          some kids

3. Do you like to play store?_____

Name: _____

# Comprehension: Singing Whales

**Directions:** Read about singing whales. Then follow the instructions.

Some whales can sing! We cannot understand the words. But we can hear the tune of the humpback whale. Each season, humpback whales sing a different song.

1. Circle the main idea:

   All whales can sing.

   Some whales can sing.

2. Name the kind of whale that sings.

   _____

3. How many different songs does the humpback whale sing each year?

       1           2           3           4

# Comprehension: Paper-Bag Puppets

**Directions:** Read about paper-bag puppets. Then follow the instructions.

It is easy to make a hand puppet. You need a small paper bag. You need colored paper. You need glue. You need scissors. Are you ready?

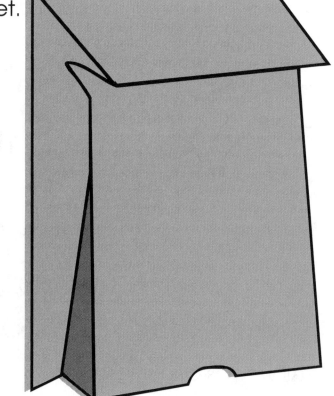

1. Circle the main idea:

   You need scissors.

   Making a hand puppet is easy.

2. Write the four objects you need to make a paper-bag puppet.

   1) _____

   2) _____

   3) _____

   4) _____

3. Draw a face on the paper-bag puppet.

# Comprehension: Sea Horses Look Strange!

**Directions:** Read about sea horses. Then answer the questions.

Sea horses are fish, not horses. A sea horse's head looks like a horse's head. It has a tail like a monkey's tail. A sea horse looks very strange!

1. (Circle the correct answer.)
   A sea horse is a kind of

   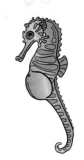

   horse.

   monkey.

   fish.

2. What does a sea horse's head look like?

   _____

   _____

3. What makes a sea horse look strange?

   a. _____

   b. _____

# Comprehension: Carla and Tony Jump Rope

**Directions:** Read about jumping rope. Then follow the instructions.

Carla and Tony like to jump rope. Carla likes to jump rope alone. Tony likes to have two people turn the rope for him. Carla and Tony can jump slowly. They can also jump fast.

1. Name another way to jump rope.

   a. Have two people turn the rope.

   b. _____

   _____

2. Name two speeds for jumping rope.

   1)_____  2)_____

3. Do you like to jump rope? _____

   _____

Name: _____

# Comprehension: How to Stop a Dog Fight

**Directions:** Read about how to stop a dog fight. Then answer the questions.

Sometimes dogs fight. They bark loudly. They may bite. Do not try to pull apart fighting dogs. Turn on a hose and spray them with water. This will stop the fight.

1. Name some things dogs may do if they are mad.

_____

_____

2. Why is it unwise to pull on dogs that are fighting?

_____

_____

3. Do you think dogs like to get wet?

_____

**Grade 2 - Comprehensive Curriculum**

# Comprehension: Training a Dog

**Directions:** Read about how to train dogs. Then answer the questions.

A dog has a ball in his mouth. You want the ball. What should you do? Do not pull on the ball. Hold out something else for the dog. The dog will drop the ball to take it!

1. Circle the main idea:

   Always get a ball away from a dog.

   Offer the dog something else to get him to drop the ball.

2. What should you **not** do if you want the dog's ball?

   _____

3. What could you hold out for the dog to take?

   _____

# Comprehension: How to Meet a Dog

**Directions:** Read about how to meet a dog. Then follow the instructions.

Do not try to pet a dog right away. First, let the dog sniff your hand. Do not move quickly. Do not talk loudly. Just let the dog sniff.

1. Predict what the dog will let you do if it likes you.

_____

_____

2. What should you let the dog do?_____

_____

3. Name three things you should not do when you meet a dog.

1)_____

2)_____

3)_____

Name: _____

# Comprehension: Dirty Dogs

**Directions:** Read about dogs. Then answer the questions.

Like people, dogs get dirty. Some dogs get a bath once a month. Baby soap is a good soap for cleaning dogs. Fill a tub with warm water. Get someone to hold the dog still in the tub. Then wash the dog fast.

1. How often do some dogs get a bath? _____

_____

2. What is a good soap to use on dogs? _____

3. Do you think most dogs like to take baths? _____

# Comprehension: Pretty Parrots

**Directions:** Read about parrots. Then follow the instructions.

Big parrots are pretty. Their feet have four toes each. Two toes are in front. Two toes are in back. Parrots use their feet to climb. They use them to hold food.

1. (Circle the correct answer.)
   A parrot's foot has

   four toes.

   two toes.

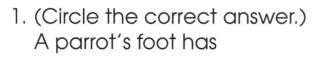

2. Name two things a parrot does with its feet.

   1) _____

   _____

   2) _____

   _____

3. Color the parrot.

# Comprehension: A Winter Story

**Directions:** Read about winter. Then follow the instructions.

It is cold in winter. Snow falls. Water freezes. Most kids like to play outdoors. Some kids make a snowman. Some kids skate. What do you do in winter?

1. Circle the main idea:

   Snow falls in winter.

   In winter, there are many things to do outside.

2. Write two things about winter weather.

   1) _____

   2) _____

3. Write what you like to do in winter.

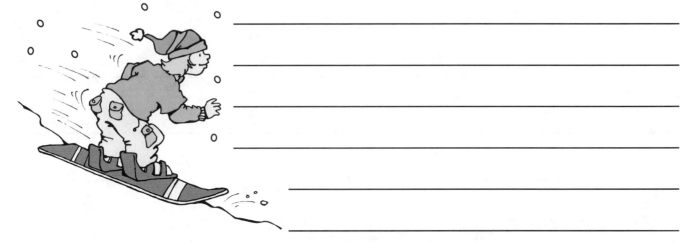

# Comprehension: The Puppet Play

**Directions:** Read the play out loud with a friend. Then answer the questions.

**Pip:** Hey, Pep. What kind of turkey eats very fast?

**Pep:** Uh, I don't know.

**Pip:** A gobbler!

**Pep:** I have a good joke for you, Pip. What kind of burger does a polar bear eat?

**Pip:** Uh, a cold burger?

**Pep:** No, an iceberg-er!

**Pip:** Hey, that was a great joke!

1. Who are the characters in the play? _____

_____

2. Who are the jokes about? _____

_____

3. What are the characters in the play doing? _____

_____

# Comprehension: Just Junk?

**Directions:** Read about saving things. Then follow the instructions.

Do you save old crayons? Do you save old buttons or cards? Some people call these things junk. They throw them out. Leah saves these things. She likes to use them for art projects. She puts them in a box. What do you do?

1. Circle the main idea:

   Everyone has junk.

   People have different ideas about what junk is.

2. Name two kinds of junk.

   1) _____

   2) _____

3. What are two things you can do with old things?

   1) _____

   2) _____

# Comprehension: Snakes!

**Directions:** Read about snakes. Then answer the questions.

There are many facts about snakes that might surprise someone. A snake's skin is dry. Most snakes are shy. They will hide from people. Snakes eat mice and rats. They do not chew them up. Snakes' jaws drop open to swallow their food whole.

1. How does a snake's skin feel? _____

2. Most snakes are _____.

3. What do snakes eat?

    a. _____

    b. _____

# Comprehension: More About Snakes!

**Directions:** Read more about snakes. Then follow the instructions.

Unlike people, snakes have cold blood. They like to be warm. They hunt for food when it is warm. They lie in the sun. When it is cold, snakes curl up into a ball.

1. What do snakes do when it is warm?

   a. _____

   b. _____

2. Why do you think snakes curl up when it is cold?_____

   _____

3. (Circle the correct answer.)
   People have:

   cold blood.                warm blood.

# Comprehension: Sean's Basketball Game

**Directions:** Read about Sean's basketball game. Then answer the questions.

Sean really likes to play basketball. One sunny day, he decided to ask his friends to play basketball at the park, but there were six people—Sean, Aki, Lance, Kate, Zac and Oralia. A basketball team only allows five to play at a time. So, Sean decided to be the coach. Sean and his friends had fun.

1. How many kids wanted to play basketball? _____

2. Write their names in ABC order:

_____     _____     _____

_____     _____     _____

3. How many players can play on a basketball team

at a time? _____

4. Where did they play basketball? _____

5. Who decided to be the coach? _____

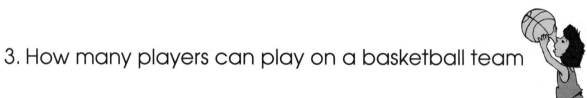

Name: _____

# Comprehension: Outdoor/Indoor Games

**Directions:** Read the story. Then answer the questions.

Derrick likes to play outdoor and indoor games. His favorite outdoor game is baseball because he likes to hit the ball with the bat and run around the bases. He plays this game in the park with the neighborhood kids.

When it rains, he plays checkers with Lorenzo on the dining-room table in his apartment. He likes the game, because he has to use his brain to think about his next move, and the rules are easy to follow.

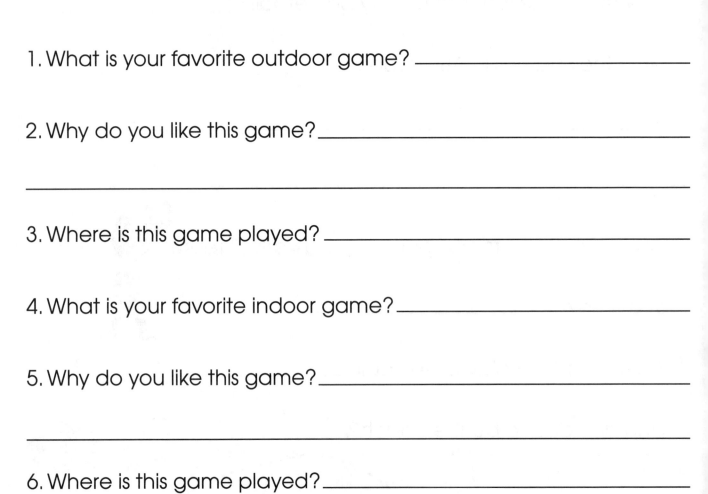

1. What is your favorite outdoor game? _____

2. Why do you like this game? _____

_____

3. Where is this game played? _____

4. What is your favorite indoor game? _____

5. Why do you like this game? _____

_____

6. Where is this game played? _____

# Reading Comprehension

**Directions:** Read the story. Then complete the sentences with words from the story.

Mike lives on a farm. There are many animals on the farm: birds, cows, pigs, goats and chickens. But Mike likes his horse the best. His horse's name is Stormy. Stormy stays in a barn. For fun, Mike rides Stormy to the lake. Stormy helps Mike, too. Stormy pulls a cart to carry weeds from the garden. After a hard day, Mike feeds Stormy corn and hay. For a treat, Stormy gets a pear.

1. Mike lives on a _____.
2. His favorite animal is a _____.
3. The horse's name is _____.
4. Stormy stays in a _____.
5. It is fun to ride to the _____.
6. Stormy eats _____ and _____.
7. Stormy's treat is a _____.

Write 5 words from the story that have an **r-controlled vowel**.

_____    _____    _____

_____    _____

Now, write 5 words from the story that have a **long vowel sound**.

_____    _____    _____

_____    _____

Name: _____

# Comprehension: Ant Farms

**Directions:** Read about ant farms. Then answer the questions.

Ant farms are sold at toy stores and pet stores. Ant farms come in a flat frame. The frame has glass on each side. Inside the glass is sand. The ants live in the sand.

1. Where are ant farms sold?_____

2. The frame has _____ on each side.

Circle the correct answer.

3. The ants live in

    water.          sand.

4. The ant farm frame is

    flat.              round.

Name: _____

# Comprehension: Amazing Ants

**Directions:** Read about ants. Then answer the questions.

Ants are insects. Ants live in many parts of the world and make their homes in soil, sand, wood and leaves. Most ants live for about 6 to 10 weeks. But the queen ant, who lays the eggs, can live for up to 15 years!

The largest ant is the bulldog ant. This ant can grow to be 5 inches long, and it eats meat! The bulldog ant can be found in Australia.

1. Where do ants make their homes? _____

_____

2. How long can a queen ant live? _____

_____

3. What is the largest ant? _____

4. What does it eat? _____

Name: _____

# Comprehension: Sharks Are Fish, Too!

**Directions:** Read the story. Then follow the instructions.

Angela learned a lot about sharks when her class visited the city aquarium. She learned that sharks are fish. Some sharks are as big as an elephant, and some can fit into a small paper bag. Sharks have no bones. They have hundreds of teeth, and when they lose them, they grow new ones. They eat animals of any kind. Whale sharks are the largest of all fish.

1. Circle the main idea:

   Angela learned a lot about sharks at the aquarium.

   Some sharks are as big as elephants.

2. When sharks lose teeth, they _____

   _____ .

3. _____ are the largest of all fish.

4. Sharks have bones. (Circle the answer.)

   Yes                         No

# Comprehension: Fish

**Directions:** Read about fish. Then follow the instructions.

Some fish live in warm water. Some live in cold water. Some fish live in lakes. Some fish live in oceans. There are 20,000 kinds of fish!

1. Name two types of water in which fish live.

   a. _____

   b. _____

2. Name another place fish live _____

   Some fish live in lakes and some live in _____ .

3. There are _____ kinds
   of fish.

Name: _____

# Comprehension: Fish Come in Many Colors

**Directions:** Read about the color of fish. Then follow the instructions.

All fish live in water. Fish that live at the top are blue, green or black. Fish that live down deep are silver or red. The colors make it hard to see the fish.

1. List the colors of fish at the top.

_____     _____     _____

2. List the two colors of fish that live down deep.

_____     _____

3. Color the top fish and the bottom fish the correct colors.

# Comprehension: Fish Can Protect Themselves

**Directions:** Read about two fish. Then follow the instructions.

Most fish have ways to protect themselves from danger. Two of these fish are the trigger fish and the porcupine fish. The trigger fish lives on the ocean reef. When it sees danger, it swims into its private hole and puts its top fin up and squeezes itself in tight. Then it cannot be taken from its hiding place. The porcupine fish also lives on the ocean reef. When danger comes, it puffs up like a balloon by swallowing air or water. When it puffs up, poisonous spikes stand out on its body. When danger is past, it deflates its body.

1. Circle the main idea:

   Trigger fish and procupine fish can be dangerous.

   Some fish have ways to protect themselves from danger.

2. Trigger fish and porcupine fish live on the _____.

3. The porcupine fish puffs up by swallowing _____

   or _____ .

# Comprehension: Ideas Come From Books

**Directions:** Read the story. Then follow the instructions.

Tonda has many books. She gets different ideas from these books. Some of her books are about fish. Some are about cardboard and paper crafts. Some are about nature. Others are about reusing junk. Tonda wants to make a paper airplane. She reads about it in one of her books. Then she asks an adult to help her.

1. Circle the main idea:

   Tonda learns about different ideas from books.

   Tonda likes crafts.

2. (Circle the correct answer.) Tonda is:

   a person who likes to read.

   a person who doesn't like books.

3. What does Tonda want to make from paper?_____

   _____

4. Write two ways to learn how to do something.

   1) _____

   2) _____

Name: _____

# Predicting: A Rainy Game

**Predicting** is telling what is likely to happen based on the facts.

**Directions:** Read the story. Then check each sentence below that tells how the story could end.

One cloudy day, Juan and his baseball team, the Bears, played the Crocodiles. It was the last half of the fifth inning, and it started to rain. The coaches and umpires had to decide what to do.

_____ They kept playing until nine innings were finished.

_____ They ran for cover and waited until the rain stopped.

_____ Each player grabbed an umbrella and returned to the field to finish the game.

_____ They canceled the game and played it another day.

_____ They acted like crocodiles and slid around the wet bases.

_____ The coaches played the game while the players sat in the dugout.

**Grade 2 - Comprehensive Curriculum**

Name: _____

# Predicting: Oops!

**Directions:** Look at the pictures on the left. On the right, draw and write what you predict will happen next.

_____
_____
_____
_____
_____

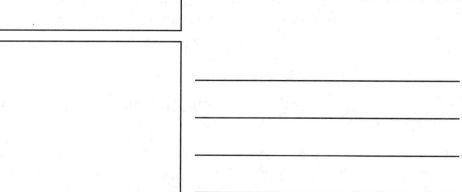

_____
_____
_____
_____

_____
_____
_____
_____
_____

# Predicting: Dog Derby

**Directions:** Read the story. Then answer the questions.

Marcy had a great idea for a game to play with her dogs, Marvin and Mugsy. The game was called "Dog Derby." Marcy would stand at one end of the driveway and hold on to the dogs by their collars. Her friend Mitch would stand at the other end of the driveway. When he said, "Go!" Marcy would let go of the dogs and they would race to Mitch. The first one there would get a dog biscuit. If there was a tie, both dogs would get a biscuit.

1. Who do you think will win the race?

_____

Why? _____

_____

2. What do you think will happen when they race again?

_____

_____

# Predicting: What Will Bobby Do?

**Directions:** Read about Bobby the cat. Then write what you think will happen.

One sunny spring day, Bobby was sleeping under her favorite tree. She was dreaming about her favorite food—tuna. Suddenly she became hungry for a treat. Bobby woke up and listened when she heard someone call her name.

1. Why do you think Bobby was being called? _____

_____

2. What do you think will happen next? _____

_____

_____

# Predicting: Dog-Gone!

**Directions:** Read the story. Then follow the instructions.

Scotty and Simone were washing their dog, Willis. His fur was wet. Their hands were wet. Willis did NOT like to be wet. Scotty dropped the soap. Simone picked it up and let go of Willis. Uh-oh!

1. Write what happened next.

_____

_____

_____

2. Draw what happened next.

# Predicting Outcome

**Directions:** Read the story. Complete the story in the last box.

1. A cat is playing with a ball of yarn.

2. A mouse peeks around the corner.

3. The mouse tiptoes past the playful cat.

4. _____
   _____
   _____

Name: _____

# Predicting Outcome

**Directions:** Read the story. Complete the story in the last box.

1. "Look at that elephant! He sure is big!"

2. "I'm hungry." "I bet that elephant is, too."

3. "Stop, Amy! Look at that sign!"

4. _____
_____
_____

# Predicting Outcome

**Directions:** Read the story. In the last box, draw what you think will happen next. Then write the words for the end of the story.

1. Do you want to go to the library with me?"
   "Yes, I want a book about seashells."

3. "Excuse me. Where can I find a book about seashells?"

2. "Have you found your book?"
   "No. I can't find it."
   "Why don't you ask someone?"

4. _____

_____

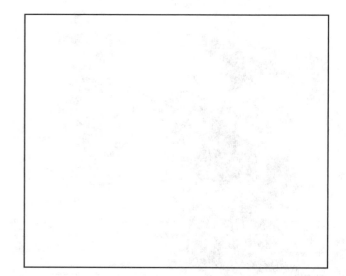

# Predicting Outcomes

**Directions:** Complete the story. Then draw pictures to match the four parts.

1. Sylvia and Marge are flying a kite.

3. _____
_____

Beginning

Middle

2. The kite gets stuck in a tree.

4. _____
_____

Middle

End

**Grade 2 - Comprehensive Curriculum**

# Predicting Outcome

**Directions:** Create your own story in the squares. Show the beginning in box 1, the middle in boxes 2 and 3 and the end in box 4.

Beginning (Setting)          Middle (Problem)

| 1. | 3. |
|---|---|
| 2. | 4. |

Middle (Problem)          End (Solution)

Name: _____

# Predicting Outcome

Kelly and Gina always have fun at the fair.

**Directions:** Read the sentences.
Write what you think will happen next.

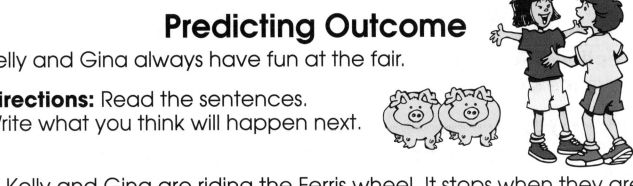

1. Kelly and Gina are riding the Ferris wheel. It stops when they are at the top.

   _____

   _____

   _____

2. As they walk into the animal barn, a little piglet runs towards them.

   _____

   _____

   _____

3. Snow cones are their favorite way to cool off. The ones they bought are made from real snow.

   _____

   _____

   _____

4. They play a "toss the ring over the bottle" game, but when the ring goes around the bottle, it disappears.

   _____

   _____

   _____

**Grade 2 - Comprehensive Curriculum**

# Predicting: Puff and Trigg

**Directions:** Read about Puff and Trigg. Then write what happens next in the story.

It was a sunny, warm day in the Pacific Ocean. Puff, the happy porcupine fish, and Trigg, the jolly trigger fish, were having fun playing fish tag. They were good friends. Suddenly, they saw the shadow of a giant fish! It was coming right at them! They knew the giant fish might like eating smaller fish! What did they do?

What did Puff and Trigg do to get away from the giant fish?

_____

_____

_____

_____

_____

# Fact and Opinion: Games!

A **fact** is something that can be proven. An **opinion** is a feeling or belief about something and cannot be proven.

**Directions:** Read these sentences about different games. Then write **F** next to each fact and **O** next to each opinion.

_____ 1. Tennis is cool!

_____ 2. There are red and black markers in a Checkers game.

_____ 3. In football, a touchdown is worth six points.

_____ 4. Being a goalie in soccer is easy.

_____ 5. A yo-yo moves on a string.

_____ 6. June's sister looks like the queen on the card.

_____ 7. The six kids need three more players for a baseball team.

_____ 8. Table tennis is more fun than court tennis.

_____ 9. Hide-and-Seek is a game that can be played outdoors or indoors.

_____ 10. Play money is used in many board games.

# Fact and Opinion: Recycling

**Directions:** Read about recycling. Then follow the instructions.

What do you throw away every day? What could you do with these things? You could change an old greeting card into a new card. You could make a puppet with an old paper bag. Old buttons make great refrigerator magnets. You can plant seeds in plastic cups. Cardboard tubes make perfect rockets. So, use your imagination!

1. Write **F** next to each fact and **O** next to each opinion.

_____ Cardboard tubes are ugly.

_____ Buttons can be made into refrigerator magnets.

_____ An old greeting card can be changed into a new card.

_____ Paper-bag puppets are cute.

_____ Seeds can be planted in plastic cups.

_____ Rockets can be made from cardboard tubes.

2. What could you do with a cardboard tube? _____

_____

Name: _____

# Fact and Opinion: An Owl Story

**Directions:** Read the story. Then follow the instructions.

My name is Owen Owl, and I am a bird. I go to Nocturnal School. Our teacher is Mr. Screech Owl. In his class I learned that owls are birds and can sleep all day and hunt at night. Some of us live in nests in trees. In North America, it is against the law to harm owls. I like being an owl!

Write **F** next to each fact and **O** next to each opinion.

_____ 1. No one can harm owls in North America.

_____ 2. It would be great if owls could talk.

_____ 3. Owls sleep all day.

_____ 4. Some owls sleep in nests.

_____ 5. Mr. Screech Owl is a good teacher.

_____ 6. Owls are birds.

_____ 7. Owen Owl would be a good friend.

_____ 8. Owls hunt at night.

_____ 9. Nocturnal School is a good school for smart owls.

_____ 10. This story is for the birds.

Name: _____

# Fact and Opinion: A Bounty of Birds

**Directions:** Read the story. Then follow the instructions.

Tashi's family likes to go to the zoo. Her favorite animals are all the different kinds of birds. Tashi likes birds because they can fly, they have colorful feathers and they make funny noises.

Write **F** next to each fact and **O** next to each opinion.

_____ 1. Birds have two feet.

_____ 2. All birds lay eggs.

_____ 3. Parrots are too noisy.

_____ 4. All birds have feathers and wings.

_____ 5. It would be great to be a bird and fly south for the winter.

_____ 6. Birds have hard beaks or bills instead of teeth.

_____ 7. Pigeons are fun to watch.

_____ 8. Some birds cannot fly.

_____ 9. Parakeets make good pets.

_____ 10. A penguin is a bird.

Name: _____

# Fact and Opinion: Henrietta the Humpback

**Directions:** Read the story. Then follow the instructions.

My name is Henrietta, and I am a humpback whale. I live in cold seas in the summer and warm seas in the winter. My long flippers are used to move forward and backward. I like to eat fish. Sometimes, I show off by leaping out of the water. Would you like to be a humpback whale?

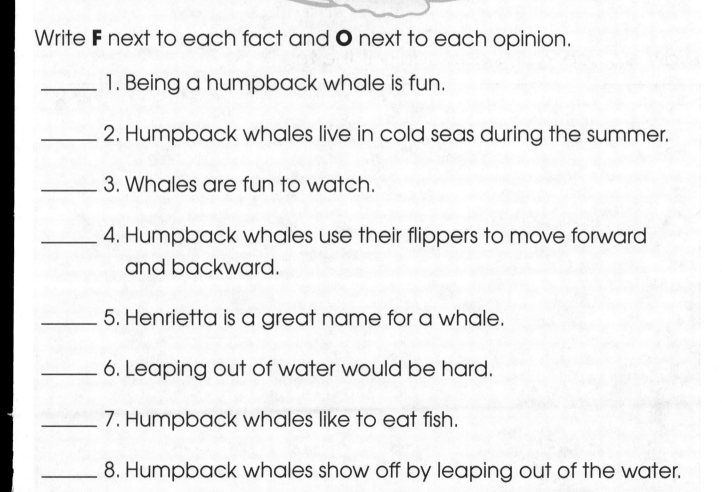

Write **F** next to each fact and **O** next to each opinion.

_____ 1. Being a humpback whale is fun.

_____ 2. Humpback whales live in cold seas during the summer.

_____ 3. Whales are fun to watch.

_____ 4. Humpback whales use their flippers to move forward and backward.

_____ 5. Henrietta is a great name for a whale.

_____ 6. Leaping out of water would be hard.

_____ 7. Humpback whales like to eat fish.

_____ 8. Humpback whales show off by leaping out of the water.

# Making Inferences: Ryan's Top

**Directions:** Read about Ryan's top. Then follow the instructions.

Ryan got a new top. He wanted to place it where it would be safe. He asked his dad to put it up high. Where can his dad put the top?

1. Write where Ryan's dad can put the top. _____

_____

Draw a place Ryan's dad can put the top.

Name: _____

# Making Inferences: Down on the Ant Farm

**Directions:** Read about ant farms. Then answer the questions.

Ants are busy on the farm. They dig in the sand. They make roads in the sand. They look for food in the sand. When an ant dies, other ants bury it.

1. Where do you think ants are buried? _____

_____

2. Is it fair to say ants are lazy? _____

3. Write a word that tells about ants. _____

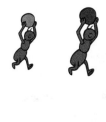

**Grade 2 - Comprehensive Curriculum**

# Inferences: Monty's Trip

**Directions:** Read Monty's answer. Then circle the answer to each question. Color the pictures.

Monty says, "I want to learn more about big cats. Someday, I would like to be an animal trainer or a zoo director. Where can we learn about big cats?"

1. What cat does Monty want to learn about?

2. Where should he go?

Name: _____

# Making Inferences

**Directions:** Read the story. Then answer the questions.

Jeff is baking cookies. He wears special clothes when he bakes. He puts flour, sugar, eggs and butter into a bowl. He mixes everything together. He puts the cookies in the oven at 11:15 A.M. It takes 15 minutes for the cookies to bake. Jeff wants something cold and white to drink when he eats his cookies.

1. Is Jeff baking a cake?      Yes  No

2. What are two things Jeff might wear when he bakes?
   hat      boots      apron      tie      raincoat      roller skates

3. What didn't Jeff put in the cookies?
   flour            eggs            milk            butter            sugar

4. What do you think Jeff does after he mixes the cookies but before he bakes them?_____

   _____

   _____

5. What time will the cookies be done? _____

6. What will Jeff drink with his cookies? _____

7. Why do you think Jeff wanted to bake cookies? _____

   _____

   _____

# Making Inferences

**Directions:** Read the story. Then answer the questions.

Shawn and his family are on a trip. It is very sunny. Shawn loves to swim. He also likes the waves. There is something else he likes even more. Shawn builds drip castles. He makes drips by using very wet sand. He lets it drip out of his hand into a tall pile. He makes the drip piles as high as he can.

1. Where is Shawn? _____

2. What does Shawn wear on his trip? _____

3. Is Shawn hot or cold? _____

4. What does Shawn like to do best? _____

5. What are drip castles made from? _____

6. What do you think happens when drip castles get too big?

_____

7. If Shawn gets too hot, what do you think he will do?

_____

Name: _____

# Making Inferences

**Directions:** Read the story. Then answer the questions.

Mrs. Sweet looked forward to a visit from her niece, Candy. In the morning, she cleaned her house. She also baked a cherry pie. An hour before Candy was to arrive, the phone rang. Mrs. Sweet said, "I understand." When she hung up the phone, she looked very sad.

1. Who do you think called Mrs. Sweet?

_____

_____

2. How do you know that?

_____

_____

3. Why is Mrs. Sweet sad?

_____

_____

# Making Inferences: Sea Horses

**Directions:** Read more about sea horses. Then answer the questions

A father sea horse helps the mother. He has a small sack, or pouch, on the front of his body. The mother sea horse lays the eggs. She does not keep them. She gives the eggs to the father.

1. What does the mother sea horse do with her eggs?

_____

2. Where does the father sea horse put the eggs?

_____

3. Sea horses can change color. Color the sea horses.

# Making Inferences: Using Pictures

**Directions:** Draw a picture for each idea. Then write two sentences that tell about it.

You and a friend are playing your favorite game.

_____

_____

You and a friend are sharing your favorite food.

_____

_____

# Making Inferences: Visualizing

**Directions:** Read this story about Ling and Bradley. Draw pictures for the beginning and middle to describe each part of the story.

**Beginning:** One sunny day, Ling and Bradley, wearing their empty backpacks, rode their bikes down the street to the park.

**Middle:** They stopped by an oak tree with many acorns under it. They picked up some and stuffed them into their backpacks.

**Directions:** Draw an ending for this story that tells what you think they did with the acorns.

**End:** With the heavy backpacks strapped on their backs, they pedaled home.

# Making Inferences: Visualizing

**Directions:** Read the story about Melinda. Then draw pictures that describe each part of the story.

**Beginning:** It was Halloween. Melinda's costume was a black cat with super-duper, polka-dot sunglasses.

**Middle:** Her little brown dog, Marco, yelped and ran under a big red chair when he saw her come into the room.

**End:** Melinda took off her black cat mask and sunglasses. Then she held out a dog biscuit. She picked Marco up and hugged him. Then he was happy.

# Making Inferences: Visualizing

**Directions:** Read the story about Chad and Leon. Then draw pictures that describe each part of the story.

**Beginning:** One chilly morning, Chad and Leon rolled two big snowballs to make a snowman in Chad's front yard.

**Middle:** Chad put his big snowball on top of the bigger one. Leon added a carrot nose, two charcoal eyes, a stick mouth and a cowboy hat. Then they went into the house.

**End:** Later, when they looked out the window, they saw the snowman dancing around. "Thank you!" he shouted to the boys.

Name: _____

# Making Inferences: Point of View

Juniper has three problems to solve. She needs your help.

**Directions:** Read each problem. Write what you think she should do.

1. Juniper is watching her favorite TV show when the power goes out.

_____

_____

_____

_____

2. Juniper is riding her bike to school when the front tire goes flat.

_____

_____

_____

_____

3. Juniper loses her father while shopping in the supermarket.

_____

_____

_____

_____

# Making Inferences: Point of View

Toran also has three problems. Now that you have helped Juniper, he would like you to help him, too.

**Directions:** Read each problem. Write what you think he should do.

1. The class is having a picnic, and Toran left his lunch at home.

_____

_____

_____

2. Toran wants to buy a special video game, but he needs three more dollars.

_____

_____

_____

3. Toran's best friend, Felix, made the third out, and their team lost the kickball game.

_____

_____

_____

Name: _____

# Making Inferences: Sequencing

**Directions:** Draw three pictures to tell a story about each topic.

1. Feeding a pet

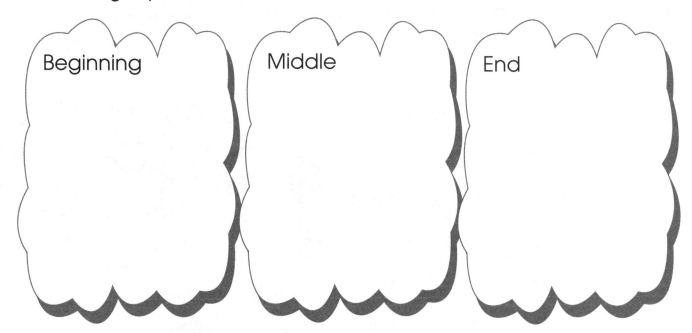

Beginning        Middle        End

2. Playing with a friend

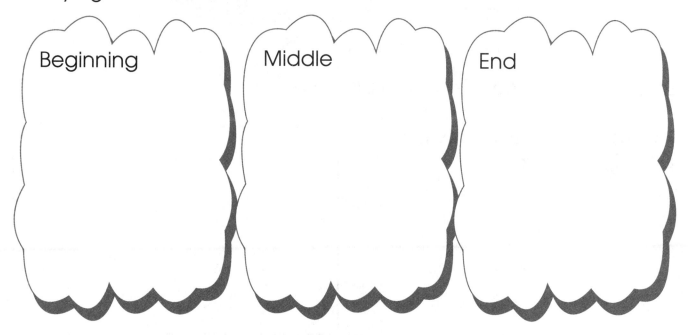

Beginning        Middle        End

# Making Inferences: Sequencing

Help make a "doggie pizza" for Spotty Dog. The steps to follow are all mixed-up. Three of the steps are not needed.

**Directions:** Number the steps in order from 1 to 7. Draw a dog bone by the 3 steps that are not needed.

_____ Place the dough on a round pan.

_____ Cover the top with cheese.

_____ Take a nap.

_____ Make the pizza dough.

_____ Run out the door.

_____ Bake it in a hot oven.

_____ Roll the dough out flat.

_____ Play ball with Spotty.

_____ Spread the sauce on the dough.

_____ Sprinkle bits of dog biscuits on top.

**Directions:** Draw Spotty Dog's pizza in the box.

# Making Deductions: Find the Books

**Directions:** Use the clues to help the children find their books. Draw a line from each child's name to the correct book.

Brett     Aki     Lorenzo     Kate     Zac     Oralia

| CHILDREN | BOOKS |
|----------|-------|
| Brett | jokes |
| Aki | cakes |
| Lorenzo | monsters |
| Kate | games |
| Zac | flags |
| Oralia | space |

## Clues

1. Lorenzo likes jokes.

2. Kate likes to bake.

3. Oralia likes far away places.

4. Aki does not like monsters or flags.

5. Zac does not like space or monsters.

6. Brett does not like games, jokes or cakes.

Name: _____

# Making Deductions: Travel

Six children from the same neighborhood each travel to school in a different way. Can you find out how each one gets to school?

**Directions:** Read the clues. Draw a dot to show how each child travels to school. Draw **X**'s on the remaining boxes.

|  | Brian | Gina | Lawrence | Luna | Taylor | Marianna |
|---|---|---|---|---|---|---|
| car |  |  |  |  |  |  |
| bus |  |  |  |  |  |  |
| walk |  |  |  |  |  |  |
| bicycle |  |  |  |  |  |  |
| truck |  |  |  |  |  |  |
| van |  |  |  |  |  |  |

## Clues:

1. Lawrence likes to walk to school.
2. Taylor hates to walk, so his mother takes him in a car.
3. Luna lives next door to Lawrence and waves to Gina as Gina goes by in a pickup truck.
4. Brian joins his pals on the bus.
5. Gina's friend, who lives next door to Lawrence, rides a bike to school.
6. Marianna likes to sit in the middle seat while riding to school.

# Making Deductions: Sports

Children all over the world like to play sports. They like many different kinds of sports: football, soccer, basketball, softball, in-line skating, swimming and more.

**Directions:** Read the clues. Draw dots and **X**'s on the chart to match the children with their sports.

|  | swimming | football | soccer | basketball | baseball | in-line skating |
|---|---|---|---|---|---|---|
| J.J. | | | | | | |
| Zoe | | | | | | |
| Andy | | | | | | |
| Amber | | | | | | |
| Raul | | | | | | |
| Sierra | | | | | | |

## Clues

1. Zoe hates football.
2. Andy likes basketball.
3. Raul likes to pitch in his favorite sport.
4. J.J. likes to play what Zoe hates.
5. Amber is good at kicking the ball to her teammates.
6. Sierra needs a pool for her favorite sport.

# Making Deductions: What Day Is It?

Dad is cooking dinner tonight. You can find out what day of the week it is.

**Directions:** Read the clues. Complete the menu. Answer the question.

## Menu

Monday _____

Tuesday _____

Wednesday _____

Thursday _____

Friday _____

Saturday _____

Sunday _____

1. Mom fixed pizza on Monday.
2. Dad fixed cheese rolls the day before that.
3. Tess made meat pie three days after Mom fixed pizza.
4. Tom fixed corn-on-the-cob the day before Tess made meat pie.
5. Mom fixed hot dogs the day after Tess made meat pie.
6. Tess cooked fish the day before Dad fixed cheese rolls.
7. Dad is making chicken today. What day is it? _____

Name: _____

# Review

**Directions:** Read the story. Then answer the questions.

Randa, Emily, Ali, Dave, Liesl and Deana all love to read. Every Tuesday, they all go to the library together and pick out their favorite books. Randa likes books about fish. Emily likes books about sports and athletes. Ali likes books about art. Dave likes books about wild animals. Liesl likes books with riddles and puzzles. Deanna likes books about cats and dogs.

1. Circle the main idea:

   Randa, Emily, Ali, Dave, Liesl and Deana are good friends.

   Randa, Emily, Ali, Dave, Liesl and Deana all like books.

2. Who do you think might grow up to be an artist?

   _____

3. Who do you think might grow up to be an oceanographer (someone who studies the ocean)?

   _____

4. Who do you think might grow up to be a veterinarian (an animal doctor)?

   _____

5. Who do you think might grow up to be a zookeeper (someone who cares for zoo animals)?

   _____

# Fiction/Nonfiction: Heavy Hitters

**Fiction** is a make-believe story. **Nonfiction** is a true story.

**Directions:** Read the stories about two famous baseball players. Then write **fiction** or **nonfiction** in the baseball bats.

In 1998, Mark McGwire played for the St. Louis Cardinals. He liked to hit home runs. On September 27, 1998, he hit home run number 70, to set a new record for the most home runs hit in one season. The old record was set in 1961 by Roger Maris, who later played for the St. Louis Cardinals (1967 to 1968), when he hit 61 home runs.

The Mighty Casey played baseball for the Mudville Nine and was the greatest of all baseball players. He could hit the cover off the ball with the power of a hurricane. But, when the Mudville Nine was behind 4 to 2 in the championship game, Mighty Casey struck out with the bases loaded. There was no joy in Mudville that day, because the Mudville Nine had lost the game.

Name: _____

# Nonfiction: Tornado Tips

**Directions:** Read about tornadoes. Then follow the instructions.

A tornado begins over land with strong winds and thunderstorms. The spinning air becomes a funnel. It can cause damage. If you are inside, go to the lowest floor of the building. A basement is a safe place. A bathroom or closet in the middle of a building can be a safe place, too. If you are outside, lie in a ditch. Remember, tornadoes are dangerous.

Write five facts about tornadoes.

1. _____

   _____

2. _____

   _____

3. _____

   _____

4. _____

   _____

5. _____

   _____

# Fiction: Hercules

The setting is where a story takes place. The characters are the people in a story or play.

**Directions:** Read about Hercules. Then answer the questions.

Hercules was born in the warm Atlantic Ocean. He was a very small and weak baby. He wanted to be the strongest hurricane in the world. But he had one problem. He couldn't blow 75-mile-per-hour winds. Hercules blew and blew in the ocean, until one day, his sister, Hola, told him it would be more fun to be a breeze than a hurricane. Hercules agreed. It was a breeze to be a breeze!

1. What is the setting of the story? _____

2. Who are the characters? _____

3. What is the problem? _____

4. How does Hercules solve his problem? _____

_____

# Fiction/Nonfiction: The Fourth of July

**Directions:** Read each story. Then write whether it is fiction or nonfiction.

One sunny day in July, a dog named Stan ran away from home. He went up one street and down the other looking for fun, but all the yards were empty. Where was everybody? Stan kept walking until he heard the sound of band music and happy people. Stan

 walked faster until he got to Central Street. There he saw men, women, children and dogs getting ready to walk in a parade. It was the Fourth of July!

Fiction or Nonfiction?_____

Americans celebrate the Fourth of July every year, because it is the birthday of the United States of America. On July 4, 1776, the United States got its independence from Great Britain. Today, Americans celebrate this holiday with parades, picnics and fireworks as they proudly wave the red, white and blue American flag.

Fiction or Nonfiction?_____

**Grade 2 - Comprehensive Curriculum**

# Fiction and Nonfiction: Which Is It?

**Directions:** Read about fiction and nonfiction books. Then follow the instructions.

There are many kinds of books. Some books have make-believe stories about princesses and dragons. Some books contain poetry and rhymes, like Mother Goose. These are fiction.

Some books contain facts about space and plants. And still other books have stories about famous people in history like Abraham Lincoln. These are nonfiction.

Write **F** for fiction and **NF** for nonfiction.

_____ 1. nursery rhyme

_____ 2. fairy tale

_____ 3. true life story of a famous athlete

_____ 4. Aesop's fables

_____ 5. dictionary entry about foxes

_____ 6. weather report

_____ 7. story about a talking tree

_____ 8. story about how a tadpole becomes a frog

_____ 9. story about animal habitats

_____ 10. riddles and jokes

# Writing: My Snake Story

**Directions:** Write a fictional (make-believe) story about a snake. Make sure to include details and a title.

_____ 
title

_____

_____

_____

_____

_____

_____

_____

_____

_____

# Review: All About You!

In this book you learned about many children and what they like to do. You have many interests, too!

**Directions:** Write a story telling what you like to do. Then draw a picture to go with your story on another sheet of paper.

_____

_____

_____

_____

_____

_____

_____

_____

_____

_____

_____

Name: _____

# ABC Order

**Directions:** Put the words in ABC order on the bags.

grapes _____

bread _____

soup _____

apples _____

napkins _____

rolls _____

ice cream _____

pizza _____

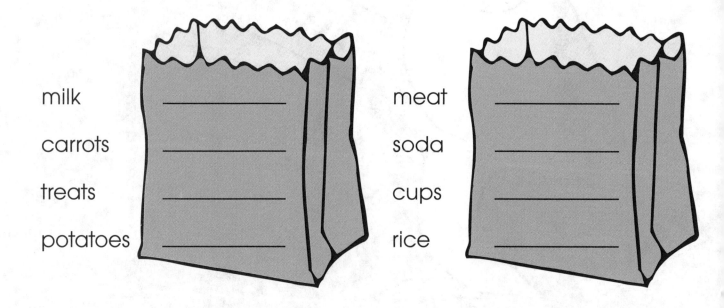

milk _____

carrots _____

treats _____

potatoes _____

meat _____

soda _____

cups _____

rice _____

# Alphabetical Order

**Directions:** Cut out the scoops of ice cream on the bottom. Place them on the correct cone in the correct alphabetical order.

cut ✂ - - - - - - - - - - - - - - - - - - - - - - - - - - - - - - - - - - - - - - - - - - - - -

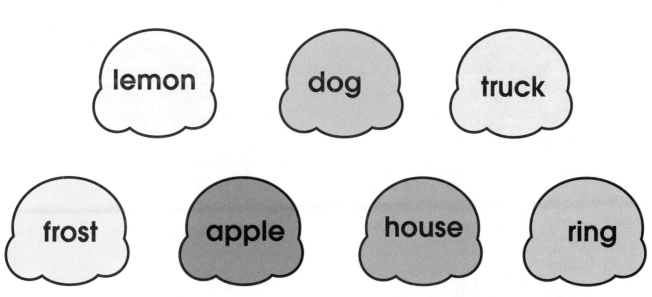

Page is blank for cutting exercise on previous page.

Name: _____

# ABC Order

**Directions:** Write these words in order. If two words start with the same letter, look at the second letter in each word.

**Example:** **lamb**      Lamb comes first because **a** comes before **i**
        **light**      in the alphabet.

tree      _____

branch      _____

leaf      _____

dish      _____

dog      _____

bone      _____

rain      _____

umbrella _____

cloud      _____

mail      _____

stamp      _____

slot      _____

**Grade 2 - Comprehensive Curriculum**

# Sequencing: ABC Order

**Directions:** Write 1, 2, 3 or 4 on the lines in each row to put the words in ABC order.

**Example:**

1. __1__ bell     __4__ well     __2__ smell     __3__ tell

2. _____ bite     _____ kite     _____ write     _____ might

3. _____ tar      _____ car      _____ far       _____ bar

4. _____ sand     _____ land     _____ band      _____ fanned

5. _____ sweet    _____ meat     _____ eat       _____ treat

6. _____ hair     _____ pear     _____ tear      _____ wear

7. _____ lake     _____ bake     _____ rake      _____ take

8. _____ round    _____ sound    _____ pound     _____ found

Name: _____

# Sequencing: ABC Order

If the first letters of two words are the same, look at the second letters in both words. If the second letters are the same, look at the third letters.

**Directions:** Write 1, 2, 3 or 4 on the lines in each row to put the words in ABC order.

**Example:**

1. __1__ candy    __2__ carrot    __4__ duck    __3__ dance

2. _____ cold    _____ hot    _____ carry    _____ hit

3. _____ flash    _____ fan    _____ fun    _____ garden

4. _____ seat    _____ sun    _____ saw    _____ sit

5. _____ row    _____ ring    _____ rock    _____ run

6. _____ truck    _____ turn    _____ twin    _____ talk

7. _____ seven    _____ shoe    _____ soup    _____ smell

# Sequencing: ABC Order

**Directions:** Write the following names in ABC order: Oscar, Ali, Lance, Kim, Zane and Bonita.

**Directions:** Write the names of six of your friends or family in ABC order.

# Sequencing: ABC Order

Kwan likes to make rhymes. Help Kwan think of rhyming words.

**Directions:** Write three words in ABC order that rhyme with each word Kwan wrote.

cap                    bet                    bill

_____            _____            _____

_____            _____            _____

_____            _____            _____

dog                    man                    hat

_____            _____            _____

_____            _____            _____

_____            _____            _____

**Directions:** Write a short poem using some of the rhyming words you wrote.

_____

_____

_____

_____

Name: _____

# Synonyms

Words that mean the same or nearly the same are called **synonyms**

**Directions:** Read the sentence that tells about the picture. Draw a circle around the word that means the same as the **bold** word.

The child is **unhappy**.

sad                    hungry

The flowers are **lovely**.

pretty                    green

The baby was very **tired**.

sleepy                    hurt

The **funny** clown made us laugh.

silly                    glad

The ladybug is so **tiny**.

small                    red

We saw a **scary** tiger.

frightening                    ugly

Name: _____

# Synonyms

**Synonyms** are words that have almost the same meaning.

**Directions:** Read the story. Then fill in the blanks with the synonyms.

| | |
|---|---|
| funny | unhappy |
| windy | little |

**A New Balloon**

It was a breezy day. The wind blew the small child's balloon away. The child was sad. A silly clown gave him a new balloon.

1. It was a _____ day.

2. The wind blew the _____ child's balloon away.

3. The child was _____ .

4. A _____ clown gave him a new balloon.

Name: _____

# Synonyms

**Directions:** Read each sentence. Fill in the blanks with the synonyms.

| friend | tired | story |
|---|---|---|
| presents | | little |

I want to go to bed because I am very <u>sleepy</u>.  _____

On my birthday I like to open my <u>gifts</u>.  _____

My <u>pal</u> and I like to play together.  _____

My favorite <u>tale</u> is *Cinderella*.  _____

The mouse was so <u>tiny</u> that it was hard to catch him.  _____

Name: _____

# Antonyms

**Antonyms** are words that mean the opposite of another word.

**Examples:**
    **hot** and **cold**
    **short** and **tall**

**Directions:** Draw a line from each word on the left to its antonym on the right.

| | |
|---|---|
| sad | white |
| bottom | stop |
| black | fat |
| tall | top |
| thin | hard |
| little | found |
| cold | short |
| lost | hot |
| go | big |
| soft | happy |

# Antonyms

**Antonyms** are words that are opposites.

**Directions:** Read the words next to the pictures. Draw a line to the antonyms.

| | | |
|---|---|---|
| | dark | empty |
| | hairy | dry |
| | closed | happy |
| | dirty | bald |
| | sad | clean |
| | full | light |
| | wet | open |

Name: _____

# Antonyms: Words

**Directions:** Read the sentences. Complete each sentence with the correct antonym. Use the clues in the picture and below each sentence. Then color the picture.

1. Spotty's suitcase is _____ .  _____
   (antonym for closed)

2. Spotty has a ___ on his face.  _____
   (antonym for frown)

3. His pillow is _____ .  _____
   (antonym for hard)

4. His coat is _____ .  _____
   (antonym for little)

5. Spotty packs his stuffed animal _____ .  _____
   (antonym for first)

**Grade 2 - Comprehensive Curriculum**

Name: _____

# Antonyms: Words and Pictures

Anna and Luke often like to do opposite things. Help them design their new white tee-shirts—using opposites, of course.

**Directions:** Think of a pair of antonyms. Write one on each shirt. Draw pictures on their shirts to match the antonyms.

Name: _____

# Antonyms

Words that mean the opposite are called **antonyms**.

**Directions:** Read the sentence. Write the word from the word box that means the opposite of the **bold** word.

| bottom | outside | black | summer | after |
|--------|---------|-------|--------|-------|
| light  | sister  | clean | last   | evening |

1. Lisa has a new baby **brother**.  _____

2. The class went **inside** for recess.  _____

3. There is a **white** car in the driveway.  _____

4. We went to the park **before** dinner.  _____

5. Joe's puppy is **dirty**.  _____

6. My name is at the **top** of the list.  _____

7. I like to play outside in the **winter**.  _____

8. I like to take walks in the **morning**.  _____

9. The sky was **dark** after the storm.  _____

10. Our team is in **first** place.  _____

Name: _____

# Antonyms

**Directions:** Look at each picture and read the sentence. Cross out the incorrect word and write its antonym in the blank.

When it is light, we go
to bed.                              _____

When I broke the vase,
it made my mom smile.        _____

The hot chocolate is
very cold, so be careful!      _____

My pants were tight, so
I needed to wear a belt.      _____

The balloon floats down
in the sky.                          _____

Name: _____

# Homophones

**Directions:** Look at each picture. Circle the correct homophone.

deer    dear

blue    blew

two    to

hi    high

by    bye

new    knew

ate    eight

red    read

Name: _____

# Homophones

**Homophones** are words that sound the same but are spelled differently and have different meanings. Sometimes homophones can be more than two words.

**Examples:**

Pear and pair are homophones.

To, too and two are three homophones.

**Directions:** Draw a line from each word on the left to its homophone on the right.

| | |
|---|---|
| blue | knight |
| night | too |
| beet | blew |
| write | see |
| hi | meet |
| two | son |
| meat | bee |
| sea | high |
| be | right |
| sun | beat |

Name: _____

# Homophones

**Homophones** are words that sound the same but are spelled differently and mean different things.

**Directions:** Write the homophone from the box next to each picture.

| so | see | blew | pear |
|----|-----|------|------|

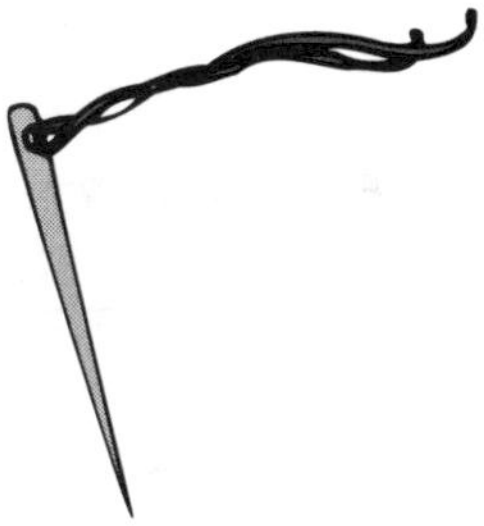

sew      _____

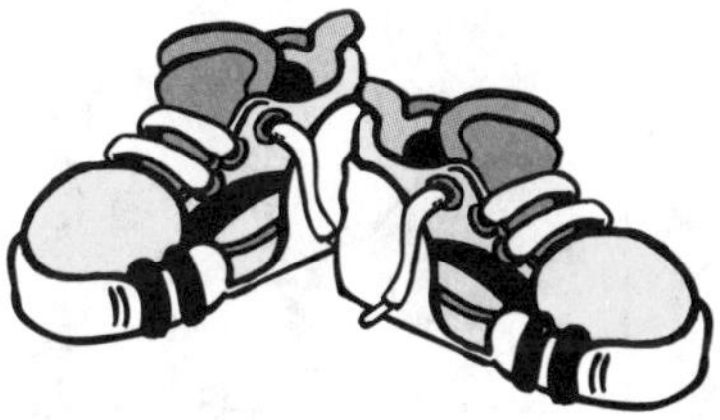

pair      _____

sea      _____

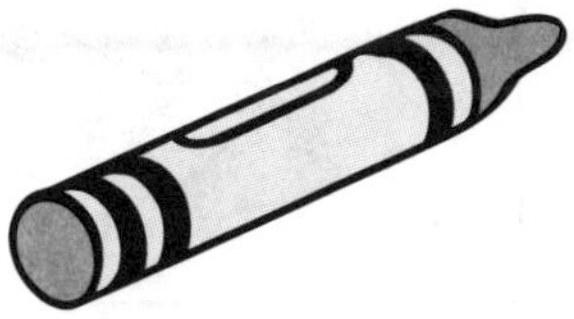

blue      _____

**Grade 2 - Comprehensive Curriculum**

Name: _____

# Homophones

**Directions:** Read each word. Circle the picture that goes with the word.

1. sun

2. ate

3. buy

4. hi

5. four

6. hear

# Homophones

**Directions:** Match each word with its homophone.

| | |
|---|---|
| eight | blew |
| buy | whole |
| pail | ate |
| red | pale |
| hole | read |
| blue | hour |
| our | by |

**Directions:** Choose 3 homophone pairs and write sentences using them.

1. _____

2. _____

3. _____

Name: _____

# Homophones: Doggy Birthday Cake

**Homophones** are words that sound alike but have different spellings and meanings.

**Directions:** Read the sentences. The bold words are homophones. Then follow the directions for a doggy birthday cake.

1. The baker **read** a recipe to bake a doggy cake. Color the plate he put it on **red**.

2. Draw a **hole** in the middle of the doggy cake. Then color the **whole** cake yellow.

3. Look **for** the top of the doggy cake. Draw **four** candles there.

4. In the hole, draw what you think the doggy would really like.

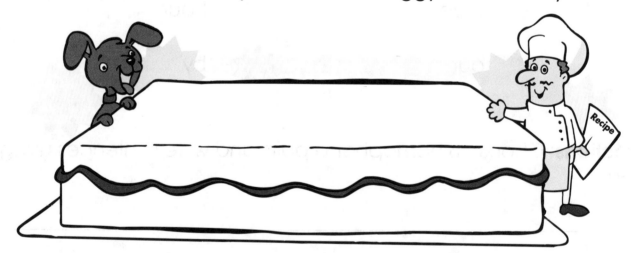

5. Write a sentence using the words **hole** and **whole**.

_____

6. Write a sentence using the words **read** and **red**.

_____

Name: _____

# Nouns

A **noun** is the name of a person, place or thing.

**Directions:** Read the story and circle all the nouns. Then write the nouns next to the pictures below.

Our family likes to go to the park.

_____

_____

We play on the swings.

_____

We eat cake.

_____

We drink lemonade.

_____

We throw the ball to our dog.

_____

Then we go home.

_____

# Nouns

**Directions:** Look through a magazine. Cut out pictures of nouns and glue them below. Write the name of the noun next to the picture.

NOUNS

Name: _____

# Proper Nouns

**Proper nouns** are the names of specific people, places and pets. Proper nouns begin with a capital letter.

**Directions:** Write the proper nouns on the lines below. Use capital letters at the beginning of each word.

logan, utah

mike smith

_____

_____

lynn cramer

buster

_____

_____

fluffy

chicago, illinois

_____

_____

**Grade 2 - Comprehensive Curriculum**

# Proper Nouns

The days of the week and the months of the year are always capitalized.

**Directions:** Circle the words that are written correctly. Write the words that need capital letters on the lines below.

| | | | | |
|---|---|---|---|---|
| sunday | July | Wednesday | may | december |
| friday | tuesday | june | august | Monday |
| january | February | March | Thursday | April |
| September | saturday | October | | |

**Days of the Week**

1. _____

2. _____

3. _____

4. _____

**Months of the Year**

1. _____

2. _____

3. _____

4. _____

5. _____

Name: _____

# Capitalization

The first word and all of the important words in a title begin with a capital letter.

**Directions:** Write the book titles on the lines below. Use capital letters.

1. _____

2. _____

3. _____

4. _____

5. _____

6. _____

**Grade 2 - Comprehensive Curriculum**

Name: _____

# Review

**Directions:** Write capital letters where they should appear in the sentences below.

**Example:** joe can play in january.

Joe can play in January.

1. we celebrate thanksgiving on the fourth thursday in november.

_____

_____

2. in june, michelle and mark will go camping every friday.

_____

_____

3. on mondays in october, i will take piano lessons.

_____

_____

Name: _____

# Plural Nouns

**Plural nouns** name more than one person, place or thing.

**Directions:** Read the words in the box. Write the words in the correct column.

| | | | | |
|---|---|---|---|---|
| hats | girl | cows | kittens | cake |
| spoons | glass | book | horse | trees |

_____    _____

_____    _____

_____    _____

_____    _____

_____    _____

**Grade 2 - Comprehensive Curriculum**

# Plurals

**Plurals** are words that mean more than one. You usually add an **s** or **es** to the word. In some words ending in **y**, the **y** changes to an **i** before adding **es**. For example, **baby** changes to **babies**.

**Directions:** Look at the following lists of plural words. Write the word that means one next to it. The first one has been done for you.

| | | | |
|---|---|---|---|
| foxes | **fox** | balls | _____ |
| bushes | _____ | candies | _____ |
| dresses | _____ | wishes | _____ |
| chairs | _____ | boxes | _____ |
| shoes | _____ | ladies | _____ |
| stories | _____ | bunnies | _____ |
| puppies | _____ | desks | _____ |
| matches | _____ | dishes | _____ |
| cars | _____ | pencils | _____ |
| glasses | _____ | trucks | _____ |

# Pronouns

**Pronouns** are words that can be used instead of nouns. **She**, **he**, **it** and **they** are pronouns.

**Directions:** Read the sentence. Then write the sentence again, using **she**, **he**, **it** or **they** in the blank.

1. Dan likes funny jokes.     _____ likes funny jokes.

2. Peg and Sam went to the zoo. _____ went to the zoo.

3. My dog likes to dig in the yard. _____ likes to dig in the yard.

4. Sara is a very good dancer. _____ is a very good dancer.

5. Fred and Ted are twins.    _____ are twins.

Name: _____

# Subjects

The **subject** of a sentence is the person, place or thing the sentence is about.

**Directions:** Underline the subject in each sentence.

**Example:**   Mom read a book.

(Think: Who is the sentence about?  <u>Mom</u>)

1. The bird flew away.

2. The kite was high in the air.

3. The children played a game.

4. The books fell down.

5. The monkey climbed a tree.

# Compound Subjects

Two similar sentences can be joined into one sentence if the predicate is the same. A **compound subject** is made up of two subjects joined together by the word **and**.

**Example:** Jamie can sing.
Sandy can sing.

Jamie **and** Sandy can sing.

**Directions:** Combine the sentences. Write the new sentence on the line.

1. The cats are my pets.
   The dogs are my pets.

_____

2. Chairs are in the store.
   Tables are in the store.

_____

3. Tom can ride a bike.
   Jack can ride a bike.

_____

**Grade 2 - Comprehensive Curriculum**

Name: _____

# Verbs

A **verb** is the action word in a sentence. Verbs tell what something does or that something exists.

**Example: Run, sleep** and **jump** are verbs.

**Directions:** Circle the verbs in the sentences below.

1. We play baseball everyday.

2. Susan pitches the ball very well.

3. Mike swings the bat harder than anyone.

4. Chris slides into home base.

5. Laura hit a home run.

# Verbs

We use verbs to tell when something happens. Sometimes we add an **ed** to verbs that tell us if something has already happened.

**Example:** Today, we will **play**. Yesterday, we **played**.

**Directions:** Write the correct verb in the blank.

1. Today, I will _____ my dog, Fritz.
   wash      washed

2. Last week, Fritz _____ when we said, "Bath time, Fritz."
   cry      cried

3. My sister likes to _____ wash Fritz.
   help      helped

4. One time she _____ Fritz by herself.
   clean      cleaned

5. Fritz will _____ a lot better after his bath.
   look      looked

Name: _____

# Verbs

**Directions:** Write each verb in the correct column.

| rake | talked | look | hopped | skip |
| cooked | fished | call | clean | sewed |

## Yesterday

_____

_____

_____

_____

_____

## Today

_____

_____

_____

_____

_____

Name: _____

# Predicates

The **predicate** is the part of the sentence that tells about the action.

**Directions:** Circle the predicate in each sentence.

**Example:**  The boys ran on the playground.

(Think: The boys did what? (Ran))

1. The woman painted a picture.

2. The puppy chases his ball.

3. The students went to school.

4. Butterflies fly in the air.

5. The baby wants a drink.

**Grade 2 - Comprehensive Curriculum**

Name: _____

# Compound Predicates

A **compound predicate** is made by joining two sentences that have the same subject. The predicates are joined together by the word **and**.

**Example:** Tom can jump.
　　　　　　Tom can run.

　　Tom can run **and** jump.

**Directions:** Combine the sentences. Write the new sentence on the line.

1. The dog can roll over.
　 The dog can bark.

_____

2. My mom plays with me.
　 My mom reads with me.

_____

3. Tara is tall.
　 Tara is smart.

_____

Name: _____

# Subjects and Predicates

The **subject** part of the sentence is the person, place or thing the sentence is about. The **predicate** is the part of the sentence that tells what the subject does.

**Directions:** Draw a line between the subject and the predicate. Underline the noun in the subject and circle the verb.

**Example:**      The furry <u>cat</u> | (ate) food.

1. Mandi walks to school.

2. The bus drove the children.

3. The school bell rang very loudly.

4. The teacher spoke to the students.

5. The girls opened their books.

Name: _____

# Compound Subjects and Predicates

The following sentences have either a compound subject or a compound predicate.

**Directions:** If the sentence has a compound subject (more than one thing doing the action), **underline** the subject. If it has a compound predicate (more than one action), **circle** the predicate.

**Example:** <u>Bats and owls</u> like the night.

The fox (slinks and spies.)

1. Raccoons and mice steal food.

2. Monkeys and birds sleep in trees.

3. Elephants wash and play in the river.

4. Bears eat honey and scratch trees.

5. Owls hoot and hunt.

# Compound Subjects and Predicates

**Directions:** Write one new sentence using a compound subject or predicate.

**Example:** The boy will jump. The girl will jump.

The <u>boy and girl</u> will jump.

1. The clowns run. The clowns play.

_____

2. The dogs dance. The bears dance.

_____

3. Seals bark. Seals clap.

_____

4. The girls play. The girls laugh.

_____

Name: _____

# Parts of a Sentence

**Directions:** Draw a circle around the noun, the naming part of the sentence. Draw a line under the verb, the action part of the sentence.

**Example:**  (John) <u>drinks</u> juice every morning.

1. Our class skates at the roller-skating rink.

2. Mike and Jan go very fast.

3. Fred eats hot dogs.

4. Sue dances to the music.

5. Everyone likes the skating rink.

# Parts of a Sentence

**Directions:** Look at the pictures. Draw a line from the naming part of the sentence to the action part to complete the sentence.

The boy                    delivered the mail.

A small dog                threw a football.

The mailman                fell down.

The goalie                 chased the ball.

Name: _____

# Adjectives

**Adjectives** are words that tell more about a person, place or thing.

**Examples:** cold, fuzzy, dark

**Directions:** Circle the adjectives in the sentences.

1. The juicy apple is on the plate.

2. The furry dog is eating a bone.

3. It was a sunny day.

4. The kitten drinks warm milk.

5. The baby has a loud cry.

Name: _____

# Adjectives

**Directions:** Choose an adjective from the box to fill in the blanks.

| | | | |
|---|---|---|---|
| hungry | sunny | busy | funny |
| fresh | deep | pretty | cloudy |

1. It is a _____ day on Farmer Brown's farm.

2. Farmer Brown is a very _____ man.

3. Mrs. Brown likes to feed the _____ chickens.

4. Every day she collects the _____ eggs.

5. The ducks swim in the _____ pond.

**Grade 2 - Comprehensive Curriculum**

Name: _____

# Adjectives

**Directions:** Think of your own adjectives. Write a story about Fluffy the cat.

1. Fluffy is a _____ cat.

2. The color of his fur is _____ .

3. He likes to chew on my_____ shoes.

4. He likes to eat _____ cat food.

5. I like Fluffy because he is so _____.

# Articles

**Articles** are small words that help us to better understand nouns. **A** and **an** are articles. We use **an** before a word that begins with a vowel. We use **a** before a word that begins with a consonant.

**Example:** We looked in **a** nest. It had **an** eagle in it.

**Directions:** Read the sentences. Write **a** or **an** in the blank.

1. I found _____ book.

2. It had a story about _____ ant in it.

3. In the story, _____ lion gave three wishes to _____ ant.

4. The ant's first wish was to ride _____ elephant.

5. The second wish was to ride _____ alligator.

6. The last wish was _____ wish for three more wishes.

# Sentences and Non-Sentences

A **sentence** tells a complete idea. It has a noun and a verb. It begins with a capital letter and has punctuation at the end.

**Directions:** Circle the group of words if it is a sentence.

1. Grass is a green plant.

2. Mowing the lawn.

3. Grass grows in fields and lawns.

4. Tickle the feet.

5. Sheep, cows and horses eat grass.

6. We like to play in.

7. My sister likes to mow the lawn.

8. A picnic on the grass.

9. My dog likes to roll in the grass.

10. Plant flowers around.

Name: _____

# Sentences and Non-Sentences

**Directions:** Circle the group of words if it tells a complete idea.

1. A secret is something you know.

2. My mom's birthday gift is a secret.

3. No one else.

4. If you promise not to.

5. I'll tell you a secret.

6. Something nobody knows.

# Statements

**Statements** are sentences that tell us something. They begin with a capital letter and end with a period.

**Directions:** Write the sentences on the lines below. Begin each sentence with a capital letter and end it with a period.

1. we like to ride our bikes

_____

2. we go down the hill very fast

_____

3. we keep our bikes shiny and clean

_____

4. we know how to change the tires

_____

Name: _____

# Surprising Sentences

**Surprising sentences** tell a strong feeling and end with an exclamation point. A surprising sentence may be only one or two words showing fear, surprise or pain. **Example: Oh, no!**

**Directions:** Put a period at the end of the sentences that tell something. Put an exclamation point at the end of the sentences that tell a strong feeling. Put a question mark at the end of the sentences that ask a question.

1. The cheetah can run very fast

2. Wow

3. Look at that cheetah go

4. Can you run fast

5. Oh, my

6. You're faster than I am

7. Let's run together

8. We can run as fast as a cheetah

9. What fun

10. Do you think cheetahs get tired

Name: _____

# Commands

**Commands** tell someone to do something. **Example:** "**Be careful.**"
It can also be written as "Be careful!" if it tells a strong feeling.

**Directions:** Put a period at the end of the command sentences.
Use an exclamation point if the sentence tells a strong feeling. Write
your own commands on the lines below.

1. Clean your room

2. Now

3. Be careful with your goldfish

4. Watch out

5. Be a little more careful

_____

_____

Name: _____

# Questions

**Questions** are sentences that ask something. They begin with a capital letter and end with a question mark.

**Directions:** Write the questions on the lines below. Begin each sentence with a capital letter and end it with a question mark.

1. will you be my friend

_____

2. what is your name

_____

3. are you eight years old

_____

4. do you like rainbows

_____

Name: _____

# Making Inferences: Writing Questions

Tommy likes to answer questions. He knows the answers, but you need to write the questions.

**Directions:** Write two questions for each answer.

Answer: It has four legs.

1. _____?

_____?

Answer: It lives on a farm.

2. _____?

_____?

Answer: It is soft.

3. _____?

_____?

Name: _____

# Making Inferences: Writing Questions

Toban and Sean use many colors when they paint.

**Directions:** Write two questions for each answer.

Answer: It is red.

1. _____ ?

_____ ?

Answer: It is purple.

2. _____ ?

_____ ?

Answer: It is green.

3. _____ ?

_____ ?

**Grade 2 - Comprehensive Curriculum**

Name: _____

# Making Inferences: Writing Questions

Ron likes sports. He enjoys meeting athletes. He would like to be a sports reporter someday.

**Directions:** Write a question Ron could ask each of these athletes.

1. An Olympic champion skier _____

_____

2. An All-Star basketball player _____

_____

3. The Quarterback of the Year _____

_____

4. The winner of the Indy 500 _____

_____

5. The top home-run hitter _____

_____

6. An Olympic champion runner _____

_____

7. A first place winner in diving _____

_____

Name: _____

# Making Inferences: Writing Questions

Erin found many solid shapes in her house.

**Directions:** Write two questions for each answer.

Answer: It is a cube.

1. _____?

_____?

Answer: It is a cylinder.

2. _____?

_____?

Answer: It is a sphere.

3. _____?

_____?

Name: _____

# Making Inferences: Point of View

Chelsea likes to pretend she will meet famous people someday. She would like to ask them many questions.

**Directions:** Write a question you think Chelsea would ask if she met these people.

1. an actor in a popular, new film _____

_____?

2. an Olympic gold medal winner _____

_____?

3. an alien from outer space _____

_____?

**Directions:** Now, write the answers these people might have given to Chelsea's questions.

4. an actor in a popular, new film _____

_____

5. an Olympic Gold medal winner _____

_____

6. an alien from outer space _____

_____

Name: _____

# Making Inferences: Point of View

Ellen likes animals. Someday she might want to be an animal doctor.

**Directions:** Write one question you think Ellen would ask each of these animals if she could speak their language.

1. a giraffe _____?

2. a mouse _____?

3. a shark _____?

4. a hippopotamus _____?

5. a penguin _____?

6. a gorilla _____?

7. an eagle _____?

**Directions:** Now, write the answers you think these animals might have given Ellen.

9. a giraffe _____

10. a mouse _____

11. a shark _____

12. a hippopotamus _____

13. a penguin _____

14. a gorilla _____

15. an eagle _____

# Creative Writing

**Directions:** Look at the picture below. Write a story about the picture.

_____

_____

_____

_____

_____

_____

Name: _____

# Ownership

We add **'s** to nouns (people, places or things) to tell who or what owns something.

**Directions:** Read the sentences. Fill in the blanks to show ownership.

**Example:** The doll belongs to **Sara**.

It is **Sara's** doll.

1. Sparky has a red collar.

_____ collar is red.

2. Jimmy has a blue coat.

_____ coat is blue.

3. The tail of the cat is short.

The _____ tail is short.

4. The name of my mother is Karen.

My _____ name is Karen.

# Ownership

**Directions:** Read the sentences. Choose the correct word and write it in the sentences below.

1. The _____ lunchbox is broken.        boys      boy's

2. The _____ played in the cage.        gerbil's    gerbils

3. _____ hair is brown.        Anns      Ann's

4. The _____ ran in the field.        horse's    horses

5. My _____ coat is torn.        sister's    sisters

6. The _____ fur is brown.        cats      cat's

7. Three _____ flew past our window.        birds      bird's

8. The _____ paws are muddy.        dogs      dog's

9. The _____ neck is long.        giraffes    giraffe's

10. The _____ are big and powerful.        lion's      lions

Name: _____

# Is, Are and Am

**Is, are** and **am** are special action words that tell us something is happening now.

Use **am** with **I**. **Example: I am**.
Use **is** to tell about one person or thing. **Example: He is**.
Use **are** to tell about more than one. **Example: We are**.
Use **are** with **you**. **Example: You are**.

**Directions:** Write **is, are** or **am** in the sentences below.

1. My friends _____ helping me build a tree house.

2. It _____ in my backyard.

3. We _____ using hammers, wood and nails.

4. It _____ a very hard job.

5. I _____ lucky to have good friends.

Name: _____

# Was and Were

**Was** and **were** tell us about something that already happened.

Use **was** to tell about one person or thing. **Example:** I **was**, he **was**.
Use **were** to tell about more than one person or thing or when using the word you. **Example:** We **were**, you **were**.

**Directions:** Write **was** or **were** in each sentence.

1. Lily _____ eight years old on her birthday.

2. Tim and Steve _____ happy to be at the party.

3. Megan _____ too shy to sing "Happy Birthday."

4. Ben _____ sorry he dropped his cake.

5. All of the children _____ happy to be invited.

Name: _____

# Go, Going and Went

We use **go** or **going** to tell about now or later. Sometimes we use **going** with the words **am** or **are**. We use **went** to tell about something that already happened.

**Directions:** Write **go**, **going** or **went** in the sentences below.

1. Today, I will _____ to the store.

2. Yesterday, we _____ shopping.

3. I am _____ to take Muffy to the vet.

4. Jan and Steve _____ to the party.

5. They are _____ to have a good day.

# Have, Has and Had

We use **have** and **has** to tell about now. We use **had** to tell about something that already happened.

**Directions:** Write **has**, **have** or **had** in the sentences below.

1. We _____ three cats at home.

2. Ginger _____ brown fur.

3. Bucky and Charlie _____ gray fur.

4. My friend Tom _____ one cat, but he died.

5. Tom _____ a new cat now.

# See, Saw and Sees

We use **see** or **sees** to tell about now. We use **saw** to tell about something that already happened.

**Directions:** Write **see**, **sees** or **saw** in the sentences below.

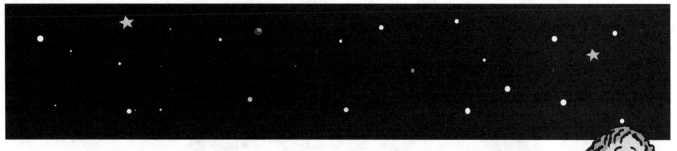

1. Last night, we _____ the stars.

2. John can _____ the stars from his window.

3. He _____ them every night.

4. Last week, he _____ the Big Dipper.

5. Can you _____ it in the night sky, too?

6. If you _____ it, you would remember it!

7. John _____ it often now.

8. How often do you _____ it?

Name: _____

# Eat, Eats and Ate

We use **eat** or **eats** to tell about now. We use **ate** to tell about what already happened.

**Directions:** Write **eat**, **eats** or **ate** in the sentences below.

1. We like to _____ in the lunchroom.

2. Today, my teacher will _____ in a different room.

3. She _____ with the other teachers.

4. Yesterday, we _____ pizza, pears and peas.

5. Today, we will _____ turkey and potatoes.

Name: _____

# Leave, Leaves and Left

We use **leave** and **leaves** to tell about now. We use **left** to tell about what already happened.

**Directions:** Write **leave**, **leaves** or **left** in the sentences below.

1. Last winter, we _____ seeds in the bird feeder everyday.

2. My mother likes to _____ food out for the squirrels.

3. When it rains, she _____ bread for the birds.

4. Yesterday, she _____ popcorn for the birds.

**Grade 2 - Comprehensive Curriculum**

Name: _____

# Learning Dictionary Skills

A dictionary is a book that gives the meaning of words. It also tells how words sound. Words in a dictionary are in ABC order. That makes them easier to find. A picture dictionary lists a word, a picture of the word and its meaning.

**Directions:** Look at this page from a picture dictionary. Then answer the questions.

**baby**

A very young child.

**band**

A group of people who play music.

**bank**

A place where money is kept.

**bark**

The sound a dog makes.

**berry**

A small, juicy fruit.

**board**

A flat piece of wood.

1. What is a small, juicy fruit? _____

2. What is a group of people who play music? _____

3. What is the name for a very young child? _____

4. What is a flat piece of wood called? _____

Name: _____

# Learning Dictionary Skills

**Directions:** Look at this page from a picture dictionary. Then answer the questions.

**safe**

A metal box.

**sea**

A body of water.

**seed**

The beginning of a plant.

**sheep**

An animal that has wool.

**store**

A place where items are sold.

**skate**

A shoe with wheels or a blade on it.

**snowstorm**

A time when much snow falls.

**squirrel**

A small animal with a bushy tail.

**stone**

A small rock.

1. What kind of animal has wool? _____

2. What do you call a shoe with wheels on it? _____

3. When a lot of snow falls, what is it called? _____

4. What is a small animal with a bushy tail? _____

5. What is a place where items are sold? _____

6. When a plant starts, what is it called? _____

Name: _____

# Learning Dictionary Skills

**Directions:** Look at this page from a picture dictionary. Then answer the questions.

**table**

Furniture with legs and a flat top.

**tail**

A slender part that is on the back of an animal.

**teacher**

A person who teaches lessons.

**telephone**

A machine that sends and receives sounds.

**ticket**

A paper slip or card.

**tiger**

An animal with stripes.

1. Who is a person who teaches lessons? _____

2. What is the name of an animal with stripes? _____

3. What is a piece of furniture with legs and a flat top? _____

4. What is the definition of a ticket?

_____

5. What is a machine that sends and receives sounds?

_____

Name: _____

# Learning Dictionary Skills

The guide words at the top of a page in a dictionary tell you what the first and last words on the page will be. Only words that come in ABC order between those two words will be on that page. Guide words help you find the page you need to look up a word.

**Directions:** Write each word from the box in ABC order between each pair of guide words.

| | | | | |
|---|---|---|---|---|
| faint | far | fence | feed | farmer |
| fan | feet | farm | family | face |

**face**                                                                 **fence**

_____        _____

_____        _____

_____        _____

_____        _____

**Grade 2 - Comprehensive Curriculum**

Name: _____

# Learning Dictionary Skills

**Directions:** Write each word from the box in ABC order between each pair of guide words.

| | | | | |
|---|---|---|---|---|
| fierce | fix | fight | first | few |
| fish | fill | flush | flat | finish |

**few**                          **flush**

_____      _____

_____      _____

_____      _____

_____      _____

_____      _____

Name: _____

# Learning Dictionary Skills

**Directions:** Create your own dictionary page. Include guide words at the top. Write the words with their meanings in ABC order.

_____
guide word

1. _____
word

_____

_____

_____

2. _____
word

_____

_____

_____

3. _____
word

_____

_____

_____

_____
guide word

4. _____
word

_____

_____

_____

5. _____
word

_____

_____

_____

6. _____
word

_____

_____

_____

Name: _____

# Learning Dictionary Skills

When words have more than one meaning, the meanings are numbered in a dictionary.

**Directions:** Read the meanings of **tag**. Write the number of the correct definition after each sentence.

## tag

1. A small strip or tab attached to something else.

2. To label.

3. To follow closely and constantly.

4. A game of chase.

1. We will play a game of tag after we study. _____

2. I will tag this coat with its price. _____

3. My little brother will tag along with us. _____

4. My mother already took off the price tag. _____

5. The tag on the puppy said, "For Sale." _____

6. Do not tag that tree. _____

Name: _____

# Silly Sentences!

**Directions:** Cut out the binoculars. Cut out the beginning and ending sentence strips on the next page. Thread the strips through the lenses to make sentences. Write each sentence on a piece of paper. Draw a picture to illustrate your silly sentences. Staple your sentences and illustrations into a book to share.

cut ✂ - - - - - - - - - - - - - - - - - - - - - - - - - - - - - - - - - - - - - - - - - - - -

cut _____

cut _____

cut _____

cut _____

Page is blank for cutting exercise on previous page.

| | |
|---|---|
| Cats | live in nests. |
| Boats | read books. |
| Flowers | have apples. |
| Birds | smell pretty. |
| Horses | can slither. |
| Garbage cans | are playful. |
| Some trees | smell stinky. |
| Children | float in water. |
| Snakes | eat hay. |

Page is blank for cutting exercise on previous page.

# SPELLING

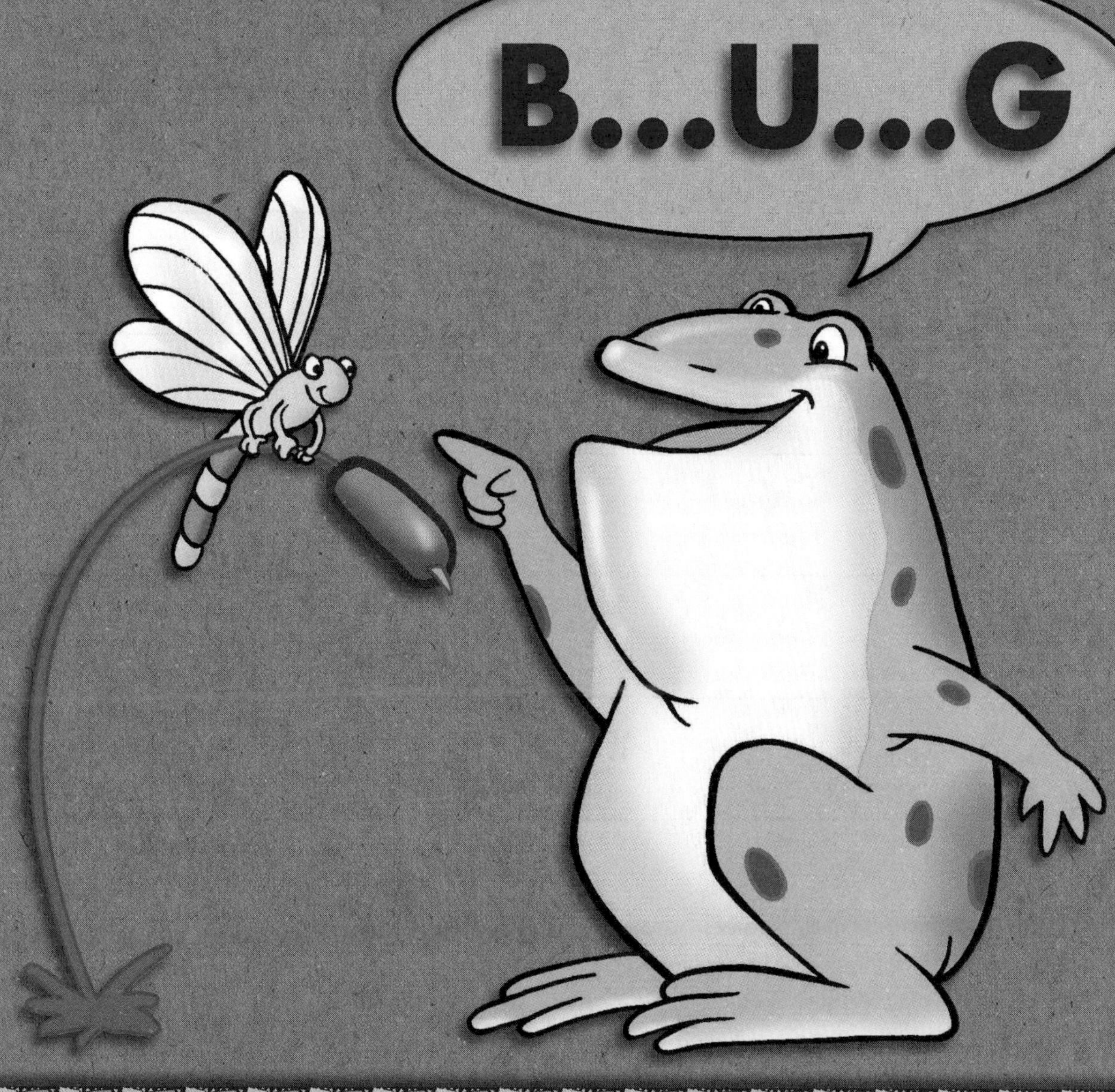

Name: _____

# Number Words

**Directions:** Write each number word beside the correct picture. Then write it again.

**Example:**

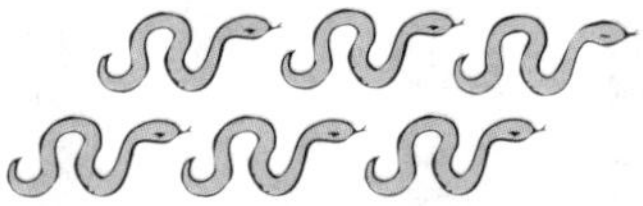

<u>six  six</u>

| one | two | three | four | five | six | seven | eight | nine | ten |
|-----|-----|-------|------|------|-----|-------|-------|------|-----|

_____

_____

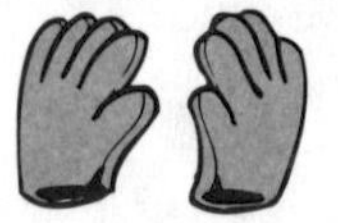

_____

_____

_____

_____

_____

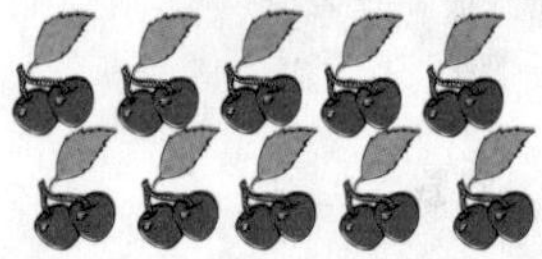

_____

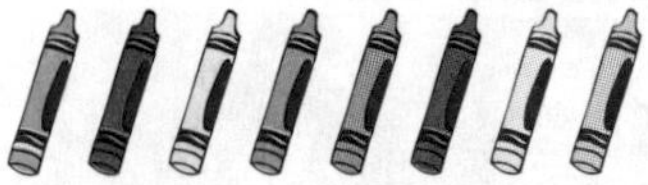

Name: _____

# Number Words

**Directions:** Write the correct number words in the blanks.

| one | two | three | four | five | six | seven | eight | nine | ten |
|-----|-----|-------|------|------|-----|-------|-------|------|-----|

Add a letter to each of these words to make a number word.

**Example:**

even                          on                          tree

_seven_                    _____        _____

Change a letter to make these words into number words.

**Example:**

live                          fix                          line

_five_                      _____        _____

Write the number words that sound the same as these:

**Example:**

ate                          to                          for

_eight_                    _____        _____

Write the number word you did not use:          _____

# Number Words: Asking Sentences

**Directions:** Write an asking sentence about each picture. Begin each sentence with **How many**. Then answer your question. Begin each sentence with a capital letter and end it with a period or a question mark.

| one | two | three | four | five | six | seven | eight | nine | ten |
|-----|-----|-------|------|------|-----|-------|-------|------|-----|

**Example:**

How many cookies
does the boy have?
He has six cookies.

_____

_____

_____

_____

_____

Name: _____

# Number Words: Sentences

**Directions:** Change the telling sentences into asking sentences. Change the asking sentences into telling sentences. Begin each one with a capital letter and end it with a period or a question mark.

**Examples:**

Is she eating three cookies?

## She is eating three cookies.

He is bringing one truck.

## Is he bringing one truck?

1. Is he painting two blue birds?

_____

2. Did she find four apples?

_____

3. She will be six on her birthday.

_____

# Short a Words: Rhyming Words

**Short a** is the sound you hear in the word **math**.

**Directions:** Use the **short a** words in the box to write rhyming words.

| | | | |
|---|---|---|---|
| lamp | fat | bat | van |
| path | can | cat | Dan |
| math | stamp | fan | sat |

1. Write four words that rhyme with **mat**.

_____     _____

_____     _____

2. Write two words that rhyme with **bath**.

_____     _____

3. Write two words that rhyme with **damp**.

_____     _____

4. Write four words that rhyme with **pan**.

_____     _____

_____     _____

Name: _____

# Short a Words: Sentences

**Directions:** Use a word from the box to complete each sentence.

| | | | |
|---|---|---|---|
| fat | path | lamp | can |
| van | stamp | Dan | math |
| sat | cat | fan | bat |

**Example:**

1. The _____**lamp**_____ had a pink shade.

2. The bike _____ led us to the park.

3. I like to add in _____ class.

4. The cat is very _____.

5. The _____ of beans was hard to open.

6. The envelope needed a _____.

7. He swung the _____ and hit the ball.

8. The _____ blew air around.

9. My mom drives a blue _____.

10. I _____ in the backseat.

# Long a Words

**Long a** is the vowel sound which says its own name. **Long a** can be spelled **ai** as in the word **mail, ay** as in the word **say** and **a** with a **silent e** at the end of a word as in the word **same**.

**Directions:** Say each word and listen for the **long a** sound. Then write each word and underline the letters that make the **long a** vowel sound.

| | | |
|---|---|---|
| mail | bake | train |
| game | day | sale |
| paint | play | name |
| made | gray | tray |

1. _____

2. _____

3. _____

4. _____

5. _____

6. _____

7. _____

8. _____

9. _____

10. _____

11. _____

12. _____

Name: _____

# Long a Words: Rhyming Words

**Long a** is the vowel sound you hear in the word **cake**.

**Directions:** Use the **long a** words in the box to write rhyming words.

| | | | |
|---|---|---|---|
| paint | gray | train | tray |
| mail | day | sale | play |
| game | made | name | bake |

1. Write the word that rhymes with **make**.

_____

2. Write the words that rhyme with **hail**.

_____     _____

3. Write the words that rhyme with **say**.

_____     _____

_____     _____

4. Write the word that rhymes with **shade**.

_____

5. Write the words that rhyme with **same**.

_____     _____

**Grade 2 - Comprehensive Curriculum**

Name: _____

# Long a Words: Sentence Order

**Directions:** Write the words in order so that each
sentence tells a complete idea. Begin each
sentence with a capital letter and end it
with a period or a question mark.

1. plate was on the cake a

_____

2. like you would to play a game

_____

3. gray around the a corner train came

_____

4. was on mail Bob's name the

_____

5. sail for on day we went a nice a

_____

Name: _____

# Short o Words

**Short o** is the vowel sound you hear in the word **pot**.

**Directions:** Say each word and listen for the **short o** sound. Then write each word and underline the letter that makes the **short o** sound.

| | | | |
|---|---|---|---|
| hot | box | sock | mop |
| stop | not | fox | cot |
| Bob | rock | clock | lock |

1. _____

2. _____

3. _____

4. _____

5. _____

6. _____

7. _____

8. _____

9. _____

10. _____

11. _____

12. _____

Grade 2 - Comprehensive Curriculum

Name: _____

# Short o Words: Rhyming Words

**Short o** is the vowel sound you hear in the word **got**.

**Directions:** Use the **short o** words in the box to write rhyming words.

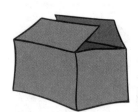

| | | | |
|---|---|---|---|
| hot | rock | lock | cot |
| stop | sock | fox | mop |
| box | mob | clock | Bob |

1. Write the words that rhyme with **dot**.

_____     _____

2. Write the words that rhyme with **socks**.

_____     _____

3. Write the words that rhyme with **hop**.

_____     _____

4. Write the words that rhyme with **dock**.

_____     _____

5. Write the words that rhyme with **cob**.

_____     _____

Name: _____

# Long o Words

**Long o** is the vowel sound which says its own name. **Long o** can be spelled **oa** as in the word **float** or **o** with a **silent e** at the end as in **cone**.

**Directions:** Say each word and listen for the **long o** sound. Then write each word and underline the letters that make the **long o** sound.

| | | | |
|---|---|---|---|
| rope | coat | soap | wrote |
| note | hope | boat | cone |
| bone | pole | phone | hole |

1. _____

2. _____

3. _____

4. _____

5. _____

6. _____

7. _____

8. _____

9. _____

10. _____

11. _____

12. _____

**Grade 2 - Comprehensive Curriculum**

# Long o Words: Rhyming Words

**Long o** is the vowel sound you hear in the word **home**.

**Directions:** Use the **long o** words in the box to write rhyming words.

| | | | |
|---|---|---|---|
| rope | soap | coat | wrote |
| note | boat | hope | cone |
| bone | phone | pole | hole |

1. Write the words that rhyme with **mope**.

_____  _____  _____

2. Write the words that rhyme with **tote**.

_____  _____


_____  _____

3. Write the words that rhyme with **lone**.

_____  _____  _____

4. Write the words that rhyme with **goal**.

_____  _____

# Long o Words: Sentences

**Directions:** Draw a line from the first part of the sentence to the part which completes the sentence.

1. Do you know

2. The dog

3. The boat floats

4. I hope the phone

5. Carol's ice-cream cone

6. The rope swing

7. I had to wear

in the water.

was in the tree.

who wrote the note?

has a bone.

rings soon for me!

a coat in the cold.

was melting.

**Grade 2 - Comprehensive Curriculum**

Name: _____

# Animal Words

**Directions:** Write the animal names twice beside each picture.

| fox | rabbit | bear | squirrel | mouse | deer |

**Example:**

squirrel          squirrel

_____

_____

_____

_____

_____

Name: _____

# Animal Words

**Directions:** Circle the word in each sentence that is not spelled correctly. Then write it correctly.

| squirrel | bears | rabbit | deer | fox | mouse |

**Example:**

Animals like to live in (threes.)

___trees___

1. Bares do not eat people.

_____

2. The squirel found a nut.

_____

3. Sometimes a little moose might get into your house.

_____

4. Dear eat leaves and grass.

_____

5. A focks has a bushy tail.

_____

6. One day, a rabitt came into our yard.

_____

Name: _____

# Animal Words: More Than One

To show more than one of something, we add **s** to most words.

**Example:** one dog – **two dogs**        one book – **two books**

But some words are different. For words that end with **x**, use **es** to show two.

**Example:** one fox – **two foxes**        one box – **two boxes**

The spelling of some words changes a lot when there are two.

**Example:** one mouse – **two mice**

Some words stay the same, even when you mean two of something.

**Example:** one deer – **two deer**        one fish – **two fish**

**Directions:** Complete the sentences below with the correct word.

1. The  run fast.        _____

2. The  are eating.        _____

3. Have you seen any  today?   _____

4. Where do the  live?        _____

5. Did you ever have  for pets? _____

Name: _____

# Animal Words: More Than One

**Directions:** Write the two sentences below as one sentence. Remember the special spelling of **fox**, **mouse** and **deer** when there are more than one.

**Example:**

I saw a mouse. You saw a mouse.

## We saw two mice.

1. Julie petted a deer.
   Matt petted a deer.

_____

_____

2. Mike colored a fox.
   Kim colored a fox.

_____

_____

**313**

# Animal Words: Kinds of Sentences

Another name for an asking sentence is a **question**.

**Directions:** Use the words in the box to write a telling sentence. Then use the words to write a question.

**Example:**

| a | mouse | I | see |
|---|---|---|---|
| the | bed | under | do |

Telling sentence:

## I see a mouse under the bed.

Question:

## Do I see a mouse under the bed?

| in | live |
|---|---|
| these | woods |
| bears | do |

Telling sentence:

_____

Question:

_____

_____

Name: _____

# Animal Words: Sentences

**Directions:** Read the sentences on each line and draw a line between them. Then write each sentence again on the lines below. Begin each one with a capital letter and put a period or question mark at the end.

**Example:**

why do squirrels hide nuts | they eat them in the winter

## Why do squirrels hide nuts?
## They eat them in the winter.

1. bears sleep in the winter they don't need food then

_____

_____

2. he said he saw a fox do you think he did

_____

_____

# Review

**Directions:** Complete each line of tho poem below with a word from the box. Make sure each line rhymes.

| deer | fox | house | here | mouse | box |

A little gray _____

Once ran through my _____.

Then a bushy-tailed _____

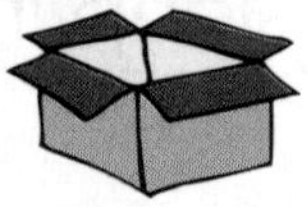

Ran into a _____.

Last came a _____.

What was he doing _____?

Now make your own poem using the words **bear** and **there**.

_____

_____

Name: _____

# Family Words

**Directions:** This is Andy's **family tree**. It shows all the people in his family. Use the words in the box to finish writing the names in Andy's family tree.

| | |
|---|---|
| grandmother | mother |
| grandfather | father |
| aunt | uncle |
| brother | sister |

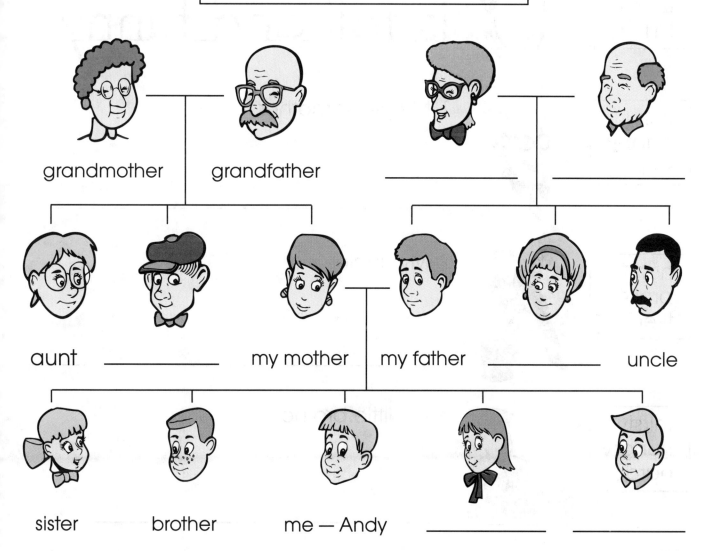

**Grade 2 - Comprehensive Curriculum**

# Family Words

Some words tell how a person looks or feels. These are called **describing** words or **adjectives**.

**Directions:** Help Andy write about the people in his family. Cross out the **describing** word that does not tell about each picture. Write a sentence that uses the other two describing words.

**Example:**

~~asleep~~
funny
tall

My aunt

is tall and funny.

fast
happy
smiling

1. My grandmother

_____

hot
broken
tired

2. My uncle

_____

thirsty
hungry
hard

3. My little brother

_____

# Family Words: Joining Words

**Joining words** join two ideas to make one long sentence. Three words help do this:

**and** — if both sentences are much the same.
**Example:** I took my dog for a walk, **and** I played with my cat.

**but** — if the second sentence says something different than the first sentence. Sometimes the second sentence tells why you can't do the first sentence.
**Example:** I want to play outside, **but** it is raining.

**or** — if each sentence names a different thing you could do.
**Example:** You could eat your cookie, **or** you could give it to me.

**Directions:** Use the word given to join the two short sentences into one longer sentence.

**(but)**
My aunt lives far away. She calls me often.

My aunt lives far away, but she calls me often.

1. **(and)**
My sister had a birthday. She got a new bike.

_____

_____

2. **(or)**
We can play outside. We can play inside.

_____

_____

Name: _____

# Family Words: Joining Words

**Directions:** Read each pair of sentences. Then join them with **and**, **but** or **or**.

1. My uncle likes popcorn.
   He does not like peanuts.

_____

_____

2. He could read a book.
   He could tell me his own story.

_____

_____

3. My little brother is sleepy.
   He wants to go to bed.

_____

_____

Name: _____

# Family Words: Completing a Story

**Directions:** Write the family words in the blanks to complete the story.

One day, my family had a picnic. My _____

baked chicken. _____ baked some rolls.

My _____ Jack brought corn. My

_____ made something green and white in a big dish.

I ate the chicken my _____ brought. I had two

rolls made by my _____ . My

_____ gave me some corn. I liked it all! Then my

_____ and I looked in the dish my

_____ had brought. "Did you try it?" I asked him.

"You're my big _____," he said. "You try it!" I put a

tiny bit in my mouth. It tasted good! But the dish was almost empty.

"It's terrible!" I said. "I'll eat the rest of it so you won't have to. That's

what a big _____ is for!" My _____

watched me eat it all. I tried not to look too happy!

Name: _____

# Short e Words

**Short e** is the vowel sound you hear in the word **pet**.

**Directions:** Say each word and listen for the **short e** sound. Then write each word and underline the letter that makes the **short e** sound.

| get | Meg | rest | tent |
|-----|------|------|------|
| red | spent | test | help |
| bed | pet | head | best |

1. _____

2. _____

3. _____

4. _____

5. _____

6. _____

7. _____

8. _____

9. _____

10. _____

11. _____

12. _____

Name: _____

# Short e Words: Rhyming Words

**Short e** is the vowel sound you hear in the word **egg**.

**Directions:** Use the **short e** words in the box to write rhyming words.

| | | | |
|---|---|---|---|
| get | test | pet | help |
| let | head | spent | red |
| best | tent | rest | bed |

1. Write the words that rhyme with **fed**.

_____    _____    _____

2. Write the words that rhyme with **bent**.

_____    _____

3. Write the words that rhyme with **west**.

_____    _____    _____

4. Write the words that rhyme with **bet**.

_____    _____    _____

**Grade 2 - Comprehensive Curriculum**

Name: _____

# Short e Words: Sentences

**Directions:** Write the correct **short e** word in each sentence.

| get | Meg | rest | bed | spent | best |
|-----|-----|------|-----|-------|------|
| test | help | head | pet | red | tent |

1. Of all my crayons, I like the color _____

   the _____ !

2. I always make my _____ when I _____ up.

3. My new hat keeps my _____ warm.

4. _____ wanted a dog for a _____ .

5. When we go camping, my job is to _____ put up

   the _____ .

6. I have a _____ in math tomorrow, so I want to get

   a good night's _____ .

Name: _____

# Long e Words

**Long e** is the vowel sound which says its own name. **Long e** can be spelled **ee** as in the word **teeth, ea** as in the word **meat** or **e** as in the word **me**.

**Directions:** Say each word and listen for the **long e** sound. Then write the words and underline the letters that make the **long e** sound.

| | | | |
|---|---|---|---|
| street | neat | treat | feet |
| sleep | keep | deal | meal |
| mean | clean | beast | feast |

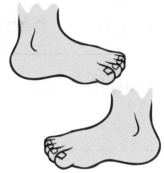

1. _____

2. _____

3. _____

4. _____

5. _____

6. _____

7. _____

8. _____

9. _____

10. _____

11. _____

12. _____

**Grade 2 - Comprehensive Curriculum**

Name: _____

# Long e Words: Rhyming Words

**Long e** is the vowel sound you hear in the word **meet**.

**Directions:** Use the **long e** words in the box to write rhyming words.

| | | | |
|---|---|---|---|
| street | feet | neat | treat |
| keep | deal | sleep | meal |
| mean | beast | clean | feast |

1. Write the words that rhyme with **beat**.

_____    _____

_____    _____

2. Write the words that rhyme with **deep**.

_____    _____

3. Write the words that rhyme with **feel**.

_____    _____

4. Write the words that rhyme with **bean**.

_____    _____

5. Write the words that rhyme with **least**.

_____    _____

# Long e Words: Sentences

**Directions:** Write a word from the box to complete each sentence.

| | | | |
|---|---|---|---|
| street | feet | neat | treat |
| keep | deal | sleep | meal |
| mean | beast | clean | feast |

1. I went to _____ late last night.

2. One of my favorite stories is "Beauty and

   the _____ ."

3. Look both ways when you cross the _____ .

4. It would be _____ to kick someone.

5. I wear socks and shoes on my_____ .

6. The most important _____ of the day

   is breakfast.

Name: _____

# Verbs

**Verbs** are words that tell the action in the sentence.

**Directions:** Draw a line from each sentence to its picture. Then finish the sentence with the verb or action word that is under each picture.

**Example:**
He will ___ help ___ the baby.

1. I can _____ my book.

2. It is time to _____ up.

3. That chair might _____ .

4. They _____ houses.

5. I _____ this out myself.

6. Is that too heavy to _____ ?

**help**

**carry**

**cut**

**build**

**clean**

**fix**

**break**

Name: _____

# Verbs: Sentences

**Directions:** Read the two sentences in each story below. Then write one more sentence to tell what happened next. Use the verbs from the box.

| break | build | fix | clean | cut | carry |
|---|---|---|---|---|---|

Today is Mike's birthday.

Mike asked four friends to come.

_____

Edith's dog walked in the mud.

He got mud in the house.

_____

# Verbs: Sentences

**Dirctions:** Join each pair of sentences to make one longer sentence. Use one of the **joining** words: **and**, **but** or **or**. In the second part of the sentence, use **he**, **she** or **they** in place of the person's name.

**Example:** I asked Tim to help me. Tim wanted to play.

I asked Tim to help me, but he wanted to play.

1. Kelly dropped a glass. Kelly cut her finger.

_____

_____

2. Linda and Allen got a new dog. Linda and Allen named it Baby.

_____

_____

# Verbs: Word Endings

Most **verbs** end with **s** when the sentence tells about one thing. The **s** is taken away when the sentence tells about more than one thing.

**Example:**

One dog walks.
Two dogs **walk**.

One boy runs.
Three boys **run**.

The spelling of some **verbs** changes when the sentence tells about only one thing.

**Example:**

One girl carries her lunch.
Two girls **carry** their lunches.

The boy fixes his car.
Two boys **fix** their cars.

**Directions:** Write the missing verbs in the sentences.

**Example:**

Pam works hard. She and Peter work all day.

1. The father bird builds a nest.

   The mother and father _____ it together.

2. The girls clean their room. Jenny_____under her bed.

3. The children cut out their pictures. Henry _____ his slowly.

4. These workers fix things. This man _____ televisions.

5. Two trucks carry horses. One truck _____ pigs.

# Verbs: Completing a Story

**Directions:** Write a sentence that tells what happens in each picture. Use the **verb** under the picture.

**Example:**

**fall**

**break**

**clean**

## A glass falls off the table.

_____

_____

**fix**

**cut**

**carry**

_____

_____

_____

# Verbs

**Directions:** Circle the words in each sentence which are not spelled correctly. Then write the sentence correctly.

**Example:**

I need to (klean) the cage my (mouses) live in.

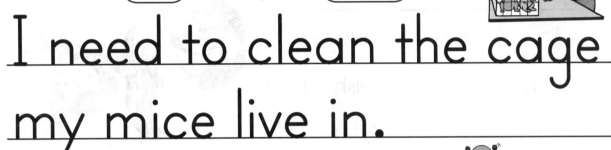

I need to clean the cage my mice live in.

2. The chair will brake if tree of us sit on it.

_____

_____

3. A muther bare carries her baby in hir mouth.

_____

_____

Name: _____

# Short i Words

**Short i** is the vowel sound you hear in the word **pig**.

**Directions:** Say each word and listen for the **short i** sound. Then write each word and underline the letter that makes the **short i** sound.

| | | | |
|---|---|---|---|
| pin | fin | dip | dish |
| kick | rich | ship | wish |
| win | fish | sick | pitch |

1. _____

2. _____

3. _____

4. _____

5. _____

6. _____

7. _____

8. _____

9. _____

10. _____

11. _____

12. _____

# Short i Words: Rhyming Words

**Short i** is the sound you hear in the word **pin**.

**Directions:** Use the **short i** words in the box to write rhyming words.

| pin | fin | win | fish |
|-----|-----|-----|------|
| pitch | wish | rich | kick |
| ship | dip | dish | sick |

1. Write the words that rhyme with **spin**.

_____   _____   _____

2. Write the words that rhyme with **ditch**.

_____   _____

3. Write the words that rhyme with **rip**.

_____   _____

4. Write the words that rhyme with **squish**.

_____   _____   _____

5. Write the words that rhyme with **lick**.

_____   _____

Name: _____

# Short i Words: Sentences

**Directions:** Complete the sentences by matching the words to the correct sentence.

1. I made a _____ on a star.                          fin

2. All we could see was the shark's _____
   above the water.                                             fish

3. I like to eat vegetables with _____ .                 kick

4. We saw lots of _____ in the water.                 win

5. The soccer player will _____the
   ball and score a goal.                                       dish

6. If you feel _____, see a doctor.                   dip

7. Did Bob _____ the race?                            wish

8. The _____ was full of candy.                       sick

Name: _____

# Long i Words

**Long i** is the vowel sound which says its own name. **Long i** can be spelled **igh** as in **sight**, **i** with a **silent e** at the end as in **mine** and **y** at the end as in **fly**.

**Directions:** Say each word and listen for the **long i** sound. Then write each word and underline the letters that make the **long i** sound.

| | | | |
|---|---|---|---|
| bike | hike | ride | line |
| glide | ripe | nine | pipe |
| fight | high | light | sigh |

1. _____

2. _____

3. _____

4. _____

5. _____

6. _____

7. _____

8. _____

9. _____

10. _____

11. _____

12. _____

**Grade 2 - Comprehensive Curriculum**

Name: _____

# Long i Words: Rhyming Words

**Long i** is the sound you hear in the word **fight**.

**Directions:** Use the **long i** words in the box to write rhyming words.

| | | | |
|---|---|---|---|
| hide | ride | line | my |
| by | nine | high | light |
| sight | fly | | |

1. Write the words that rhyme with **sigh**.

_____  _____  _____

2. Write the words that rhyme with **side**.

_____  _____

3. Write the words that rhyme with **fine**.

_____  _____

4. Write the words that rhyme with **fight**.

_____  _____

# Review

**Directions:** Write **igh** in each blank below. Then read the words.

**Example:**

_sight_   f_____t   t_____t

m_____t   l_____t   br_____t

n_____t   r_____t   fl_____t

Choose two of the **igh** words above. Draw, label and color a picture for each word.

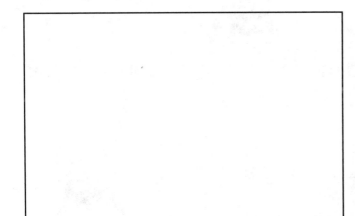 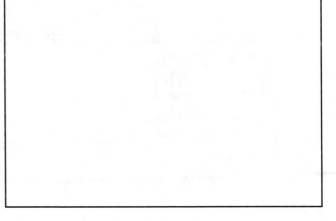

_____   _____

# Location Words

**Directions:** Use one of the location words from the box to complete each sentence.

| between | around | inside | outside | beside | across |
|---|---|---|---|---|---|

**Example:**

She will hide ___**under**___ the basket.

1. In the summer, we like to play _____ .

2. She can swim _____ the lake.

3. Put the bird _____ its cage so it won't fly away.

4. Sit _____ Bill and me so we can all work together.

5. Your picture is right _____ mine on the wall.

6. The fence goes _____ the house.

Name: _____

# Location Words

**Directions:** Draw a line from each sentence to its picture. Then complete each sentence with the word under the picture.

**Example:**

He is walking __**behind**__ the tree.

**outside**

1. We stay _____ when it rains.

**behind**

2. She drew a dog _____ his house.

**between**

3. She stands _____ her friends.

**across**

4. They walked _____ the bridge.

**around**

5. Let the cat go _____ .

**beside**

6. Draw a circle _____ the fish.

**inside**

Grade 2 - Comprehensive Curriculum

Name: _____

# Location Words

**Directions:** Write the location words that answer the questions.

| between | around | inside | outside | beside | across |

1. Write all the smaller words you find in the location words.

_____

_____

2. Which two words begin with the same sound as  ?

_____     _____

3. Put these clues together to write a location word.

a + ⭕     _____

a + ✝     _____

4. Write three words that rhyme with **hide**.

_____     _____     _____

# Location Words: Sentences

**Directions:** Use a location word from the first box and other words from the second box to complete each sentence.

| between | around | inside | outside | beside | across |
|---------|--------|--------|---------|--------|--------|

| the yard | the house | the table | the school | the box |
|----------|-----------|-----------|------------|---------|
| the hill | the picture | the field | the puddle | the park |

**Example:**

Our garden grows _outside in the yard._

1. We like to play _____

2. The street goes _____

3. Can you run _____

4. Let's ride bikes _____

# Location Words: Sentences

**Directions:** Join each pair of sentences to make a longer sentence. Use one of the **joining** words **and**, **but** or **or**.

**Example:** We play outside when it is sunny.
Today it is raining.

We play outside when it is sunny, but today it is raining.

1. We could walk between the buildings. We could walk around them.

_____

_____

2. I drew a tree beside the house. I drew flowers beside the house.

_____

_____

# Location Words: Sentences

**Directions:** Use a location word to tell where the cat is in each sentence.

 The cat is behind the box.

_____

_____

_____

_____

_____

_____

_____

_____

Name: _____

# Short u Words

**Short u** is the sound you hear in the word **bug**.

**Directions:** Say each word and listen for the **short u** sound. Then write each word and underline the letter that makes the **short u** sound.

| dust | must | nut | bug |
| bump | pump | tub | jump |
| cut | hug | rug | cub |

1. _____

2. _____

3. _____

4. _____

5. _____

6. _____

7. _____

8. _____

9. _____

10. _____

11. _____

12. _____

Name: _____

# Short u Words: Sentences

**Directions:** Circle the words in each sentence which are not correct. Then write the correct **short u** words from the box on the lines.

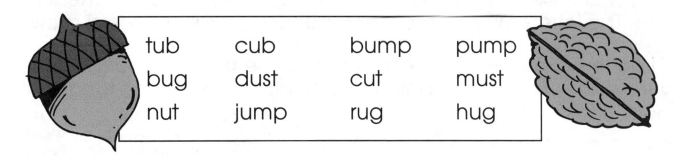

| | | | |
|---|---|---|---|
| tub | cub | bump | pump |
| bug | dust | cut | must |
| nut | jump | rug | hug |

1. The crust made me sneeze. _____

2. I need to take a bath in the cub. _____

3. The mug bite left a big pump on my arm.

_____    _____

4. It is time to get my hair hut. _____

5. The mother bear took care of her shrub. _____

6. We need to jump more gas into the car. _____

Name: _____

# Long u Words

**Long u** is the vowel sound which says its own name. **Long u** is spelled **u** with a silent **e** at the end as in **cute**. The letters **oo** make a sound very much like long **u**. They make the sound you hear in the word **zoo**. The letters **ew** also make the **oo** sound as in the word **grew**.

**Directions:** Say the words and listen for the **u** and **oo** sounds. Then write each word and underline the letters that make the **long u** and **oo** sounds.

| | | | |
|---|---|---|---|
| choose | blew | moon | fuse |
| cube | Ruth | tooth | use |
| flew | loose | goose | noon |

1. _____

2. _____

3. _____

4. _____

5. _____

6. _____

7. _____

8. _____

9. _____

10. _____

11. _____

12. _____

Name: _____

# Long u Words: Rhyming Words

**Long u** is the vowel sound you hear in the word **cube**. Another vowel sound which is very much like the **long u** sound is the **oo** sound you hear in the word **boot**.

**Directions:** Use the **long u** and **oo** words in the box to write rhyming words.

| | | | |
|---|---|---|---|
| moon | tooth | use | blew |
| flew | loose | Ruth | choose |
| fuse | noon | goose | |

1. Write the words that rhyme with **soon**.

_____   _____

2. Write the words that rhyme with **lose**.

_____   _____   _____

3. Write the words that rhyme with **grew**.

_____   _____

4. Write the words that rhyme with **moose**.

_____   _____

5. Write the words that rhyme with **booth**.

_____   _____

**Grade 2 - Comprehensive Curriculum**

Name: _____

# Long u Words: Sentences

**Directions:** Write the words in the sentences below in the correct order. Begin each sentence with a capital letter and end it with a period or a question mark.

1. the pulled dentist tooth my loose

_____

2. ice cubes I choose in my drink to put

_____

3. a Ruth fuse blew yesterday

_____

4. loose the got in garden goose the

_____

5. flew the goose winter for the south

_____

6. is full there a moon tonight

_____

# Spelling Concentration Game

Play this game with a friend. Cut out each word card below and on pages 353 and 355. Lay the cards facedown on a flat surface. Take turns turning over two cards at a time. If the cards match, give the pair to your friend. Then spell the word from memory. If you spelled it correctly, you can keep the pair. If not, put the cards back facedown. When all of the word cards have been matched and spelled correctly, the players count their pairs. Whoever has the most pairs, wins.

You can also play this by yourself—or with more than one friend!

| | | dust |
|---|---|---|
| **light** | **clean** | **bump** |
| **dust** | **sleep** | **clean** |
| **bump** | **light** | **sleep** |

**Grade 2 - Comprehensive Curriculum**

Page is blank for cutting exercise on previous page.

Name: _____

| note | head | write |
|------|------|-------|
| soap | made | nine |
| stop | play | grew |
| clock | stamp | cute |
| tent | math | choose |

**Grade 2 - Comprehensive Curriculum**

Page is blank for cutting exercise on previous page.

| note | head | write |
|------|------|-------|
| soap | made | nine |
| stop | play | grew |
| clock | stamp | cute |
| tent | math | choose |

**Grade 2 - Comprehensive Curriculum**

Page is blank for cutting exercise on previous page.

Name: _____

# Opposite Words

**Directions: Opposites** are words which are different in every way.
Use the opposite word from the box to complete these sentences.

| hard | hot | bottom | quickly | happy |
|------|-----|--------|---------|-------|
| sad | slowly | cold | soft | top |

**Example:**

My new coat is blue on __top__ and

red on the __bottom__ .

1. Snow is _____ , but fire is _____ .

2. A rabbit runs_____ , but a turtle

   moves _____ .

3. A bed is _____ , but a floor is _____ .

4. I feel _____ when my friends come

   and _____ when they leave.

Grade 2 - Comprehensive Curriculum

Name: _____

# Opposite Words

**Directions:** Draw a line from each sentence to its picture. Then complete each sentence with the word under the picture.

**Example:**

She bought a ___new___ bat.

**hard**

1. I like my _____ pillow.

**new**

2. Birthdays make me _____.

**top**

3. Put that book on _____.

**sad**

4. Jenny runs _____.

**slowly**

5. A rock makes a _____ seat.

**quickly**

6. I feel _____ when it rains.

**happy**

7. He eats _____.

**soft**

Name: _____

# Opposite Words: Sentences

**Directions:** Cross out the word in each box that does not tell about the picture. Write a sentence about the picture using the other two words.

**Example:**

| ~~teeth~~ | garden | digs |
|---|---|---|

<u>She digs in her garden.</u>

| swims | quickly | five |
|---|---|---|

_____

_____

| soft | fly | happy |
|---|---|---|

_____

_____

| popcorn | bottom | sad |
|---|---|---|

_____

_____

Name: _____

# Opposite Words: Sentences

**Directions:** Look at each picture. Then write a sentence that uses the word under the picture and tells how something is the same as the picture.

**Example:**

**cold**

My hands are as cold as ice.

**hard**

_____

_____

**slow**

_____

_____

**soft**

_____

_____

**happy**

_____

_____

# Opposite Words: Completing a Story

**Directions:** Write opposite words in the blanks to complete the story.

| | | | | |
|---|---|---|---|---|
| hot | hard | top | cold | bottom |
| soft | quickly | happy | slowly | sad |

One day, Grandma came for a visit. She gave my sister Jenny and me a box of chocolate candy. We said, "Thank you!" Then Jenny _____ took the _____ off the box. The pieces all looked the same! I couldn't tell which pieces were _____ inside and which were _____ ! I only liked the _____ ones. Jenny didn't care. She was _____ to get any kind of candy!

I _____ looked at all the pieces. I didn't know which one to pick. Just then Dad called us. Grandma was going home. He wanted us to say good-bye to her. I hurried to the front door where they were standing. Jenny came a minute later.

I told Grandma I hoped I would see her soon. I always feel _____ when she leaves. Jenny stood behind me and didn't say anything. After Grandma went home, I found out why. Jenny had most of our candy in her mouth! Only a few pieces were left in the _____ of the box! Then I was _____ ! That Jenny!

**Grade 2 - Comprehensive Curriculum**

# Review

**Directions:** Tell a story about the picture by following the directions. Write one or two sentences for each answer.

1. Write about something that is happening **quickly** or **slowly** in the picture.

_____

_____

2. Use **top** or **bottom** in a sentence about the picture.

_____

_____

3. Tell about something **hard** and something **soft** in the picture. Use the word **but** in your sentence.

_____

_____

# Learning Words

**Directions:** Write a learning word to complete each sentence. Use each word only once.

| start | watch | listen | teach | finish | write |
|-------|-------|--------|-------|--------|-------|

1. You see with your eyes, but you _____ with your ears.

2. After you think of an idea, _____ it on your paper.

3. She will _____ you how to write your name.

4. To see what to do, you have to _____ the teacher.

5. Show me your picture after you _____ drawing it.

6. When you have everything you need, you can _____ working.

# Learning Words

**Directions:** Circle the words in each sentence which are not spelled correctly. Then write each word correctly on the line.

| start | watch | listen | teach | finish | write |
|-------|-------|--------|-------|--------|-------|

1. Do you like to wach television? _____

2. Right your name at the bottom. _____

3. I will teech you to ride a bike. _____

4. You have to lisen to me. _____

5. Did you finnish reading your book? _____

6. Everyone will strat running at the _____
   same time.

Change one letter in each word below to make one of the learning words. Write the new word on the line.

reach                    white                    match

_____   _____   _____

# Learning Words: Verb Endings

Remember: Verbs end with **s** when the sentence tells about only one thing.

**Example:**  One girl **reads**.        Two girls **read**.

But when an action word ends with **ch** or **sh**, add **es**.

**Example:**  We **watch** the baby.        She **watches** the baby.
Jane and Sue **finish** their work.    Peter **finishes** his work.

| start | watch | listen | teach | finish | write |
|-------|-------|--------|-------|--------|-------|

**Directions:** Write the verb from the box which completes each sentence. Add **s** or **es** to the end of the verb if you need to.

**Example:**
Carrie reads the book. She and Chris ___read___ it together.

1. Todd listens to the teacher. We all _____ to her.

2. Joy finishes the race first. We _____ after her.

3. They write letters to our class. Tony _____ back to them.

4. We watch the puppet show.

   She _____ with us.

5. He starts at the top of the page. We _____ in the middle.

Name: _____

# Learning Words: Completing a Story

**Directions:** Write learning words to complete this story.

"How can I _____ you anything if you don't _____?"

James asked his little sister Wendy. He was trying to show her how

to _____ her name. Wendy smiled up at James. "I'll

_____ now," she said. "Okay. Let's _____ again.

_____ what I do," he said. "First, you make a big **W**." "Up

and down," Wendy said. She tried to _____

a **W** like James, but it looked like a row of upside-down

mountains. "That's better," James said. "But you have to know when

to stop." He showed her how to _____ the **e, n** and **d**. "Now,

I'll _____ you how to _____ your name,"

he said. He wrote a **y** for her. Wendy made the tail on her **y** go down

to the bottom of the page. "I can do it!" she said. "I can _____

my name from _____ to _____!" She smiled at her

brother again. "Would you _____ me how to read now,

James?" He smiled back at her. "Maybe later, okay?"

# Time Words

The time between breakfast and lunch is **morning**.

The time between lunch and dinner is **afternoon**.

The time between dinner and bedtime is **evening**.

**Directions:** Write a time word from the box to complete each sentence. Use each word only once.

| evening | morning | today | tomorrow | afternoon |
|---------|---------|-------|----------|-----------|

1. What did you eat for breakfast

   this _____?

2. We came home from school in the _____ .

3. I help wash the dinner dishes in

   the _____ .

4. I feel a little tired _____ .

5. If I rest tonight, I will feel better _____ .

# Time Words: Sentences

**Directions:** Make each pair of short sentences into one long sentence. Use the joining words **and, or, but** or **because**.

**Example:**

This morning, I am sleepy. I stayed up late last night.

<u>This morning I am sleepy because</u>
<u>I stayed up late last night.</u>

1. Do you want to go in the morning?
   Do you want to go in the afternoon?

_____

_____

2. Mom asked me to clean my room today. I forgot.

_____

_____

# Time Words: Sentences

**Directions:** Write a sentence for these time words.
Tell something you do at that time.

**Example:**

day

## Every day I walk to school.

morning

_____

_____

afternoon

_____

_____

evening

_____

_____

Name: _____

# Review

**Directions:** Write the story below again and correct all the mistakes. Watch for words that are not spelled correctly, missing periods and question marks, question marks at the end of telling sentences and sentences with the wrong joining words.

One mourning, my granmother said I could have a pet mouse. That evenening, we got my mouse at the pet store, or the next afernoon my mouse had babies! Now, I had nyne mouses! I really liked to wach them? I wanted to pick the babies up, and they were too little. When they get bigger, I have to give too mouses to my sisster.

_____

_____

_____

_____

_____

_____

_____

_____

# MATH

# Less Than, Greater Than

**Directions:** The open mouth points to the larger number. The small point goes to the smaller number. Draw the symbol **<** or **>** to the correct number.

**Example:** 5  3    This means that 5 is greater than 3, and 3 is less than 5.

12 ◯ 2            16 ◯ 6

16 ◯ 15          1 ◯ 2

7 ◯ 1            19 ◯ 5

9 ◯ 6            11 ◯ 13

Name: _____

# Counting

**Directions:** Write the numbers that are:

| next in order | one less | one greater |
|---|---|---|
| 22, 23, ____ , ____ | ____ , 16 | 6, ____ |
| 674, ____ , ____ | ____ , 247 | 125, ____ |
| 227, ____ , ____ | ____ , 550 | 499, ____ |
| 199, ____ , ____ | ____ , 333 | 750, ____ |
| 329, ____ , ____ | ____ , 862 | 933, ____ |

**Directions:** Write the missing numbers.

13  14

163  166

821  823

**Grade 2 - Comprehensive Curriculum**

# Counting by 2's

**Directions:** Each basket the players make is worth 2 points. Help your team win by counting by 2's to beat the other team's score.

**2**

___

___

**8**

___

___

**16**

___

**20**

___

___

___

**28**

___

**32**

*Winner!*

| Final Score | |
|---|---|
| **Home** | **Visitor** |
| ☐ | **30** |

Name: _____

# Counting: 2's, 5's, 10's

**Directions:** Write the missing numbers.

Count by 2's:

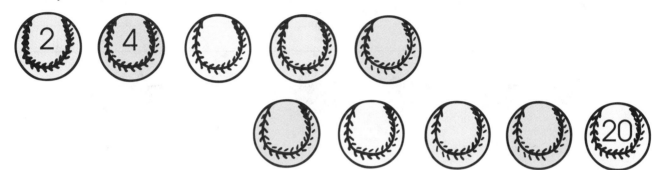

Count by 5's:

Count by 10's:

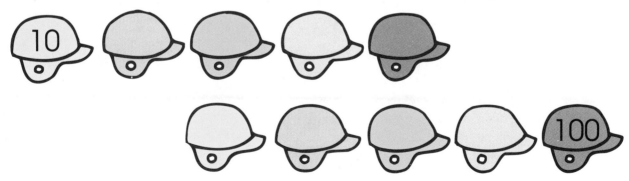

Name: _____

# Patterns

**Directions:** Write or draw what comes next in the pattern.

**Example:** 1, 2, 3, 4, __5__

---

1.      _____

2. A, 1, B, 2, C _____

3. 2, 4, 6, 8, _____

4. A, C, E, G, _____

5. 5, 10, 15, 20, _____

Name: _____

# Finding Patterns: Numbers

Mia likes to count by twos, threes, fours, fives, tens and hundreds.

**Directions:** Complete the number patterns.

1. 5, ____, ____, 20, ____, ____, 35, ____, ____, 50

2. 100, ____, ____, 400, ____, ____, ____, 800, ____

3. ____, 4, 6, ____, ____, 12, ____, 16, ____, ____

4. 10, ____, ____, 40, ____, ____, 70, ____, 90

5. 4, ____, 12, ____, ____, 24, ____, 32, ____, 40

6. ____, 6, 9, ____, ____, 18, ____, 24, ____, 30

**Directions:** Make up two of your own number patterns.

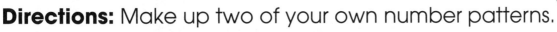

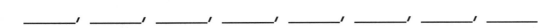

**Grade 2 - Comprehensive Curriculum**

# Finding Patterns: Shapes

**Directions:** Complete each row by drawing the correct shape.

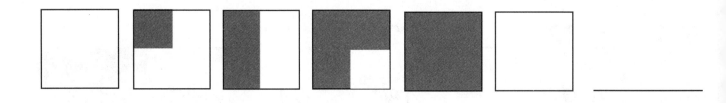

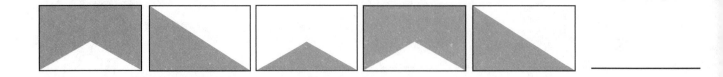

# Ordinal Numbers

Ordinal numbers indicate order in a series, such as **first**, **second** or **third**.

**Directions:** Follow the instructions to color the train cars. The first car is the engine.

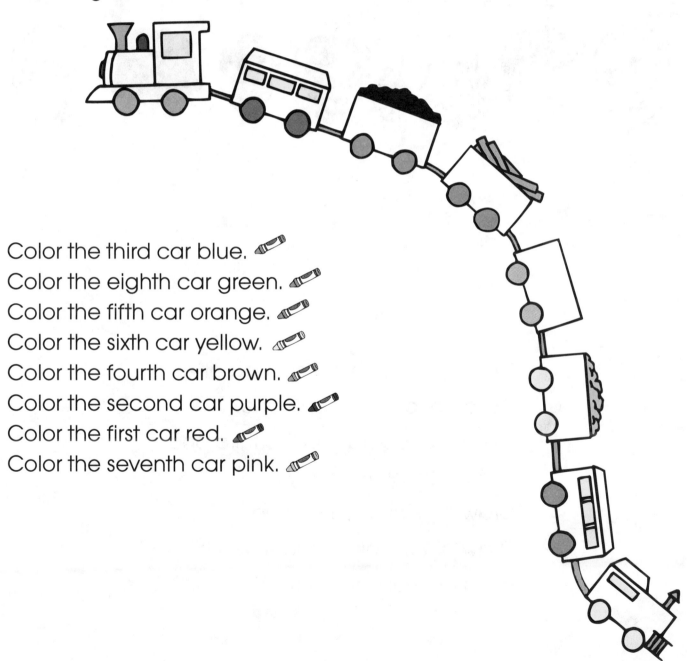

Color the third car blue.
Color the eighth car green.
Color the fifth car orange.
Color the sixth car yellow.
Color the fourth car brown.
Color the second car purple.
Color the first car red.
Color the seventh car pink.

Name: _____

# Ordinal Numbers

**Directions:** Follow the instructions.

Draw glasses on the second one.

Put a hat on the fourth one.

Color blonde hair on the third one.

Draw a tie on the first one.

Draw ears on the fifth one.

Draw black hair on the seventh one.

Put a bow on the head of the sixth one.

Name: _____

# Addition

Addition is "putting together" or adding two or more numbers to find the sum.

**Directions:** Add.

**Example:**

$$\begin{array}{r} 2 \\ +5 \\ \hline 7 \end{array}$$

| | | | | | |
|---|---|---|---|---|---|
| 3 | 6 | 7 | 8 | 5 | 3 |
| +4 | +2 | +1 | +2 | +4 | +1 |

| | | | | | |
|---|---|---|---|---|---|
| 8 | 9 | 10 | 6 | 4 | 7 |
| +2 | +5 | +3 | +6 | +9 | +7 |

| | | | | | |
|---|---|---|---|---|---|
| 9 | 8 | 6 | 7 | 7 | 9 |
| +3 | +7 | +5 | +9 | +6 | +9 |

**Grade 2 - Comprehensive Curriculum**

# Addition: Commutative Property

The commutative property of addition states that even if the order of the numbers is changed in an addition sentence, the sum will stay the same.

**Example:**     2 + 3 = 5
                 3 + 2 = 5

**Directions:** Look at the addition sentences below. Complete the addition sentences by writing the missing numerals.

5 + 4 = 9          3 + 1 = 4          2 + 6 = 8
4 + __ = 9         1 + __ = 4         6 + __ = 8


6 + 1 = 7          4 + 3 = 7          1 + 9 = 10
1 + __ = 7         3 + __ = 7         9 + __ = 10


**Now try these:**

6 + 3 = 9          10 + 2 = 12        8 + 3 = 11
__ + __ = 9        __ + __ = 12       __ + __ = 11


Look at these sums. Can you think of two number sentences that would show the commutative property of addition?

__ + __ = 7        __ + __ = 11       __ + __ = 9


__ + __ = 7        __ + __ = 11       __ + __ = 9

Name: _____

# Adding 3 or More Numbers

**Directions:** Add all the numbers to find the sum. Draw pictures to help or break up the problem into two smaller problems.

**Example:**

$$
\begin{array}{r}
1 \\
2 \\
+3 \\
\hline
6
\end{array}
$$

$$
\begin{array}{r}
+\begin{array}{c}2\\5\end{array} \longrightarrow 7 \\
+\begin{array}{c}2\\4\end{array} \longrightarrow +6 \\
\hline
13
\end{array}
$$

$$
\begin{array}{r}
3 \\
6 \\
+2 \\
\hline
\end{array}
\qquad
\begin{array}{r}
8 \\
5 \\
+4 \\
\hline
\end{array}
\qquad
\begin{array}{r}
3 \\
1 \\
+5 \\
\hline
\end{array}
\qquad
\begin{array}{r}
8 \\
2 \\
+9 \\
\hline
\end{array}
$$

$$
\begin{array}{r}
2 \\
8 \\
4 \\
+3 \\
\hline
\end{array}
\qquad
\begin{array}{r}
3 \\
6 \\
5 \\
+2 \\
\hline
\end{array}
\qquad
\begin{array}{r}
4 \\
1 \\
2 \\
+5 \\
\hline
\end{array}
\qquad
\begin{array}{r}
6 \\
7 \\
3 \\
+1 \\
\hline
\end{array}
$$

**Grade 2 - Comprehensive Curriculum**

# Subtraction

Subtraction is "taking away" or subtracting one number from another to find the difference.

**Directions:** Subtract.

**Example:**

$$\begin{array}{r} 4 \\ -3 \\ \hline 1 \end{array}$$

$$\begin{array}{r} 5 \\ -3 \\ \hline \end{array} \qquad \begin{array}{r} 6 \\ -1 \\ \hline \end{array} \qquad \begin{array}{r} 4 \\ -3 \\ \hline \end{array} \qquad \begin{array}{r} 3 \\ -1 \\ \hline \end{array} \qquad \begin{array}{r} 2 \\ -0 \\ \hline \end{array} \qquad \begin{array}{r} 1 \\ -1 \\ \hline \end{array}$$

$$\begin{array}{r} 9 \\ -2 \\ \hline \end{array} \qquad \begin{array}{r} 7 \\ -4 \\ \hline \end{array} \qquad \begin{array}{r} 10 \\ -5 \\ \hline \end{array} \qquad \begin{array}{r} 14 \\ -6 \\ \hline \end{array} \qquad \begin{array}{r} 15 \\ -9 \\ \hline \end{array} \qquad \begin{array}{r} 12 \\ -3 \\ \hline \end{array}$$

$$\begin{array}{r} 18 \\ -8 \\ \hline \end{array} \qquad \begin{array}{r} 13 \\ -5 \\ \hline \end{array} \qquad \begin{array}{r} 14 \\ -7 \\ \hline \end{array} \qquad \begin{array}{r} 11 \\ -4 \\ \hline \end{array} \qquad \begin{array}{r} 17 \\ -9 \\ \hline \end{array} \qquad \begin{array}{r} 16 \\ -8 \\ \hline \end{array}$$

Name: _____

# Addition and Subtraction

Addition is "putting together" or adding two or more numbers to find the sum. Subtraction is "taking away" or subtracting one number from another to find the difference.

**Directions:** Add or subtract. Circle the answers that are less than 10.

**Examples:**

3
+1
(4)

3
−1
(2)

| 9 | 6 | 12 | 18 | 15 |
| +3 | −2 | − 1 | +1 | −6 |

| 7 | 16 | 10 | 14 | 16 |
| + 6 | − 9 | − 3 | + 5 | − 8 |

| 8 | 12 | 13 | 17 | 9 |
| +7 | + 2 | − 4 | + 2 | +9 |

**Grade 2 - Comprehensive Curriculum**

# Place Value: Ones, Tens

The place value of a digit or numeral is shown by where it is in the number. For example, in the number **23**, **2** has the place value of **tens**, and **3** is **ones**.

**Directions:** Add the tens and ones and write your answers in the blanks.

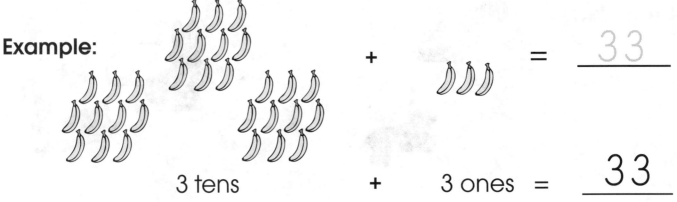

**Example:**

3 tens        +        3 ones  =  _33_

|  | tens | ones |  |  | tens | ones |
|---|---|---|---|---|---|---|

7 tens + 5 ones =  _____        4 tens + 0 ones  =  _____

2 tens + 3 ones =  _____        8 tens + 1 one   =  _____

5 tens + 2 ones =  _____        1 ten + 1 one    =  _____

5 tens + 4 ones =  _____        6 tens + 3 ones  =  _____

9 tens + 5 ones =  _____

**Directions:** Draw a line to the correct number.

6 tens + 7 ones                    73

4 tens + 2 ones                    67

8 tens + 0 ones                    51

7 tens + 3 ones                    80

5 tens + 1 one                     42

Name: _____

# Place Value: Ones, Tens

**Directions:** Write the numbers for the tens and ones. Then add.

**Example:**

2 tens + 7 ones
20 + 7
27

6 tens + 2 ones
___ + ___
___

3 tens + 4 ones
___ + ___
___

8 tens + 3 ones
___ + ___
___

5 tens + 0 ones
___ + ___
___

**Grade 2 - Comprehensive Curriculum**

# 2-Digit Addition

**Directions:** Study the example. Follow the steps to add.

**Example:**
```
  33
+41
```

**Step 1:** Add the ones.

| tens | ones |
|------|------|
| 3    | 3    |
| +4   | 1    |
|      | 4    |

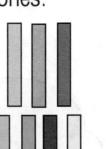 

**Step 2:** Add the tens.

| tens | ones |
|------|------|
| 3    | 3    |
| +4   | 1    |
| 7    | 4    |

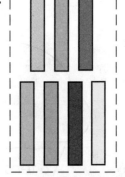

| tens | ones |
|------|------|
| 4    | 2    |
| +2   | 4    |
| 6    | 6    |

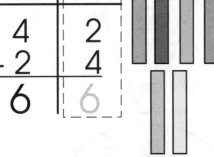

| tens | ones |
|------|------|
| 5    | 0    |
| +4   | 7    |
| 9    | 7    |

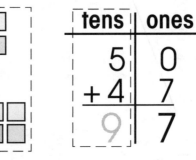 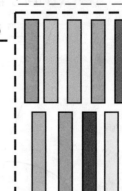 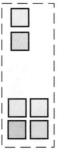

```
  24        15        38        11        37        72        33        10
+62       +23       +61       +26       +42       +11       +51       +30
```

```
  25        62        32        25        82        91        16        55
+42       +14       +44       +13       + 6       + 5       +71       + 3
```

Name: _____

# 2-Digit Addition

**Directions:** Add the total points scored in each game. Remember to add **ones** first and **tens** second.

**Example:**

Total __39__

Total _____

Total _____

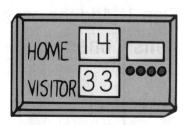

Total _____

Total _____

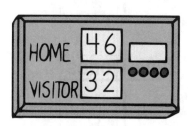

Total _____

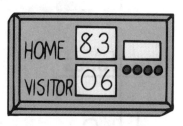

Total _____

Total _____

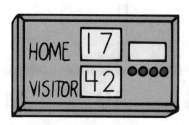

Total _____

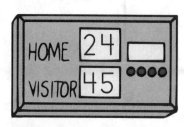

Total _____

**Grade 2 - Comprehensive Curriculum**

# 2-Digit Addition: Regrouping

Addition is "putting together" or adding two or more numbers to find the sum. Regrouping is using **ten ones** to form **one ten, ten tens** to form **one 100, fifteen ones** to form **one ten** and **five ones** and so on.

**Directions:** Study the examples. Follow the steps to add.

**Example:**
$$\begin{array}{r} 14 \\ +\ 8 \\ \hline \end{array}$$

**Step 1:** Add the ones.

| tens | ones |
|------|------|
| 1 | 4 |
| + | 8 |
| 1 | 2 |

**Step 2:** Regroup the tens.

| tens | ones |
|------|------|
| 1 | 4 |
| + | 8 |
| | 2 |

**Step 3:** Add the tens.

| tens | ones |
|------|------|
| 1 | 4 |
| + | 8 |
| 2 | 2 |

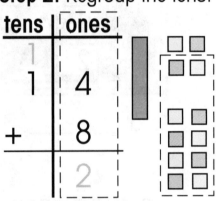
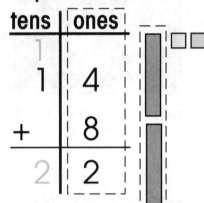

| tens | ones |
|------|------|
| 1 | 6 |
| +3 | 7 |
| 5 | 3 |

| tens | ones |
|------|------|
| 3 | 8 |
| +5 | 3 |
| 9 | 1 |

| tens | ones |
|------|------|
| 2 | 4 |
| +4 | 7 |
| 7 | 1 |

$$\begin{array}{r} 28 \\ +17 \\ \hline \end{array} \quad \begin{array}{r} 32 \\ +38 \\ \hline \end{array} \quad \begin{array}{r} 54 \\ +25 \\ \hline \end{array} \quad \begin{array}{r} 19 \\ +55 \\ \hline \end{array} \quad \begin{array}{r} 44 \\ +48 \\ \hline \end{array} \quad \begin{array}{r} 25 \\ +64 \\ \hline \end{array} \quad \begin{array}{r} 29 \\ +33 \\ \hline \end{array} \quad \begin{array}{r} 79 \\ +15 \\ \hline \end{array}$$

Name: _____

# 2-Digit Addition: Regrouping

**Directions:** Add the total points scored in the game.
Remember to add the ones, regroup, and then add the tens.

**Example:**

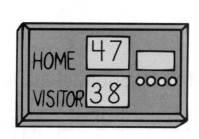

Total __85__

Total _____

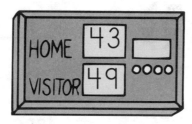

Total _____

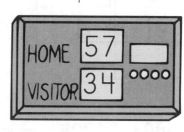

Total _____

Total _____

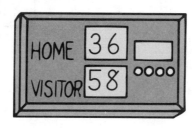

Total _____

Total _____

Total _____

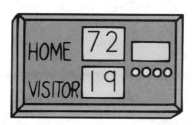

Total _____

Total _____

**Grade 2 - Comprehensive Curriculum**

Name: _____

# 2-Digit Subtraction

**Directions:** Study the example. Follow the steps to subtract.

**Example:**
$$\begin{array}{r} 28 \\ -14 \end{array}$$

**Step 1:** Subtract the ones.

| tens | ones |
|------|------|
| 2 | 8 |
| -1 | 4 |
| | 4 |

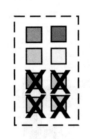

**Step 2:** Subtract the tens.

| tens | ones |
|------|------|
| 2 | 8 |
| -1 | 4 |
| 1 | 4 |

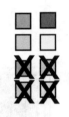

| tens | ones |
|------|------|
| 2 | 4 |
| -1 | 2 |
| 1 | 2 |

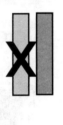 

| tens | ones |
|------|------|
| 3 | 8 |
| -1 | 5 |
| 2 | 3 |

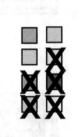

| | | | | | | | |
|---|---|---|---|---|---|---|---|
| 24 | 61 | 77 | 85 | 57 | 87 | 59 | 96 |
| − 12 | − 30 | − 44 | − 24 | − 23 | − 33 | − 34 | − 16 |

| | | | | | | | |
|---|---|---|---|---|---|---|---|
| 29 | 74 | 46 | 69 | 95 | 33 | 78 | 22 |
| − 15 | − 51 | − 32 | − 35 | − 32 | − 33 | − 26 | − 11 |

Name: _____

# 2-Digit Subtraction: Regrouping

Subtraction is "taking away" or subtracting one number from another to find the difference. Regrouping is using **one ten to form ten ones, one 100 to form ten tens** and so on.

**Directions:** Study the examples. Follow the steps to subtract.

**Example:**
$$37$$
$$-19$$

**Step 1:** Regroup.

| tens | ones |
|------|------|
| 2 | 17 |
| 3 | 7 |
| -1 | 9 |

**Step 2:** Subtract the ones.

| tens | ones |
|------|------|
| 2 | 17 |
| 3 | 7 |
| -1 | 9 |
|  | 8 |

**Step 3:** Subtract the tens.

| tens | ones |
|------|------|
| 2 | 17 |
| 3 | 7 |
| -1 | 9 |
| 1 | 8 |

| tens | ones |
|------|------|
| 0 | 12 |
| 1 | 2 |
| - | 9 |
|  | 3 |

| tens | ones |
|------|------|
| 2 | 14 |
| 3 | 4 |
| -1 | 6 |
| 1 | 8 |

| tens | ones |
|------|------|
| 3 | 15 |
| 4 | 5 |
| -2 | 9 |
| 1 | 6 |

| | | | | | | | |
|--|--|--|--|--|--|--|--|
| 28 | 46 | 12 | 30 | 52 | 47 | 21 | 45 |
| − 19 | − 18 | − 8 | − 12 | − 25 | − 35 | − 13 | − 25 |

Name: _____

# 2-Digit Subtraction: Regrouping

**Directions:** Study the steps for subtracting. Solve the problems using the steps.

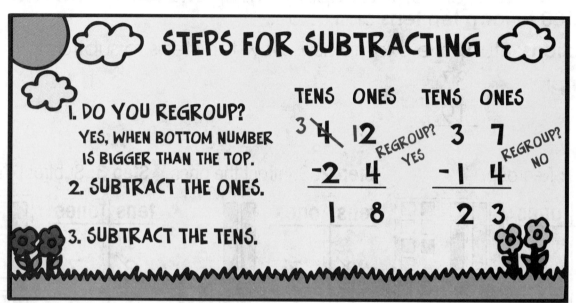

STEPS FOR SUBTRACTING

1. DO YOU REGROUP?
   YES, WHEN BOTTOM NUMBER IS BIGGER THAN THE TOP.
2. SUBTRACT THE ONES.
3. SUBTRACT THE TENS.

| TENS | ONES | | TENS | ONES | |
|------|------|---|------|------|---|
| 3 4̶ | 12 | REGROUP? YES | 3 | 7 | REGROUP? NO |
| -2 | 4 | | -1 | 4 | |
| 1 | 8 | | 2 | 3 | |

| tens | ones | | tens | ones | | tens | ones |
|------|------|---|------|------|---|------|------|
| 4 | 7 | | 6 | 4 | | 5 | 3 |
| - 2 | 8 | | - 3 | 4 | | - 3 | 9 |

```
  56        83        43        75        91
- 27      - 47      - 39      - 53      - 18
```

```
  73        35        67        26        68
- 66      - 14      - 58      -  7      - 45
```

# Review

Name: _____

**Directions:** Add or subtract. Use regrouping when needed. Always do ones first and tens last.

| tens | ones | | tens | ones | | tens | ones | | tens | ones |
|------|------|---|------|------|---|------|------|---|------|------|
| 9 | 3 | | 3 | 0 | | 6 | 5 | | 7 | 1 |
| −2 | 5 | | +2 | 7 | | +1 | 7 | | −3 | 6 |

| 7 | 6 | | 8 | 2 | | 5 | 6 | | 2 | 5 |
|---|---|---|---|---|---|---|---|---|---|---|
| −2 | 8 | | +1 | 9 | | −2 | 8 | | −1 | 6 |

| 4 | 3 | | 5 | 3 | | 2 | 4 | | 4 | 8 |
|---|---|---|---|---|---|---|---|---|---|---|
| −1 | 4 | | −1 | 5 | | +5 | 7 | | +2 | 8 |

```
  33         52         46         97
+47        +29        -37        -68
```

# 2-Digit Addition and Subtraction

Addition is "putting together" or adding two or more numbers to find the sum. Subtraction is "taking away" or subtracting one number from another to find the difference. Regrouping is using **one ten** to form **ten ones**, **one 100** to form **ten tens**, and so on.

**Directions:** Add or subtract using regrouping.

**Example:**

```
tens  ones
  2    15
  3     5
 -2     7
 ───────
        8
```

| | | | | | | | |
|---|---|---|---|---|---|---|---|
| 56 | 40 | 35 | 42 | 53 | 97 | 44 | 93 |
| − 27 | − 16 | + 27 | − 14 | +38 | − 48 | + 27 | − 39 |

| | | | | | | | |
|---|---|---|---|---|---|---|---|
| 56 | 44 | 68 | 73 | 33 | 49 | 77 | 27 |
| − 17 | + 28 | − 49 | − 24 | + 18 | + 32 | − 68 | + 19 |

Name: _____

# 2-Digit Addition and Subtraction

**Directions:** Add or subtract using regrouping.

```
  23
+ 48
_____
```
```
  84
- 56
_____
```
```
  69
+ 29
_____
```
```
  41
- 17
_____
```

```
  52
- 28
_____
```
```
  73
+ 18
_____
```
```
  84
- 27
_____
```
```
  57
- 39
_____
```

```
  33
- 15
_____
```
```
  64
+ 17
_____
```
```
  37
+ 58
_____
```
```
  36
- 19
_____
```

```
  65
- 28
_____
```
```
  48
- 30
_____
```
```
  33
+ 18
_____
```
```
  25
+ 35
_____
```

**Grade 2 - Comprehensive Curriculum**

Name: _____

# Place Value: Hundreds

The place value of a digit or numeral is shown by where it is in the number. For example, in the number **123, 1** has the place value of **hundreds, 2** is **tens** and **3** is **ones.**

**Directions:** Study the examples. Then write the missing numbers in the blanks.

**Examples:**

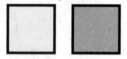      

2 hundreds + 3 tens + 6 ones =          1 hundreds + 4 tens + 9 ones =

| hundreds | tens | ones |   | | hundreds | tens | ones | |
|:---:|:---:|:---:|:---:|---|:---:|:---:|:---:|:---:|
| 2 | 3 | 6 | = 236 | | 1 | 4 | 9 | = 149 |

| | hundreds | tens | ones | total |
|---|:---:|:---:|:---:|:---:|
| 3 hundreds + 4 tens + 8 ones = | 3 | 4 | 8 | = _____ |
| _ hundreds + _ ten + _ ones = | 2 | 1 | 7 | = _____ |
| _ hundreds + _ tens + _ ones = | 6 | 3 | 5 | = _____ |
| _ hundreds + _ tens + _ ones = | 4 | 7 | 9 | = _____ |
| _ hundreds + _ tens + _ ones = | 2 | 9 | 4 | = _____ |
| _ hundreds + 5 tens + 6 ones = | 4 | ____ | ____ | = _____ |
| 3 hundreds + 1 ten + 3 ones = | ____ | ____ | ____ | = _____ |
| 3 hundreds + _ tens + 7 ones = | ____ | 5 | ____ | = _____ |
| 6 hundreds + 2 tens + _ ones = | ____ | ____ | 8 | = _____ |

# Place Value: Hundreds

**Directions:** Write the numbers for hundreds, tens and ones.
Then add.

**Example:**

1 hundred + 4 tens + 6 ones
100 + 40 + 6
146

7 hundreds + 3 tens + 5 ones
_____ + _____ + _____
_____

3 hundreds + 1 ten + 9 ones
_____ + _____ + _____
_____

5 hundreds + 8 tens + 0 ones
_____ + _____ + _____
_____

9 hundreds + 0 tens + 7 ones
_____ + _____ + _____
_____

**Grade 2 - Comprehensive Curriculum**

# 3-Digit Addition: Regrouping

**Directions:** Study the examples. Follow the steps to add.

**Example:**

**Step 1:** Add the ones.  **Step 2:** Add the tens.  **Step 3:** Add the hundreds.

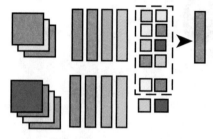   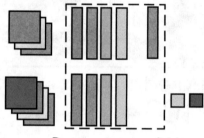   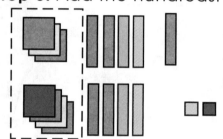

Do you regroup? Yes     Do you regroup? No

| hundreds | tens | ones | hundreds | tens | ones | hundreds | tens | ones |
|----------|------|------|----------|------|------|----------|------|------|
|          | 1    |      |          | 1    |      |          | 1    |      |
| 3        | 4    | 8    | 3        | 4    | 8    | 3        | 4    | 8    |
| +4       | 4    | 4    | +4       | 4    | 4    | +4       | 4    | 4    |
|          |      | 2    |          | 9    | 2    | 7        | 9    | 2    |

| hundreds | tens | ones | hundreds | tens | ones | hundreds | tens | ones |
|----------|------|------|----------|------|------|----------|------|------|
|          | 1    |      |          | 1    |      |          | 1    |      |
| 2        | 1    | 4    | 3        | 6    | 8    | 1        | 1    | 9    |
| +2       | 3    | 8    | +2       | 1    | 3    | +5       | 6    | 5    |
| 4        | 5    | 2    |          | 8    | 1    |          |      | 4    |

$$
\begin{array}{r} 418 \\ +323 \\ \hline \end{array}
\quad
\begin{array}{r} 471 \\ +319 \\ \hline \end{array}
\quad
\begin{array}{r} 334 \\ +528 \\ \hline \end{array}
\quad
\begin{array}{r} 659 \\ +127 \\ \hline \end{array}
\quad
\begin{array}{r} 736 \\ +145 \\ \hline \end{array}
\quad
\begin{array}{r} 426 \\ +165 \\ \hline \end{array}
\quad
\begin{array}{r} 567 \\ +228 \\ \hline \end{array}
\quad
\begin{array}{r} 327 \\ +354 \\ \hline \end{array}
$$

Name: _____

# 3-Digit Addition: Regrouping

**Directions:** Study the example. Follow the steps to add. Regroup when needed.

**Step 1:** Add the ones.
**Step 2:** Add the tens.
**Step 3:** Add the hundreds.

| hundreds | tens | ones |
|----------|------|------|
| 1 | 1 | |
| 3 | 4 | 8 |
| +4 | 5 | 4 |
| 8 | 0 | 2 |

$10 = 1$ ten $+ 0$ ones

```
 348      172      575      623      369      733
+214     +418     +329     +268     +533     +229
```

```
 411      423      639      624      272      393
+299     +169     +177     +368     +469     +418
```

# 3-Digit Subtraction: Regrouping

**Directions:** Study the example. Follow the steps to subtract.

**Step 1:** Regroup ones.
**Step 2:** Subtract ones.
**Step 3:** Subtract tens.
**Step 4:** Subtract hundreds.

**Example:**

| hundreds | tens | ones |
|---|---|---|
| | 5 | 12 |
| 4 | 6̸ | 2̸ |
| -2 | 5 | 3 |
| 2 | 0 | 9 |

$$423 - 114$$

$$562 - 349$$

$$478 - 239$$

$$651 - 333$$

**Directions:** Draw a line to the correct answer. Color the kites.

$$347 - 218$$

$$144 - 135$$

$$963 - 748$$

$$762 - 553$$

$$287 - 179$$

$$427 - 398$$

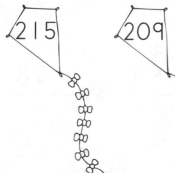 215
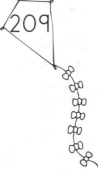 209
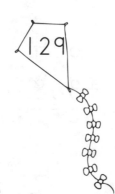 129
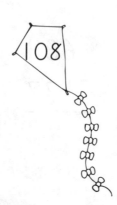 108
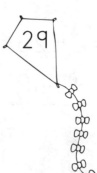 29
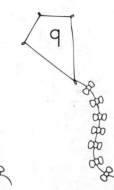 9

Name: _____

# 3-Digit Subtraction: Regrouping

**Directions:** Subtract. Circle the **7's** that appear in the **tens place**.

score
257

```
  492          184
 -221         -129
 ─────        ─────
  2⑦1
```

```
  358      765      584      693      921
 -238     -326     -435     -314     -362
 ─────    ─────    ─────    ─────    ─────
```

```
  128      744      835      248      635
 -109     -674     -217     -199     -428
 ─────    ─────    ─────    ─────    ─────
```

**Grade 2 - Comprehensive Curriculum**

# Place Value: Thousands

**Directions:** Study the example. Write the missing numbers.

**Example:**

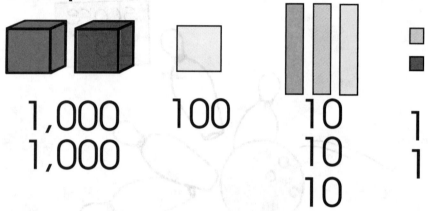

1,000  100  10  1
1,000       10  1
            10

2 thousands + 1 hundred + __3__ tens + 2 ones = __2,132__

5,286 = ____ thousands + ____ hundreds + ____ tens + ____ ones

1,831 = ____ thousands + ____ hundreds + ____ tens + ____ ones

8,972 = ____ thousands + ____ hundreds + ____ tens + ____ ones

4,528 = ____ thousands + ____ hundreds + ____ tens + ____ ones

3,177 = ____ thousands + ____ hundreds + ____ tens + ____ ones

**Directions:** Draw a line to the number that has:

| | |
|---|---|
| 8 hundreds | 7,103 |
| 5 ones | 2,862 |
| 9 tens | 5,996 |
| 7 thousands | 1,485 |

Name: _____

# Place Value: Thousands

6 , 4 3 1

thousands | hundreds | tens | ones

**Directions:** Tell which number is in each place.

 Thousands place:

2,456                4,621                3,456

_____          _____          _____

 Tens place:

4,286                1,234                5,678

_____          _____          _____

 Hundreds place:

6,321                3,210                7,871

_____          _____          _____

⭐ Ones place:

5,432                6,531                9,980

_____          _____          _____

**Grade 2 - Comprehensive Curriculum**

# Place Value: Thousands

**Directions:** Use the code to color the fan.

**If the answer has:**

9 thousands, color it pink.
6 thousands, color it green.
5 hundreds, color it orange.

8 tens, color it red.
3 ones, color it blue.

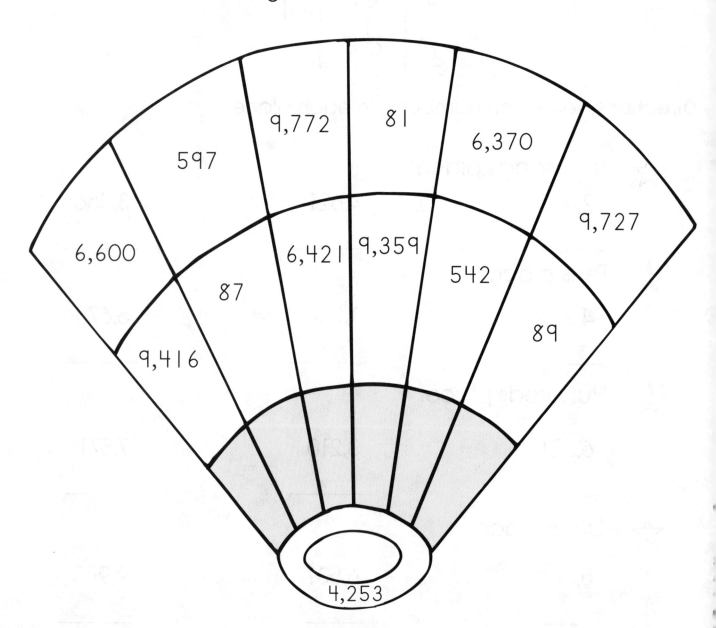

Name: _____

# Graphs

A graph is a drawing that shows information about numbers.

**Directions:** Count the apples in each row. Color the boxes to show how many apples have bites taken out of them.

**Example:**

| 1 | 2 | 3 | 4 | 5 | 6 | 7 | 8 |
|---|---|---|---|---|---|---|---|
| ▓ | ▓ | ▓ |   |   |   |   |   |

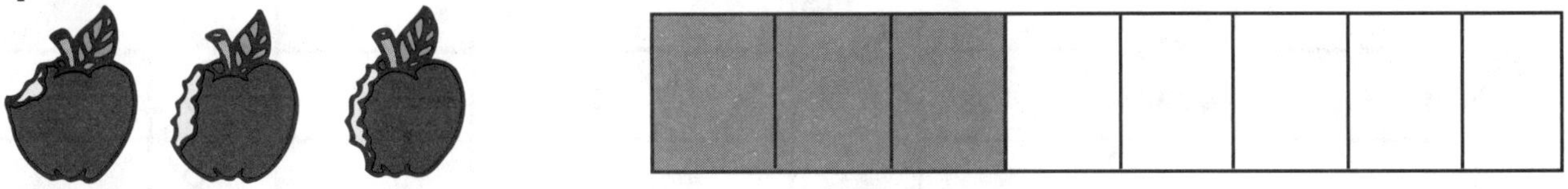

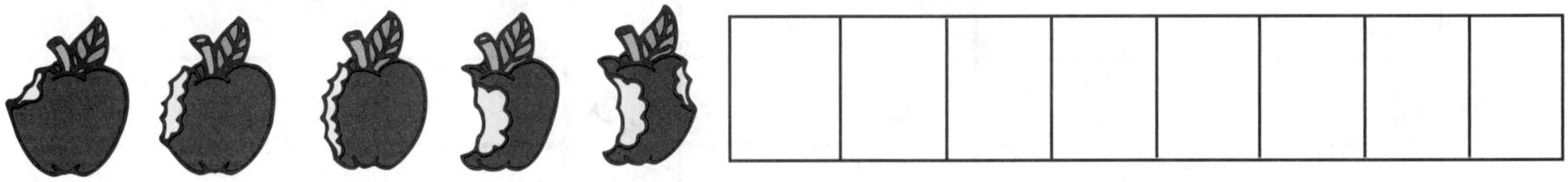

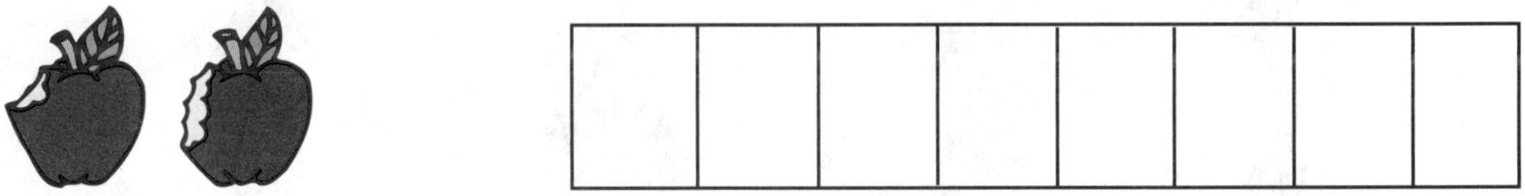

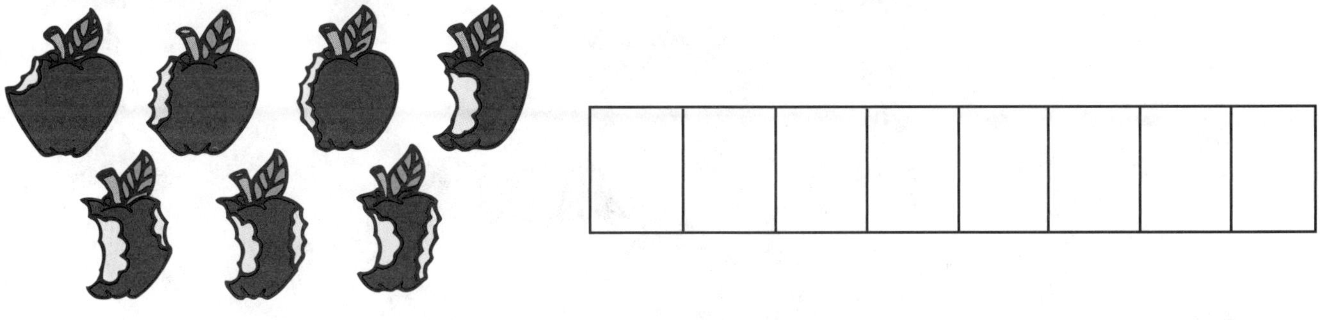

# Graphs

**Directions:** Count the bananas in each row. Color the boxes to show how many have been eaten by the monkeys.

Name: _____

# Graphs

**Directions:** Count the fish. Color the bowls to make a graph that shows the number of fish.

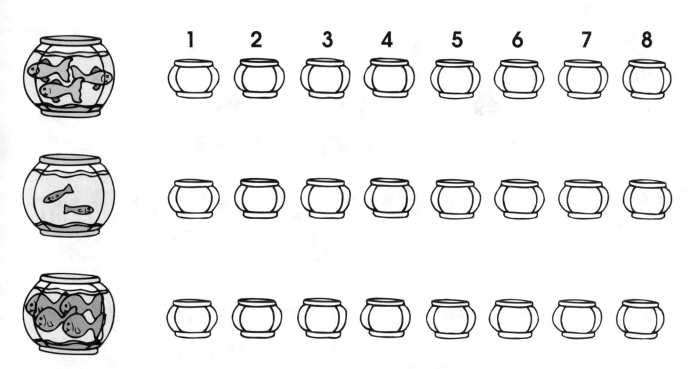

**Directions:** Use your fishbowl graphs to find the answers to the following questions. Draw a line to the correct bowl.

The most fish

The fewest fish

Name: _____

# Multiplication

Multiplication is a short way to find the sum of adding the same number a certain amount of times. For example, **4 x 7 = 28** instead of **7 + 7 + 7 + 7 = 28**.

**Directions:** Study the example. Solve the problems.

**Example:**

3 + 3 + 3 = 9
3 threes = 9
3 x 3 = 9

7 + 7 = __14__
2 sevens = __14__
2 x 7 = __14__

4 + 4 + 4 + 4 = ____
4 fours = ____
4 x ____ = ____

5 + 5 = ____
2 fives = ____
2 x ____ = ____

2 + 2 + 2 + 2 = ____
4 twos = ____
4 x ____ = ____

6 + 6 = ____
2 sixes = ____
2 x ____ = ____

Name: _____

# Multiplication

Multiplication is repeated addition.

**Directions:** Draw a picture for each problem. Then write the missing numbers.

**Example:**

Draw 2 groups of three apples.

$$3 + 3 = 6$$
$$\text{or} \quad 2 \times 3 = 6$$

---

| Draw 3 groups of four hearts. | Draw 2 groups of five boxes. |
|---|---|
|  | |
| $4 + 4 + 4 =$ ____ | $5 +$ ____ $=$ ____ |
| or $3 \times$ ____ $=$ ____ | or $2 \times$ ____ $=$ ____ |

---

Draw 6 groups of two circles.

$2 +$ ____ $+$ ____ $+$ ____ $+$ ____ $+$ ____ $=$ ____

or $6 \times$ ____ $=$ ____

---

Draw 7 groups of three triangles.

$3 +$ ____ $+$ ____ $+$ ____ $+$ ____ $+$ ____ $+$ ____ $=$ ____

or ____ $\times$ ____ $=$ ____

**Grade 2 - Comprehensive Curriculum**

# Multiplication

**Directions:** Study the example. Draw the groups and write the total.

**Example:**

$3 \times 2$

$2 + 2 + 2$ = 6

•• •• ••

$3 \times 4$

___ + ___ + ___ = _____

$2 \times 5$

___ + ___ = _____

$5 \times 3$

___ + ___ + ___ + ___ + ___ = _____

# Multiplication

**Directions:** Solve the problems.

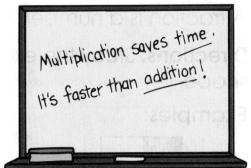

Multiplication saves time.
It's faster than addition!

$9 + 9 =$ __18__

2 nines = ____

$2 \times 9 =$ ____

$7 + 7 =$ ____

2 sevens = ____

$2 \times$ __7__ $=$ ____

$4 + 4 + 4 + 4 =$ ____

__4__ fours = ____

____ $\times 4 =$ ____

$8 + 8 + 8 + 8 + 8 =$ ____

____ eights = ____

____ $\times 8 =$ ____

$5 + 5 + 5 =$ ____

____ fives = ____

____ $\times 5 =$ ____

$9 + 9 =$ ____

____ nines = ____

____ $\times 9 =$ ____

$6 + 6 + 6 =$ ____

____ sixes = ____

____ $\times 6 =$ ____

$3 + 3 =$ ____

____ threes = ____

____ $\times 3 =$ ____

$7 + 7 + 7 + 7 =$ ____

____ sevens = ____

____ $\times 7 =$ ____

$2 + 2 =$ ____

____ twos = ____

____ $\times 2 =$ ____

**Grade 2 - Comprehensive Curriculum**

Name: _____

# Fractions: Half, Third, Fourth

A fraction is a number that names part of a whole, such as $\frac{1}{2}$ or $\frac{1}{3}$.

**Directions:** Study the examples. Color the correct fraction of each shape.

**Examples:**

shaded part 1
equal parts 2
$\frac{1}{2}$ (one-half) shaded

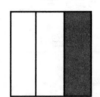

shaded part 1
equal parts 3
$\frac{1}{3}$ (one-third) shaded

shaded part 1
equal parts 4
$\frac{1}{4}$ (one-fourth) shaded

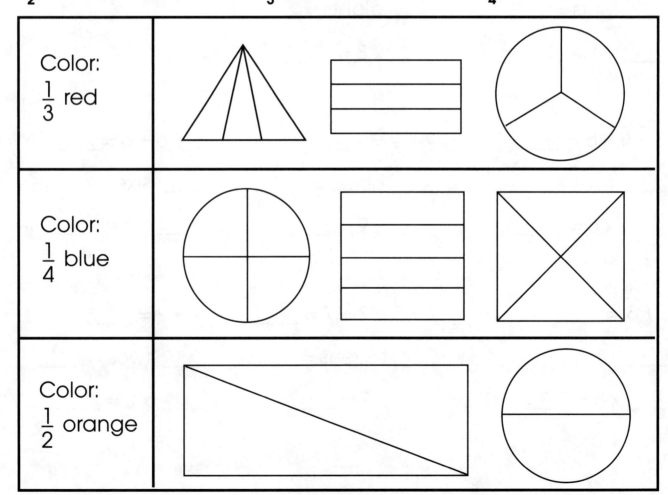

| Color: $\frac{1}{3}$ red | |
| Color: $\frac{1}{4}$ blue | |
| Color: $\frac{1}{2}$ orange | |

Name: _____

# Fractions: Half, Third, Fourth

**Directions:** Study the examples. Circle the fraction that shows the shaded part. Then circle the fraction that shows the white part.

**Examples:**

**shaded**   **white**
$\frac{1}{4}$ $\frac{1}{3}$ $\boxed{\frac{1}{2}}$   $\frac{1}{3}$ $\boxed{\frac{1}{2}}$ $\frac{1}{4}$

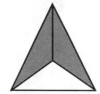

**shaded**   **white**
$\frac{1}{2}$ $\boxed{\frac{2}{3}}$ $\frac{3}{4}$   $\frac{2}{3}$ $\frac{1}{2}$ $\boxed{\frac{1}{3}}$

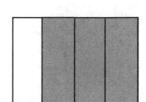

**shaded**   **white**
$\frac{1}{4}$ $\frac{1}{2}$ $\boxed{\frac{3}{4}}$   $\boxed{\frac{1}{4}}$ $\frac{2}{3}$ $\frac{1}{2}$

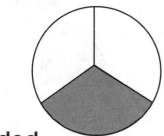

**shaded**   **white**
$\frac{1}{4}$ $\frac{1}{3}$ $\frac{1}{2}$   $\frac{2}{4}$ $\frac{2}{3}$ $\frac{2}{2}$

**shaded**   **white**
$\frac{3}{4}$ $\frac{1}{3}$ $\frac{3}{2}$   $\frac{1}{2}$ $\frac{1}{4}$ $\frac{1}{3}$

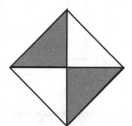

**shaded**   **white**
$\frac{2}{3}$ $\frac{2}{4}$ $\frac{2}{2}$   $\frac{1}{3}$ $\frac{2}{4}$ $\frac{2}{2}$

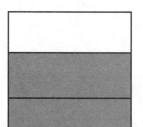

**shaded**   **white**
$\frac{2}{4}$ $\frac{2}{3}$ $\frac{2}{2}$   $\frac{1}{2}$ $\frac{1}{4}$ $\frac{1}{3}$

Name: _____

# Fractions: Half, Third, Fourth

**Directions:** Draw a line from the fraction to the correct shape.

$\frac{1}{4}$ shaded

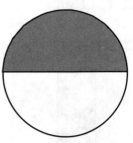

$\frac{2}{4}$ shaded

$\frac{1}{2}$ shaded

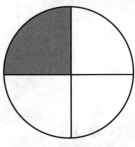

$\frac{1}{3}$ shaded

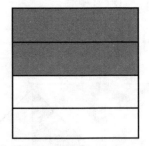

$\frac{2}{3}$ shaded

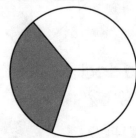

Name: _____

# Geometry

Geometry is mathematics that has to do with lines and shapes.

**Directions:** Color the shapes.

Color the triangles blue.
Color the circles red.
Color the squares green.
Color the rectangles pink.

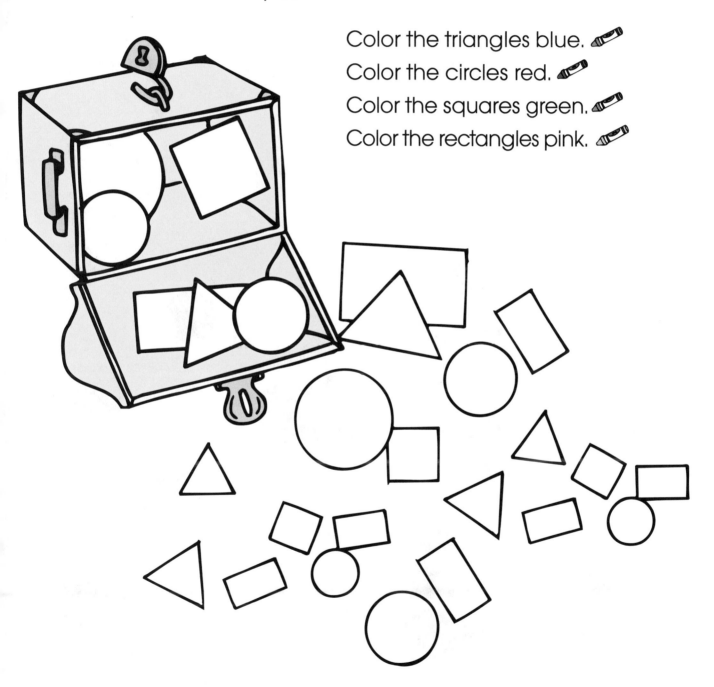

# Geometry

**Directions:** Draw a line from the word to the shape.

Use a red line for circles. Use a yellow line for rectangles.
Use a blue line for squares. Use a green line for triangles.

**Circle**        **Square**        **Triangle**        **Rectangle**

# Geometry

**Directions:** Cut out the tangram below. Mix up the pieces. Try to put it back together into a square.

Page is blank for cutting exercise on previous page.

# Measurement: Inches

**Directions:** Cut out the ruler. Measure each object to the nearest inch.

_____ inches

_____ inches

_____ inches

# Measurement

**Directions:** Measure objects around your house. Write the measurement to the nearest inch.

| | |
|---|---|
| can of soup | _____ inches |
| pen | _____ inches |
| toothbrush | _____ inches |
| paper clip | _____ inches |
| small toy | _____ inches |

cut out

8 7 6 5 4 3 2 1

Page is blank for cutting exercise on previous page.

Name: _____

# Measurement: Inches

An inch is a unit of length in the standard measurement system.

**Directions:** Use a ruler to measure each object to the nearest inch.

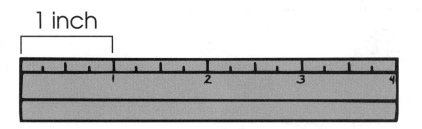

about __1__ inches

about _____ inches

about _____ inches

about _____ inches

about _____ inches

about _____ inches

about _____ inches

# Measurement: Inches

**Directions:** Use the ruler to measure the fish to the nearest inch.

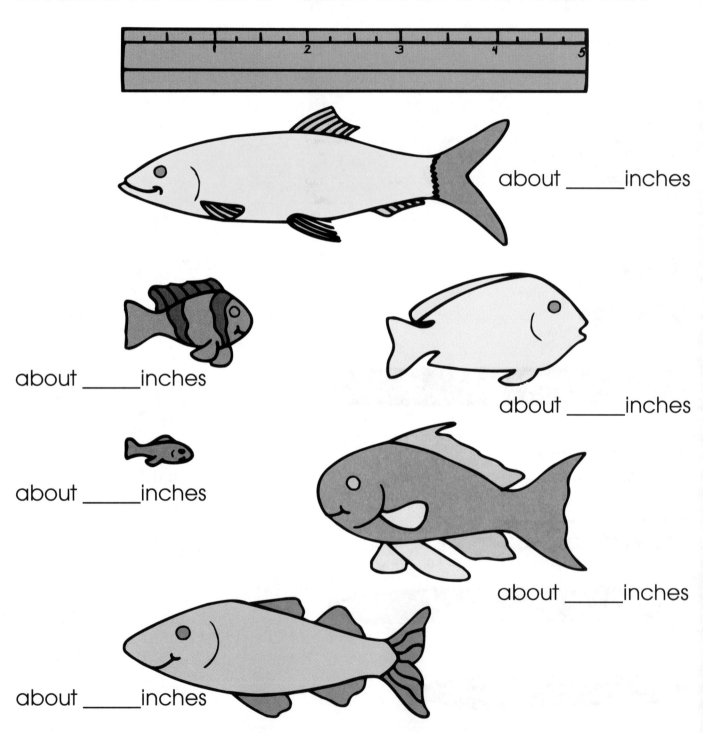

about _____ inches

about _____ inches

about _____ inches

about _____ inches

about _____ inches

about _____ inches

about _____ inches

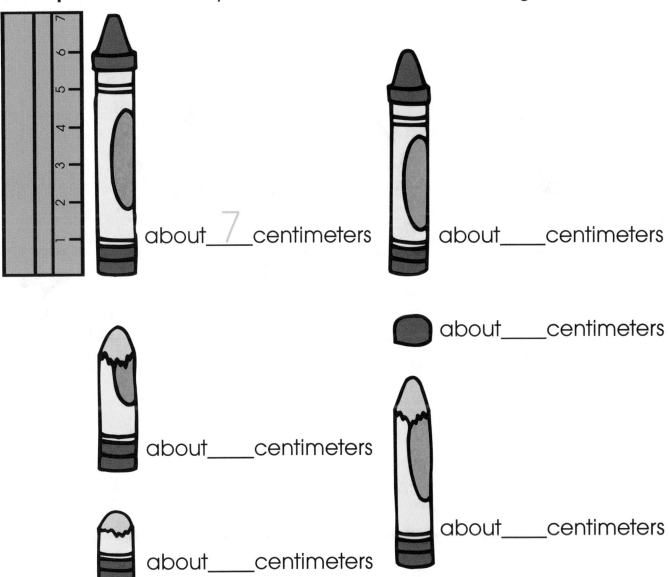

# Measurement: Centimeters

A centimeter is a unit of length in the metric system. There are 2.54 centimeters in an inch.

**Directions:** Use a centimeter ruler to measure the crayons to the nearest centimeter.

**Example:** The first crayon is about 7 centimeters long.

about__7__centimeters

about____centimeters

about____centimeters

about____centimeters

about____centimeters

about____centimeters

# Measurement: Centimeters

**Directions:** The giraffe is about 8 centimeters high. How many centimeters (cm) high are the trees? Write your answers in the blanks.

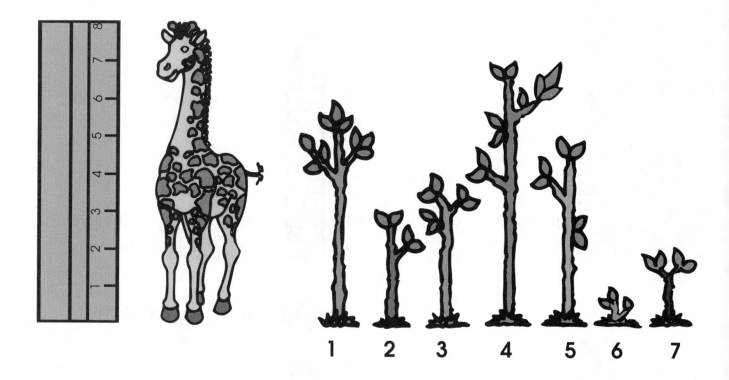

1)_____cm          2)_____cm          3)_____cm

4)_____cm          5)_____cm          6)_____cm          7)_____cm

# Time: Hour, Half-Hour

An hour is sixty minutes. The short hand of a clock tells the hour. It is written **0:00**, such as **5:00**. A half-hour is thirty minutes. When the long hand of the clock is pointing to the six, the time is on the half-hour. It is written **:30**, such as **5:30**.

**Directions:** Study the examples.
Tell what time it is on each clock.

**Examples:**

 9:00

The minute hand is on the 12.
The hour hand is on the 9.
It is 9 o'clock.

 4:30

The minute hand is on the 6.
The hour hand is *between*
the 4 and 5.
It is 4:30.

_____   _____   _____   _____   _____

_____   _____   _____   _____   _____

# Time: Hour, Half-Hour

**Directions:** Draw lines between the clocks that show the same time.

 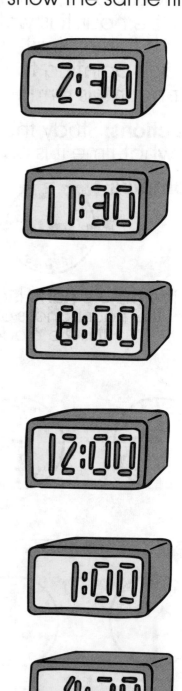

Name: _____

# Time: Counting by 5's

The minute hand of a clock takes 5 minutes to move from one number to the next. Start at the 12 and count by fives to tell how many minutes it is past the hour.

**Directions:** Study the examples. Tell what time is on each clock.

**Examples:**

  9:10     8:25

  _____     _____     _____

  _____     _____     _____

  _____     _____     _____

**Grade 2 - Comprehensive Curriculum**

Name: _____

# Time: Quarter-Hours

Time can also be shown as fractions. 30 minutes = $\frac{1}{2}$ hour.

**Directions:** Shade the fraction of each clock and tell how many minutes you have shaded.

**Example:**

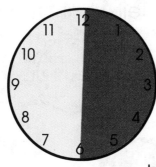

$\frac{1}{2}$ hour

<u>30</u> minutes

$\frac{1}{4}$ hour

____ minutes

$\frac{2}{4}$ hour

____ minutes

$\frac{3}{4}$ hour

____ minutes

$\frac{1}{2}$ hour

____ minutes

Name: _____

# Review
## Counting

**Directions:** Write the number that is:

| next | one less | one greater |
|------|----------|-------------|
| 68, 69, ____ | ____ , 57 | 12, ____ |
| 786, 787, ____ | ____ , 650 | 843, ____ |

## Place Value: Tens & Ones

**Directions:** Draw a line to the correct number.

| | |
|---|---|
| 4 tens + 7 ones | 20 |
| 2 tens + 0 ones | 51 |
| 7 tens + 3 ones | 47 |
| 5 tens + 1 one | 73 |

## Addition and Subtraction

**Directions:** Add or subtract.

$$
\begin{array}{cccccc}
15 & 14 & 7 & 8 & 10 & 14 \\
+\ 5 & -\ 4 & +\ 3 & -\ 6 & +\ 7 & -\ 5 \\
\hline
\end{array}
$$

**Grade 2 - Comprehensive Curriculum**

# Review

## 2-Digit Addition and Subtraction

**Directions:** Add or subtract using regrouping, if needed.

| | | | | |
|---|---|---|---|---|
| 66<br>- 37 | 38<br>+ 18 | 87<br>- 69 | 52<br>- 15 | 40<br>+ 17 |

| | | | | |
|---|---|---|---|---|
| 84<br>+ 17 | 65<br>+ 14 | 99<br>- 48 | 61<br>- 36 | 56<br>+ 46 |

## Place Value: Hundreds and Thousands

**Directions:** Draw a line to the correct number.

| | |
|---|---|
| 4 hundreds + 3 tens + 2 ones | 7,201 |
| 6 hundreds + 7 tens + 6 ones | 290 |
| 5 thousands + 3 hundreds + 7 tens + 2 ones | 432 |
| 2 hundreds + 9 tens + 0 ones | 676 |
| 7 thousands + 2 hundreds + 0 tens + 1 one | 5,372 |

## 3-Digit Addition and Subtraction

**Directions:** Add or subtract, remembering to regroup, if needed.

| | | | | | |
|---|---|---|---|---|---|
| 458<br>- 248 | 793<br>- 414 | 822<br>- 460 | 528<br>+ 319 | 697<br>+ 108 | 569<br>+ 288 |

# Review

## Multiplication

**Directions:** Solve the problems. Draw groups if necessary.

$$\begin{array}{r} 2 \\ \times\ 8 \\ \hline \end{array} \qquad \begin{array}{r} 6 \\ \times\ 4 \\ \hline \end{array} \qquad \begin{array}{r} 3 \\ \times\ 2 \\ \hline \end{array} \qquad \begin{array}{r} 8 \\ \times\ 4 \\ \hline \end{array} \qquad \begin{array}{r} 5 \\ \times\ 3 \\ \hline \end{array} \qquad \begin{array}{r} 2 \\ \times\ 2 \\ \hline \end{array}$$

## Fractions

**Directions:** Circle the correct fraction of each shape's white part.

    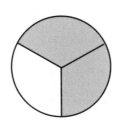    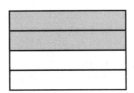

$$\frac{1}{2} \quad \frac{1}{3} \quad \frac{1}{4} \qquad\qquad \frac{1}{4} \quad \frac{1}{3} \quad \frac{1}{2} \qquad\qquad \frac{2}{3} \quad \frac{2}{4} \quad \frac{1}{3} \qquad\qquad \frac{1}{4} \quad \frac{1}{2} \quad \frac{3}{4}$$

## Graphs

**Directions:** Count the flowers. Color the pots to make a graph that shows the number of flowers.

1    2    3    4    5    6    7    8

Name: _____

# Review

## Geometry

**Directions:** Match the shapes.

rectangle

square

circle

triangle

## Measurement

**Directions:** Look at the ruler. Measure the objects to the nearest inch.

 _____ inches

 _____ inches

 _____ inches

## Time

**Directions:** Tell what time is on each clock.

_____   _____   _____   _____

Name: _____

# Money: Penny, Nickel

Penny **1¢**          Nickel **5¢**

**Directions:** Count the coins and write the amount.

**Example:**

_____8_____ ¢

5¢   1¢  1¢  1¢

_____ ¢

_____ ¢

_____ ¢

_____ ¢

Name: _____

# Money: Penny, Nickel, Dime

Penny **1¢**    Nickel **5¢**    Dime **10¢**

**Directions:** Count the coins and write the amount.

        _16_ ¢

        _____ ¢

        _____ ¢

        _____ ¢

        _____ ¢

Name: _____

# Money: Penny, Nickel, Dime

**Directions:** Draw a line from the toy to the amount of money it costs.

**Grade 2 - Comprehensive Curriculum**

Name: _____

# Money: Penny, Nickel, Dime

**Directions:** Draw a line to match the amounts of money.

# Money: Quarter

A quarter is worth 25¢.

**Directions:** Count the coins and write the amounts.

  _____ ¢

  _____ ¢

  _____ ¢

  _____ ¢

  _____ ¢

  _____ ¢

  _____ ¢

  _____ ¢

# Money: Decimal

A decimal is a number with one or more places to the right of a decimal point, such as 6.5 or 2.25. Money amounts are written with two places to the right of the decimal point.

25¢    10¢    5¢    1¢
$.25    $.10    $.05    $.01

**Directions:** Count the coins and circle the amount shown.

**Example:**

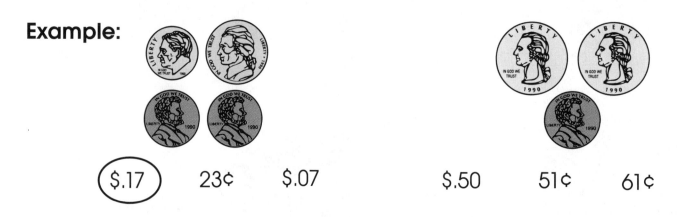

($.17)    23¢    $.07      $.50    51¢    61¢

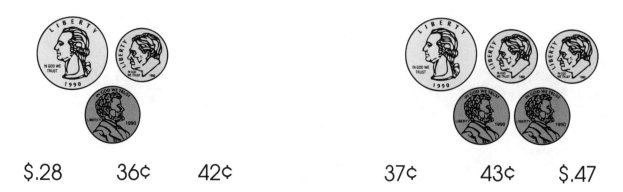

$.28    36¢    42¢      37¢    43¢    $.47

Name: _____

# Money: Decimal

**Directions:** Draw a line from the coins to the correct amount in each column.

3¢

$.55

55¢

$.41

31¢

$.37

37¢

$.31

41¢

$.03

**Grade 2 - Comprehensive Curriculum**

Name: _____

# Money: Dollar

One dollar equals 100 cents. It is written $1.00.

**Directions:** Count the money and write the amounts.

  $___.___

  $___.___

  $___.___

  $___.___

   $___.___

  $___.___

 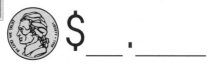  $___.___

  $___.___

Name: _____

# Adding Money

**Directions:** Write the amount of money using decimals. Then add to find the total amount.

**Example:**

$$
\begin{array}{r}
\$1.00 \\
.05 \\
+ \ .02 \\
\hline
\$1.07
\end{array}
$$

$ ___ . ___
$ ___ . ___
$ ___ . ___
+$ ___ . ___
_____
___ . ___

$ ___ . ___
$ ___ . ___
$ ___ . ___
+$ ___ . ___
_____
___ . ___

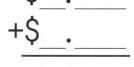
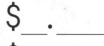

$ ___ . ___
$ ___ . ___
$ ___ . ___
_____
___ . ___

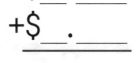

$ ___ . ___
$ ___ . ___
+$ ___ . ___
_____
___ . ___

$ ___ . ___
$ ___ . ___
$ ___ . ___
+$ ___ . ___
_____
___ . ___

**Grade 2 - Comprehensive Curriculum**

# Money: Practice

**Directions:** Draw a line from each food item to the correct amount of money.

$1.59

$.89

$1.27

$1.09

$.77

$1.95

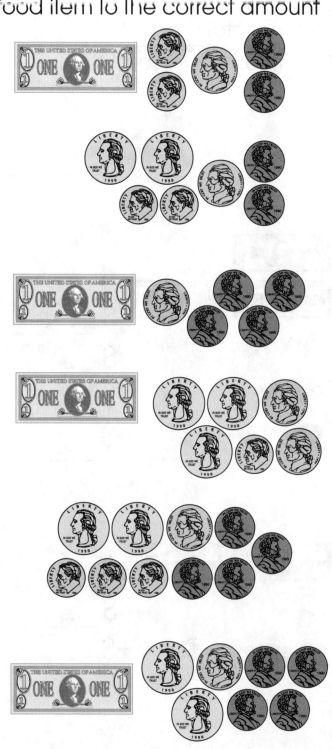

# Review

**Directions:** Add the money and write the total.

 _____ ¢

 _____ ¢

 $ _____ . _____

 _____ ¢

 $ _____ . _____

Name: _____

# Problem-Solving

**Directions:** Tell whether you should add or subtract. "In all" is a clue to add. "Left" is a clue to subtract. Draw pictures to help you.

**Example:**
Jane's dog has 5 bones. He ate 3 bones. How many bones are left?

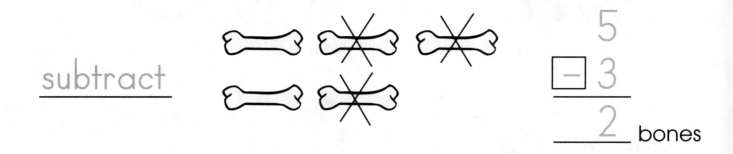

subtract

5
□ – 3
_____ 2 bones

Lucky the cat had 5 mice. She got 4 more for her birthday. How many mice did she have in all?

_____

□
_____

_____ mice

Sam bought 6 fish. She gave 2 fish to a friend. How many fish does she have left?

_____

□
_____

_____ fish

# MATH

Name: _____

# Problem-Solving: Addition, Subtraction, Multiplication

**Directions:** Tell if you add, subtract or multiply. Then write the answer.

**Example:**
There were 12 frogs sitting on a log by a pond, but 3 frogs hopped away. How many frogs are left?

_Subtract_____ __9__ frogs

There are 9 flowers growing by the pond.
Each flower has 2 leaves.
How many leaves are there?

_____ _____ leaves

A tree had 7 squirrels playing in it.
Then 8 more came along.
How many squirrels are there in all?

_____ _____ squirrels

There were 27 birds living in the trees around the pond, but 9 flew away.
How many birds are left?

_____ _____ birds

**Grade 2 - Comprehensive Curriculum**

Name: _____

# Problem-Solving: Fractions

A fraction is a number that names part of a whole, such as $\frac{1}{2}$ or $\frac{1}{3}$.

**Directions:** Read each problem. Use the pictures to help you solve the problem. Write the fraction that answers the question.

Simon and Jessie shared a pizza.
Together they ate $\frac{3}{4}$ of the pizza.
How much of the pizza is left?  _____

Sylvia baked a cherry pie. She gave $\frac{1}{3}$
to her grandmother and $\frac{1}{3}$ to a friend.
How much of the pie did she keep?  _____

Timmy erased $\frac{1}{2}$ of the blackboard
before the bell rang for recess.
How much of the blackboard does
he have left to erase?  _____

**Directions:** Read the problem. Draw your own picture to help you solve the problem. Write the fraction that answers the question.

Sarah mowed $\frac{1}{4}$ of the yard before lunch.
How much does she have left to mow?  _____

# Problem-Solving: Time

**Directions:** Solve each problem.

Tracy wakes up at 7:00. She has 30 minutes before her bus comes. What time does her bus come?

_____ : _____

Vera walks her dog for 15 minutes after supper. She finishes supper at 6:30. When does she get home from walking her dog?

_____ : _____

Chip practices the piano for 30 minutes when he gets home from school. He gets home at 3:30. When does he stop practicing?

_____ : _____

Tanya starts mowing the grass at 4:30. She finishes at 5:00. For how many minutes does she mow the lawn?

_____ minutes

Don does his homework for 45 minutes. He starts his work at 7:15. When does he stop working?

_____ : _____

**Grade 2 - Comprehensive Curriculum**

# Problem-Solving: Money

**Directions:** Read each problem. Use the pictures to help you solve the problems.

Ben bought a ball. He had 11¢ left.
How much money did he have at the start?

_____ ¢

Tara has 75¢. She buys a car.
How much money does she have left?

_____ ¢

Leah wants to buy a doll and a ball. She has 80¢.
How much more money does she need?

_____ ¢

Jacob has 95¢. He buys the car and the ball.
How much more money does he need to
buy a doll for his sister?

_____ ¢

Kim paid three quarters, one dime
and three pennies for a hat.
How much did it cost?

_____ ¢

**Addition:** Putting together or adding two or more numbers to find the sum.

**Adjectives:** Words that tell more about a person, place or thing.

**Alphabetical (ABC) Order:** Putting letters or words in the order in which they appear in the alphabet.

**Antonyms:** Words that mean the opposite. Example: big and small.

**Articles:** Small words that help us to better understand nouns. Example: a and an.

**Author:** The person who wrote the words of a book.

**Beginning Consonants:** Consonant sounds that come at the beginning of words.

**Blends:** Two consonants put together to form a single sound.

**Capital Letters:** Letters that are used at the beginning of the names of people, places, days, months and holidays. Capital letters are also used at the beginning of sentences. These letters are sometimes called uppercase or "big" letters.

**Centimeter:** A measurement of length in the metric system. There are $2\frac{1}{2}$ centimeters in an inch.

**Chapters:** Small sections of a book.

**Characters:** The people or animals in a story.

**Circle:** A figure that is round.

**Classifying:** Putting things that are alike into groups.

**Closed Figures:** Figures whose lines connect.

**Commands:** Sentences that tell someone to do something.

**Commutative Property:** The rule in addition that states that, even if the order of the numbers is changed, the sum will be the same.

**Compound Predicate:** Predicate of the sentence formed by joining two verbs that have the same subject.

**Compound Subject:** Subject of the sentence formed by joining two nouns that have the same predicate.

# GLOSSARY

**Compound Words:** Two words that are put together to make one new word. Example: house + boat = houseboat.

**Comprehension:** Understanding what you read.

**Consonants:** The letters b, c, d, f, g, h, j, k, l, m, n, p, q, r, s, t, v, w, x, y and z.

**Consonant Blends:** Two or three consonant letters in a word whose sounds combine, or blend. Examples: br, fr, gr, tr.

**Consonant Teams:** Two or three consonant letters that have the single sound. Examples: sh and tch.

**Contractions:** A short way to write two words together. Example: it is = it's.

**Decimal:** A number with one or more places to the right of a decimal point, such as 6.5 or 3.78. Money amounts are written with two places to the right of a decimal point, such as $1.30.

**Dictionary:** A reference book that gives the meaning of words and how to pronounce them.

**Difference:** The answer in a subtraction problem.

**Digit:** The symbols used to write numbers: 0, 1, 2, 3, 4, 5, 6, 7, 8 and 9.

**Dime:** Ten cents. It is written 10¢ or $.10.

**Dollar:** A dollar is equal to one hundred cents. It is written $1.00.

**Double Vowel Words:** When two vowels appear together in a word. Examples: tea, coat

**Ending Consonants:** Consonant sounds which come at the end of words.

**Fact:** Something that can be proven.

**Fiction:** A make-believe story.

**Fraction:** A number that names part of a whole, such as $\frac{1}{3}$ or $\frac{1}{2}$.

**Geometry:** Mathematics that has to do with lines and shapes.

**Glossary:** A little dictionary at the back of a book.

**Graph:** A drawing that shows information about numbers.

Grade 2 - Comprehensive Curriculum

452

**Guide Words:** The words that appear at the top of a dictionary page to tell you what the first and the last words on that page will be.

**Haiku:** An Oriental form of poetry. Most have 5 syllables in the first and third lines, and 7 syllables in the middle line.

**Half-Hour:** Thirty minutes. It is written 0:30.

**Hard and Soft c:** In words where c is followed by a or u, the c usually has a hard sound (like a k). Examples: cup, cart. When c is followed by e, i or y, it usually has a soft sound (like an s). Examples: circle, fence.

**Hard and Soft g:** When g is followed by e, i or y, it usually has a soft sound (like j). Examples: change and gentle. The hard g sounds like the g in girl or gate.

**Homophones:** Words that sound the same but are spelled differently and mean different things. Example: blue and blew.

**Hour:** Sixty minutes. The short hand of a clock tells the hour. It is written 1:00.

**Illustrator:** The person who drew pictures for a book.

**Inch:** A unit of length in the standard measurement system.

**Inference:** A conclusion arrived at by what is suggested in the text.

**Joining Words:** Words that combine ideas in a sentence, such as "and," "but," "or" and "because."

**Letter Teams:** Two letters put together to make one new sound.

**Long Vowels:** Long vowels say their names. Examples: Long a is the sound you hear in hay. Long e is the sound you hear in me. Long i is the sound you hear in pie. Long o is the sound you hear in no. Long u is the sound you hear in cute.

**Main Idea:** The most important point or idea in a story.

**Making Deductions:** Using reasoning skills to draw conclusions.

**Metric System:** A system of measuring in which length is measured in millimeters, centimeters, meters and kilometers; capacity is measured in milliliters and liters; weight is measured in grams and kilograms; and temperature is measured in degrees Celsius.

**Multiplication:** A short way to find the sum of adding the same number a certain amount of times. For example, 7 x 4 = 28 instead of 7 + 7 + 7 + 7 = 28.

**Nickel:** Five cents. It is written 5¢ or $.05.

**Nonfiction:** A true story.

**Nouns:** Words that name a person, place or thing.

**Open Figures:** Figures whose lines do not connect.

**Opinion:** A feeling or belief about something that cannot be proven.

**Opposites:** Words that are different in every way. Example: black and white.

**Ordinal Numbers:** Numbers that indicate order in a series, such as first, second or third.

**Pattern:** Similar shapes or designs.

**Penny:** One cent. It is written 1¢ or $.01.

**Place Value:** The value of a digit, or numeral, shown by where it is in the number.

**Plurals:** Words that mean more than one. Examples: shoes, ladies, dishes, foxes.

**Predicate:** The verb in the sentence that tells the main action.

**Predicting:** Telling what is likely to happen, based on the facts.

**Prefix:** A syllable added at the beginning of a word to change its meaning. Examples: disappear, misplace.

**Product:** The answer of a multiplication problem.

**Pronouns:** Words that are used in place of nouns. "She," "he," "it" and "they" are pronouns.

**Proper Nouns:** The names of specific people, places and things. Proper nouns begin with a capital letter.

**Quarter:** Twenty-five cents. It is written 25¢ or $.25.

**Questions:** Sentences that ask something. A question begins with a capital letter and ends with a question mark.

**R-Controlled Vowel:** When r follows a vowel, it gives the vowel a different sound. Examples: her, bark, bird.

**Rectangle:** A figure with four corners and four sides. Sides opposite each other are the same length.

**Regroup:** To use ten ones to form one ten, ten tens to form 100, and so on.

**Rhymes:** Words that end with the same sound.

**Rhyming Words:** Words that sound alike at the end of a word. Example: cat and rat.

**Same and Different:** Being able to tell how things are the same and how they are different.

**Sentences:** A group of words that tells a complete idea or asks a question.

**Sequencing:** Putting things in the correct order, such as 7, 8, 9 or small, medium, large.

**Short Vowels:** Vowels that make short sounds. Examples: Short a is the sound you hear in cat. Short e is the sound you hear in leg. Short i is the sound you hear in pig. Short o is the sound in box. Short u is the sound in cup.

**Silent Letters:** Letters you can't hear at all, such as the gh in night, the w in wrong and the t in listen.

**Simile:** A figure of speech that compares two things that are alike in some way. The words "like" and "as" are used in similes. Examples: as soft as a pillow, as light as a feather.

**Statements:** Sentences that tell about something. Statements begin with a capital letter and end with a period.

**Subtraction:** Taking away or subtracting one number from another to find the difference.

**Suffix:** A syllable added at the end of a word to change its meaning. Examples: smaller, helpless.

**Super Silent e:** An e that you can't hear when it appears at the end of a word. It makes the other vowel have a long sound. Examples: cape, robe, slide.

**Surprising Sentences:** Sentences that tell a strong feeling. Surprising sentences begin with a capital letter and end with an exclamation point.

**Syllables:** The parts of words that have vowel sounds.
Examples: Rab|bit has two syllables. Bas|ket|ball has three syllables.

**Synonyms:** Words that mean the same or nearly the same.
Example: sleepy and tired.

**Table of Contents:** A list at the beginning of a book, telling what is in the book and the page number.

**Telling Sentences:** Sentences that tell a strong feeling. Telling sentences begin with a capital letter and end with an exclamation point.

**Title:** The name of a book.

**Tracking:** Following a path.

**Triangle:** A figure with three corners and three sides.

**Venn Diagram:** A diagram that shows how two things are the same and how they are different.

**Verbs:** Words that tell the action in a sentence. Example: The boy ran fast.

**Vowel Team:** Vowels that appear together in words. Usually, the first one says its name and the second one is silent. Examples: leaf, soap, rain.

**Vowels:** The letters a, e, i, o, u and sometimes y.

**Y as a Vowel:** When y comes at the end of a word, it is a vowel.
Examples: my, baby.

## Page 6

**All About Me!**

**Directions:** Fill in the blanks to tell all about you!

Name ___Answers will vary.___
    (First)     (Last)
Address _____
City _____ State ____
Phone number _____
Age _____

Places I have visited: ___Answers will vary.___
_____
_____

My favorite vacation: ___Answers will vary.___
_____
_____

## Page 7

**Review: Beginning Consonants: b, c, d, f, g, h, j**

**Directions:** Fill in the beginning consonant for each word.

Example: __c__ at

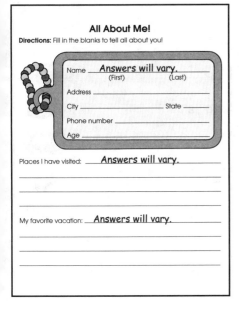

__b__ ox

__j__ acket

__g__ oat

__h__ ouse

__d__ og

__f__ ire

## Page 8

**Beginning Consonants: k, l, m, n, p, q, r**

**Directions:** Write the letter that makes the beginning sound for each picture.

__m__    __q__    __r__    __n__

__m__    __l__    __k__    __r__

__q__    __p__    __n__    __m__

__l__    __k__    __r__    __p__

## Page 9

**Beginning Consonants: k, l, m, n, p, q, r**

**Directions:** Fill in the beginning consonant for each word.

Example: __r__ ose

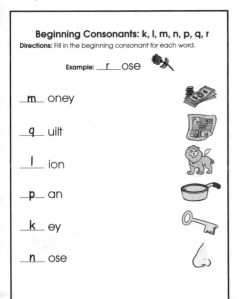

__m__ oney

__q__ uilt

__l__ ion

__p__ an

__k__ ey

__n__ ose

## Page 10

**Beginning Consonants: s, t, v, w, x, y, z**

**Directions:** Write the letter under each picture that makes the beginning sound.

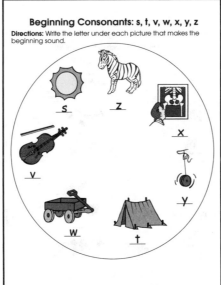

s    z    x

v    y

w    t

## Page 11

**Beginning Consonants: s, t, v, w, x, y, z**

**Directions:** Fill in the beginning consonant for each word.

Example: __s__ ock

__z__ ipper

__t__ able

__x__ ray

__v__ ase

__y__ olk

__w__ and

## Page 12

### Ending Consonants: b, d, f, g
**Directions:** Fill in the ending consonants for each word.

ma _n_

cu _b_

roo _f_

do _g_

be _d_

bi _b_

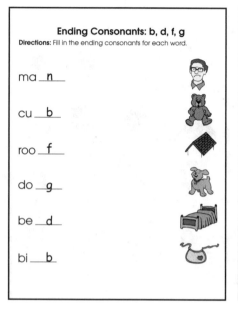

## Page 13

### Ending Consonants: k, l, m, n, p, r
**Directions:** Fill in the ending consonant for each word.

nai _l_

ca _n_

gu _m_

ca _r_

truc _k_

ca _p_

pai _l_

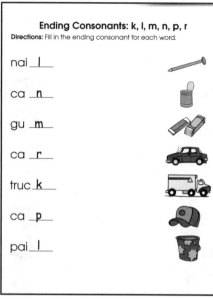

## Page 14

### Ending Consonants: s, t, x
**Directions:** Fill in the ending consonant for each word.

ca _t_

bo _x_

bu _s_

fo _x_

boa t_

ma _t_

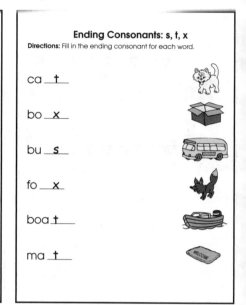

## Page 15

### Consonant Blends
**Consonant blends** are two or three consonant letters in a word whose sounds combine, or blend. **Examples:** br, fr, gr, pr, tr
**Directions:** Look at each picture. Say its name. Write the blend you hear at the beginning of each word.

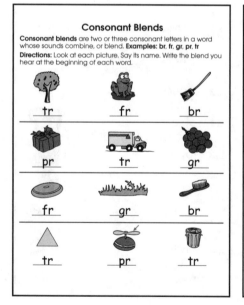

tr    fr    br

pr    tr    gr

fr    gr    br

tr    pr    tr

## Page 16

### Blends: fl, br, pl, sk, sn
**Blends** are two consonants put together to form a single sound.

**Directions:** Look at the pictures and say their names. Write the letters for the beginning sound in each word.

| _br_ | _sk_ |
| _fl_ | _br_ |
| _fl_ | _sn_ |
| _br_ | _pl_ |
| _sn_ | _fl_ |
| _sk_ | _pl_ |

## Page 17

### Blends: bl, sl, cr, cl
**Directions:** Look at the pictures and say their names. Write the letters for the beginning sound in each word.

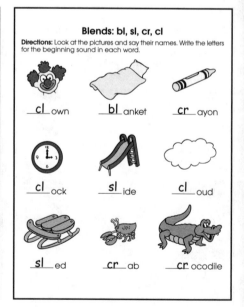

_cl_ own    _bl_ anket    _cr_ ayon

_cl_ ock    _sl_ ide    _cl_ oud

_sl_ ed    _cr_ ab    _cr_ ocodile

## Page 18

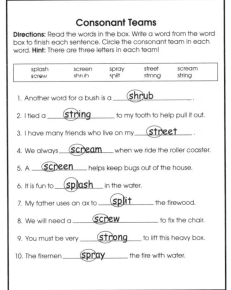

**Consonant Blends**

**Directions:** Write a word from the word box to answer each riddle.

| | | | | |
|---|---|---|---|---|
| clock | glass | blow | climb | slipper |
| sleep | gloves | clap | blocks | flashlight |

1. You need me when the lights go out. **What am I?** — flashlight
2. People use me to tell the time. **What am I?** — clock
3. You put me on your hands in the winter to keep them warm. **What am I?** — gloves
4. Cinderella lost one like me at midnight. **What am I?** — slipper
5. This is what you do with your hands when you are pleased. **What is it?** — clap
6. You can do this with a whistle or with bubble gum. **What is it?** — blow
7. These are what you might use to build a castle when you are playing. **What are they?** — blocks
8. You do this to get to the top of a hill. **What is it?** — climb
9. This is what you use to drink water or milk. **What is it?** — glass
10. You do this at night with your eyes closed. **What is it?** — sleep

## Page 19

**Consonant Teams**

**Directions:** Read the words in the box. Write a word from the word box to finish each sentence. Circle the consonant team in each word. **Hint:** There are three letters in each team!

| | | | | |
|---|---|---|---|---|
| splash | screen | spray | street | scream |
| screw | shrub | split | strong | string |

1. Another word for a bush is a shrub.
2. I tied a string to my tooth to help pull it out.
3. I have many friends who live on my street.
4. We always scream when we ride the roller coaster.
5. A screen helps keep bugs out of the house.
6. It is fun to splash in the water.
7. My father uses an ax to split the firewood.
8. We will need a screw to fix the chair.
9. You must be very strong to lift this heavy box.
10. The firemen spray the fire with water.

## Page 20

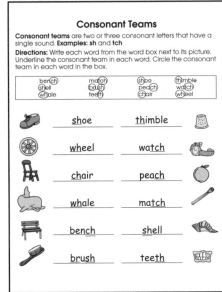

**Consonant Teams**

**Consonant teams** are two or three consonant letters that have a single sound. **Examples: sh** and **tch**

**Directions:** Write each word from the word box next to its picture. Underline the consonant team in each word. Circle the consonant team in each word in the box.

| | | | |
|---|---|---|---|
| bench | match | shoe | thimble |
| shell | brush | peach | watch |
| whale | teeth | chair | wheel |

- shoe — thimble
- wheel — watch
- chair — peach
- whale — match
- bench — shell
- brush — teeth

## Page 21

**Letter Teams: sh, ch, wh, th**

**Directions:** Look at the first picture in each row. Circle the pictures that have the same sound.

- wh / whistle
- sh / shoe
- ch / chin
- th / thumb

## Page 22

**Letter Teams: sh, ch, wh, th**

**Directions:** Look at the pictures and say the words. Write the first two letters of the word on the space below each picture.

- sh
- ch
- sh
- wh
- wh
- ch
- th
- sh
- th

## Page 23

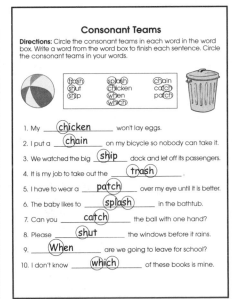

**Consonant Teams**

**Directions:** Circle the consonant teams in each word in the word box. Write a word from the word box to finish each sentence. Circle the consonant teams in your words.

| | | |
|---|---|---|
| trash | splash | chain |
| shut | chicken | catch |
| ship | when | patch |
| | which | |

1. My chicken won't lay eggs.
2. I put a chain on my bicycle so nobody can take it.
3. We watched the big ship dock and let off its passengers.
4. It is my job to take out the trash.
5. I have to wear a patch over my eye until it is better.
6. The baby likes to splash in the bathtub.
7. Can you catch the ball with one hand?
8. Please shut the windows before it rains.
9. When are we going to leave for school?
10. I don't know which of these books is mine.

**Grade 2 - Comprehensive Curriculum**

## Page 24

### Consonant Teams

**Directions:** Look at the words in the word box. Write all of the words that end with the **ng** sound in the column under the picture of the **ring**. Write all of the words that end with the **nk** sound under the picture of the **sink**. Finish the sentences with words from the word box.

| strong | rank | bring | bank | honk | hang | thank |
| long | hunk | song | stung | bunk | sang | junk |

**ng**

| | |
|---|---|
| strong | rank |
| long | hunk |
| bring | bank |
| song | honk |
| stung | bunk |
| hang | thank |
| sang | junk |

**nk**

1. __Honk__ your horn when you get to my house.
2. He was ____stung____ by a bumblebee.
3. We are going to put our money in a ____bank____.
4. I want to ____thank____ you for the birthday present.
5. My brother and I sleep in ____bunk____ beds.

## Page 25

### Silent Letters

Some words have letters you can't hear at all, such as the **gh** in **night**, the **w** in **wrong**, the **l** in **walk**, the **k** in **knee**, the **b** in **climb** and the **t** in **listen**.

**Directions:** Look at the words in the word box. Write the word under its picture. Underline the silent letters.

| knife | light | calf | wrench | lamb | eight |
| wrist | whistle | comb | thumb | knob | knee |

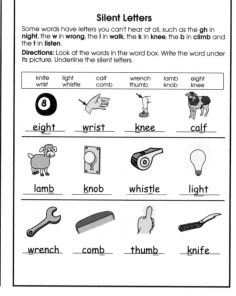

| eight | wrist | knee | calf |
|---|---|---|---|
| lamb | knob | whistle | light |
| wrench | comb | thumb | knife |

## Page 26

### Review

**Directions:** Read the story. Circle the consonant teams (two or three letters) and silent letters in the underlined words. Be sure to check for more than one team in a word! One has been done for you.

One day last Spring my family went on a picnic. My father picked out a pretty spot next to a stream. While my brother and I climbed a tree, my mother spread out a sheet and placed the food on it. But before we could eat, a skunk walked out of the woods! Mother screamed and scared the skunk. It sprayed us with a terrible smell! Now, we think it is a funny story. But that day, we ran!

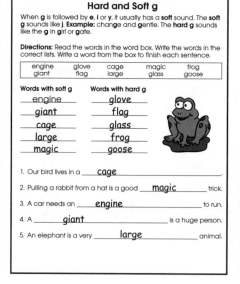

**Directions:** Write the words with three-letter blends on the lines.

__Spring__   __stream__   __spread__

__screamed__   __sprayed__

## Page 27

### Hard and Soft c

When **c** is followed by **e**, **i** or **y**, it usually has a **soft** sound. The **soft** c sounds like **s**. For example, **circle** and **fence**. When **c** is followed by **a** or **u**, it usually has a **hard** sound. The **hard** c sounds like **k**.

**Example:** **c**up and **c**art

**Directions:** Read the words in the word box. Write the words in the correct lists. Write a word from the word box to finish each sentence.

| pencil | cookie |
| dance | cent |
| popcorn | circus |
| lucky | mice |
| tractor | card |

**Words with soft c**
pencil
dance
cent
mice
circus

**Words with hard c**
circus
popcorn
lucky
tractor
cookie
card

1. Another word for a penny is a ____cent____.
2. A cat likes to chase ____mice____.
3. You will see animals and clowns at the ____circus____.
4. Will you please sharpen my ____pencil____?

## Page 28

### Hard and Soft g

When **g** is followed by **e**, **i** or **y**, it usually has a **soft** sound. The **soft** g sounds like **j**. **Example:** **change** and **gentle**. The **hard** g sounds like the **g** in **girl** or **gate**.

**Directions:** Read the words in the word box. Write the words in the correct lists. Write a word from the box to finish each sentence.

| engine | glove | cage | magic | frog |
| giant | flag | large | glass | goose |

**Words with soft g**
engine
giant
cage
large
magic

**Words with hard g**
glove
flag
glass
frog
goose

1. Our bird lives in a ____cage____.
2. Pulling a rabbit from a hat is a good ____magic____ trick.
3. A car needs an ____engine____ to run.
4. A ____giant____ is a huge person.
5. An elephant is a very ____large____ animal.

## Page 29

### Hard and Soft c and g

**Directions:** Look at the **c** and **g** words at the bottom of the page. Cut them out and glue them in the correct box below.

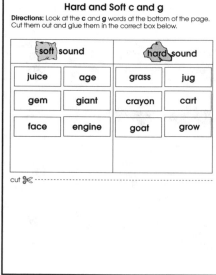

| **soft** sound | | **hard** sound | |
|---|---|---|---|
| juice | age | grass | jug |
| gem | giant | crayon | cart |
| face | engine | goat | grow |

cut ✂ --------------------------------

# ANSWER KEY

## Page 31

### Short Vowels

**Vowels** can make **short** or **long** sounds. The short **a** sounds like the **a** in **cat**. The short **e** is like the **e** in **leg**. The short **i** sounds like the **i** in **pig**. The short **o** sounds like the **o** in **box**. The short **u** sounds like the **u** in **cup**.

**Directions:** Look at each picture. Write the missing short vowel letter.

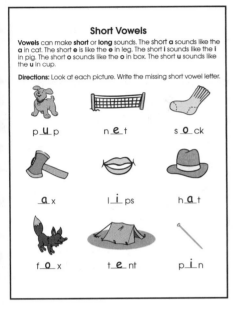

p u p          n e t          s o ck

a x          l i ps          h a t

f o x          t e nt          p i n

## Page 32

### Short Vowels

**Vowels** can make **short** or **long** sounds. The short **a** sounds like the **a** in **cat**. The short **e** is like the **e** in **leg**. The short **i** sounds like the **i** in **pig**. The short **o** sounds like the **o** in **box**. The short **u** is like the **u** in **cup**.

**Directions:** Look at the pictures. Their names all have short vowel sounds. But the vowels are missing! Fill in the missing vowels in each word.

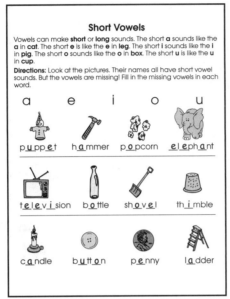

a          e          i          o          u

p u pp e t          h a mmer          p o pcorn          el e ph a nt

tel e v i sion          b o ttle          sh o v e l          th i mble

c a ndle          b u tt o n          p e nny          l a dder

## Page 33

### Short Vowels

**Directions:** Cut out the giant vowel letters. Draw pictures, write words or cut pictures from magazines with the short vowel sound and put them on both sides of the letters. Then hang the letters with string!

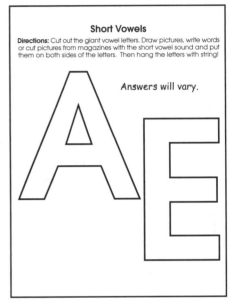

Answers will vary.

## Page 35

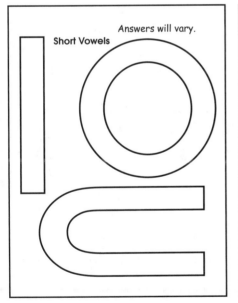

Answers will vary.

**Short Vowels**

## Page 37

### Super Silent e

Long vowel sounds have the same sound as their names. When a **Super Silent e** appears at the end of a word, you can't hear it, but it makes the other vowel have a long sound. For example: **tub** has a **short** vowel sound, and **tube** has a **long** vowel sound.

**Directions:** Look at the following pictures. Decide if the word has a short or long vowel sound. Circle the correct word. Watch for the **Super Silent e!**

can (cane)          (tub) tube          rob (robe)          (rat) rate

(pin) pine          (cap) cape          not (note)          (pan) pane

slid (slide)          dim (dime)          tap (tape)          cub (cube)

## Page 38

### Long Vowels

Long vowel sounds have the same sound as their names. When a **Super Silent e** comes at the end of a word, you can't hear it, but it changes the short vowel sound to a long vowel sound.

**Example:** rope, skate, bee, pie, cute

**Directions:** Say the name of the pictures. Listen for the long vowel sounds. Write the missing long vowel sound under each picture.

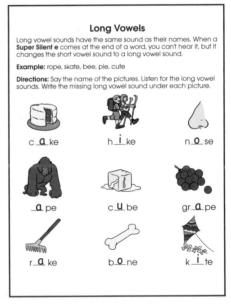

c a ke          h i ke          n o se

a pe          c u be          gr a pe

r a ke          b o ne          k i te

**Grade 2 - Comprehensive Curriculum**

## Page 39

**Review**

**Directions:** Read the words in each box. Cross out the word that does not belong.

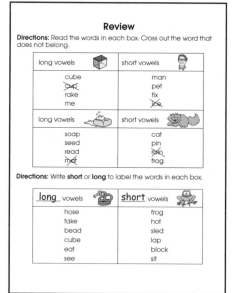

| long vowels | short vowels |
|---|---|
| cube | man |
| ~~cup~~ | pet |
| rake | fix |
| me | ~~ice~~ |

| long vowels | short vowels |
|---|---|
| soap | cat |
| seed | pin |
| read | ~~rain~~ |
| ~~mat~~ | frog |

**Directions:** Write **short** or **long** to label the words in each box.

| __long__ vowels | __short__ vowels |
|---|---|
| hose | frog |
| take | hot |
| bead | sled |
| cube | lap |
| eat | block |
| see | sit |

## Page 40

**R-Controlled Vowels**

When a vowel is followed by the letter **r**, it has a different sound.

**Example: he** and **her**

**Directions:** Write a word from the word box to finish each sentence. Notice the sound of the vowel followed by an **r**.

| park | chair | horse | bark | bird |
|---|---|---|---|---|
| hurt | girl | hair | store | ears |

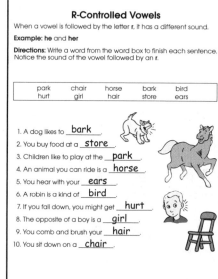

1. A dog likes to __bark__.
2. You buy food at a __store__.
3. Children like to play at the __park__.
4. An animal you can ride is a __horse__.
5. You hear with your __ears__.
6. A robin is a kind of __bird__.
7. If you fall down, you might get __hurt__.
8. The opposite of a boy is a __girl__.
9. You comb and brush your __hair__.
10. You sit down on a __chair__.

## Page 41

**R-Controlled Words**

**R-Controlled Words** are words in which the **r** that comes after the vowel changes the sound of the vowel. **Examples:** bird, star, burn

**Directions:** Write the correct word in the sentences below.

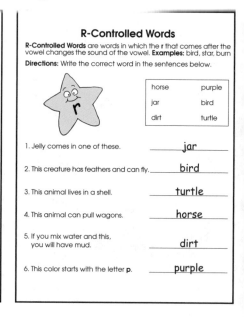

| horse | purple |
|---|---|
| jar | bird |
| dirt | turtle |

1. Jelly comes in one of these. __jar__

2. This creature has feathers and can fly. __bird__

3. This animal lives in a shell. __turtle__

4. This animal can pull wagons. __horse__

5. If you mix water and this, you will have mud. __dirt__

6. This color starts with the letter **p**. __purple__

## Page 42

**R-Controlled Vowels**

**Directions:** Answer the riddles below. You will need to complete the words with the correct vowel followed by **r**.

1. I am something you may use to eat. What am I?  f __o__ __r__ k

2. My word names the opposite of tall. What am I?  sh __o__ __r__ t

3. I can be seen high in the sky. I twinkle. What am I?  st __a__ __r__

4. I am a kind of clothing a girl might wear. What am I?  sk __i__ __r__ t

5. My word tells what a group of cows is called. What am I?  h __e__ __r__ d

6. I am part of your body. What am I?  __a__ __r__ m

## Page 43

**Double Vowel Words**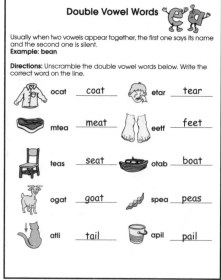

Usually when two vowels appear together, the first one says its name and the second one is silent.
**Example: bean**

**Directions:** Unscramble the double vowel words below. Write the correct word on the line.

ocat __coat__      etar __tear__

mtea __meat__      eetf __feet__

teas __seat__      otab __boat__

ogat __goat__      spea __peas__

atli __tail__      apil __pail__

## Page 44

**Vowel Teams**

The vowel teams **ou** and **ow** can have the same sound. You can hear it in the words **clown** and **cloud**. The vowel teams **au** and **aw** have the same sound. You hear it in the words **because** and **law**.

**Directions:** Look at the pictures. Write the correct vowel team to complete the words. The first one is done for you. You may need to use a dictionary to help you with the correct spelling.

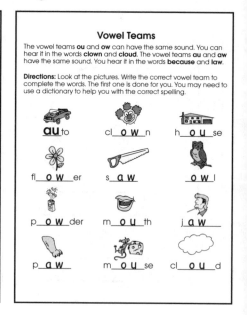

__au__ to      cl __ow__ n      h __ou__ se

fl __ow__ er      s __aw__      __ow__ l

p __ow__ der      m __ou__ th      j __aw__

p __aw__      m __ou__ se      cl __ou__ d

## Page 45

**Vowel Teams**

The vowel team **ea** can have a short **e** sound like in **head**, or a long **e** sound like in **bead**. An **ea** followed by an **r** makes a sound like the one in **ear** or like the one in **heard**.

**Directions:** Read the story. Listen for the sound **ea** makes in the bold words.

Have you ever **read** a book or **heard** a story about a **bear**? You might have **learned** that bears sleep through the winter. Some bears may sleep the whole **season**. Sometimes they look almost **dead**! But they are very much alive. As the cold winter passes and the spring **weather** comes **near**, they wake up. After such a nice rest, they must be **ready** to **eat** a **really** big **meal**!

| words with long **ea** | words with short **ea** | **ea** followed by **r** |
|---|---|---|
| season | read | heard |
| eat | dead | bear |
| really | weather | learned |
| meal | ready | near |

## Page 46

**Vowel Teams**

The vowel team **ie** makes the long **e** sound like in **believe**. The team **ei** also makes the long **e** sound like in **either**. But **ei** can also make a long **a** sound like in **eight**.

**Directions:** Circle the **ei** words with the long **a** sound.

(neighbor)   (veil)

receive   (reindeer)

(reign)   ceiling

The teams **eigh** and **ey** also make the long **a** sound.
**Directions:** Finish the sentences with words from the word box.

| chief | sleigh | obey | weigh | thief | field | ceiling |
|---|---|---|---|---|---|---|

1. Eight reindeer pull Santa's _____sleigh_____ .
2. Rules are for us to _____obey_____ .
3. The bird got out of its cage and flew up to the _____ceiling_____ .
4. The leader of an Indian tribe is the _____chief_____ .
5. How much do you _____weigh_____ ?
6. They caught the _____thief_____ who took my bike.
7. Corn grows in a _____field_____ .

## Page 47

**Letter Teams: oi, oy, ou, ow**

**Directions:** Look at the first picture in each row. Circle the pictures that have the same sound.

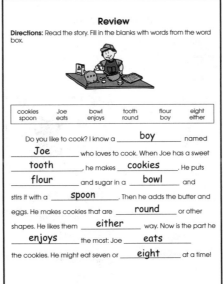

oil

toy

couch

howl

## Page 48

**Letter Teams: ai, ee**

**Directions:** Write in the letter team **ai** or **ee** to complete each word.

r a i n

f e e d

s e e d

p a i l

s a i l

cr e e k

## Page 49

**Review**

**Directions:** Read the story. Fill in the blanks with words from the word box.

| cookies | Joe | bowl | tooth | flour | eight |
|---|---|---|---|---|---|
| spoon | eats | enjoys | round | boy | either |

Do you like to cook? I know a _____boy_____ named _____Joe_____ who loves to cook. When Joe has a sweet _____tooth_____ , he makes _____cookies_____ . He puts _____flour_____ and sugar in a _____bowl_____ and stirs it with a _____spoon_____ . Then he adds the butter and eggs. He makes cookies that are _____round_____ or other shapes. He likes them _____either_____ way. Now is the part he _____enjoys_____ the most: Joe _____eats_____ the cookies. He might eat seven or _____eight_____ at a time!

## Page 50

**Y as a Vowel**

When **y** comes at the end of a word, it is a vowel. When **y** is the only vowel at the end of a one-syllable word, it has the sound of a long **i** (like in **my**). When **y** is the only vowel at the end of a word with more than one syllable, it has the sound of a long **e** (like in **baby**).

**Directions:** Look at the words in the word box. If the word has the sound of a long **i**, write it under the word **my**. If the word has the sound of a long **e**, write it under the word **baby**. Write the word from the word box that answers each riddle.

| happy | penny | fry | try | sleepy | dry |
|---|---|---|---|---|---|
| bunny | why | windy | sky | party | fly |

| my | baby |
|---|---|
| why | happy |
| fry | bunny |
| try | penny |
| sky | windy |
| dry | sleepy |
| fly | party |

1. It takes five of these to make a nickel. _____penny_____
2. This is what you call a baby rabbit. _____bunny_____
3. It is often blue and you can see it if you look up. _____sky_____
4. You might have one of these on your birthday. _____party_____
5. It is the opposite of wet. _____dry_____
6. You might use this word to ask a question. _____why_____

# ANSWER KEY

## Page 51

### Y as a Vowel

**Directions:** Read the rhyming story. Choose the words from the box to fill in the blanks.

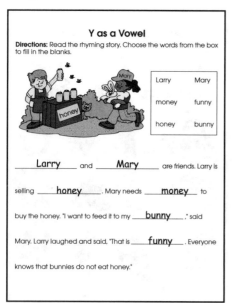

| Larry | Mary |
| money | funny |
| honey | bunny |

___Larry___ and ___Mary___ are friends. Larry is

selling ___honey___. Mary needs ___money___ to

buy the honey. "I want to feed it to my ___bunny___," said

Mary. Larry laughed and said, "That is ___funny___. Everyone

knows that bunnies do not eat honey."

## Page 52

### Y as a Vowel

**Directions:** Read the story. Choose the words from the box to fill in the blanks.

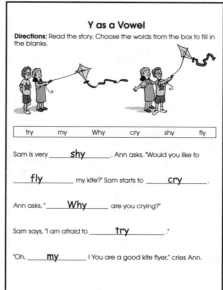

| try | my | Why | cry | shy | fly |

Sam is very ___shy___. Ann asks, "Would you like to

___fly___ my kite?" Sam starts to ___cry___.

Ann asks, "___Why___ are you crying?"

Sam says, "I am afraid to ___try___."

"Oh, ___my___! You are a good kite flyer," cries Ann.

## Page 53

### School Words

| pencil | teacher | crayons |
| recess | lunchbox | play |
| fun | math | |

**Directions:** Fill in the blanks with a word from the word box.

1. I need to sharpen my ___pencil___.
2. I like to ___play___ at recess.
3. School is ___fun___!
4. My ___teacher___ helps me learn.
5. I need to color the picture with ___crayons___.
6. I play kickball at ___recess___.
7. My sandwich is in my ___lunchbox___.
8. In ___math___ I can add and subtract.

## Page 54

### Days of the Week

**Directions:** Write the day of the week that answers each question.

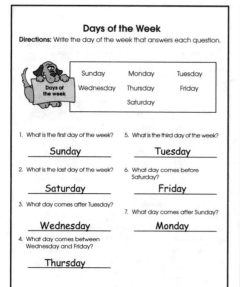

| Sunday | Monday | Tuesday |
| Wednesday | Thursday | Friday |
| | Saturday | |

1. What is the first day of the week?
   ___Sunday___

2. What is the last day of the week?
   ___Saturday___

3. What day comes after Tuesday?
   ___Wednesday___

4. What day comes between Wednesday and Friday?
   ___Thursday___

5. What is the third day of the week?
   ___Tuesday___

6. What day comes before Saturday?
   ___Friday___

7. What day comes after Sunday?
   ___Monday___

## Page 55

### Compound Words

**Compound words** are formed by putting together two smaller words.
**Directions:** Help the cook brew her stew. Mix words from the first column with words from the second column to make new words. Write your new words on the lines at the bottom.

| grand | brows |
| snow | light |
| eye | stairs |
| down | string |
| rose | book |
| shoe | mother |
| note | ball |
| moon | bud |

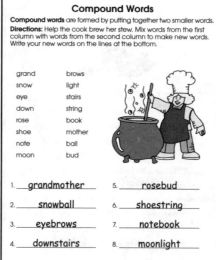

1. ___grandmother___
2. ___snowball___
3. ___eyebrows___
4. ___downstairs___
5. ___rosebud___
6. ___shoestring___
7. ___notebook___
8. ___moonlight___

## Page 56

### Compound Words

**Compound words** are two words that are put together to make one new word.

**Directions:** Read the sentences. Fill in the blank with a compound word from the box.

| raincoat | bedroom | lunchbox | hallway | sandbox |

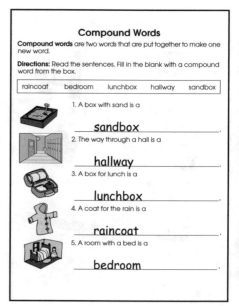

1. A box with sand is a
   ___sandbox___.

2. The way through a hall is a
   ___hallway___.

3. A box for lunch is a
   ___lunchbox___.

4. A coat for the rain is a
   ___raincoat___.

5. A room with a bed is a
   ___bedroom___.

## Page 57

### Compound Words

**Directions:** Cut out the words below. Glue them together in the box to make compound words.

**─ COMPOUND WORDS ─**

| | |
|---|---|
| sunflower | football |
| mailbox | watermelon |
| classroom | airplane |
| livingroom | bodyguard |

Can you think of any more compound words?

## Page 59

### Compound Words

**Directions:** Draw a line under the compound word in each sentence. On the line, write the two words that make up the compound word.

1. A <u>firetruck</u> came to help put out the fire.

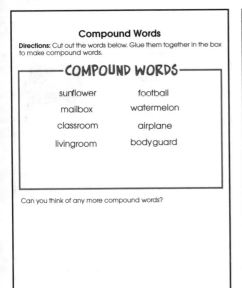

   fire   truck

2. I will be nine years old on my next <u>birthday</u>.

   birth   day

3. We built a <u>treehouse</u> at the back.

   tree   house

4. Dad put a <u>scarecrow</u> in his garden.

   scare   crow

5. It is fun to make <u>footprints</u> in the snow.

   foot   prints

6. I like to read the comics in the <u>newspaper</u>.

   news   paper

7. <u>Cowboys</u> ride horses and use lassos.

   cow   boys

## Page 60

### Contractions

**Contractions** are a short way to write two words, such as **isn't**, **I've** and **weren't**. Example: **it is = it's**

**Directions:** Draw a line from each word pair to its contraction.

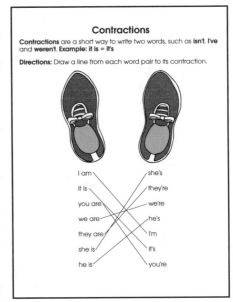

| | |
|---|---|
| I am | she's |
| it is | they're |
| you are | we're |
| we are | he's |
| they are | I'm |
| she is | it's |
| he is | you're |

## Page 61

### Contractions

**Directions:** Circle the contraction that would replace the underlined words.

**Example: were not = weren't**

1. The boy <u>was not</u> sad.
   (wasn't)   weren't

2. We <u>were not</u> working.
   wasn't   (weren't)

3. Jen and Caleb <u>have not</u> eaten lunch yet.
   (haven't)   hasn't

4. The mouse <u>has not</u> been here.
   haven't   (hasn't)

## Page 62

### Contractions

**Directions:** Match the words with their contractions.

| | |
|---|---|
| would not | I've |
| was not | he'll |
| he will | wouldn't |
| could not | wasn't |
| I have | couldn't |

**Directions:** Make the words at the end of each line into contractions to complete the sentences.

1. He __didn't__ know the answer.  **did not**
2. __It's__ a long way home.  **It is**
3. __Here's__ my house.  **Here is**
4. __We're__ not going to school today.  **We are**
5. __They'll__ take the bus home tomorrow.  **They will**

## Page 63

### Contractions

**Directions:** Cut out the two words and put them together to show what two words make the contraction. Glue them over the contraction.

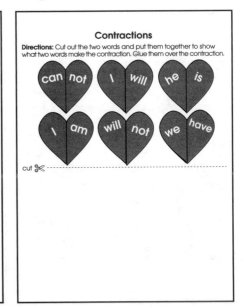

can  not    I  will    he  is

I  am    will  not    we  have

cut ✂ - - - - - - - - - - - - - - - - -

# ANSWER KEY

## Page 65

### Syllables

Words are made up of parts called **syllables**. Each syllable has a vowel sound. One way to count syllables is to clap as you say the word.

**Example:** cat    1 clap    1 syllable
table    2 claps    2 syllables
butterfly    3 claps    3 syllables

**Directions:** "Clap out" the words below. Write how many syllables each word has.

| | | | |
|---|---|---|---|
| movie | 2 | dog | 1 |
| piano | 3 | basket | 2 |
| tree | 1 | swimmer | 2 |
| bicycle | 3 | rainbow | 2 |
| sun | 1 | paper | 2 |
| cabinet | 3 | picture | 2 |
| football | 2 | run | 1 |
| television | 4 | enter | 2 |

## Page 66

### Syllables

Dividing a word into syllables can help you read a new word. You also might divide syllables when you are writing if you run out of space on a line.
Many words contain two consonants that are next to each other. A word can usually be divided between the consonants.

**Directions:** Divide each word into two syllables. The first one is done for you.

| | | |
|---|---|---|
| kitten | kit | ten |
| lumber | lum | ber |
| batter | bat | ter |
| winter | win | ter |
| funny | fun | ny |
| harder | hard | er |
| dirty | dir | ty |
| sister | sis | ter |
| little | lit | tle |
| dinner | din | ner |

## Page 67

### Syllables

One way to help you read a word you don't know is to divide it into parts called **syllables**. Every syllable has a vowel sound.

**Directions:** Say the words. Write the number of syllables. The first one is done for you.

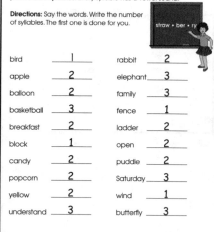
straw • ber • ry

| | | | |
|---|---|---|---|
| bird | 1 | rabbit | 2 |
| apple | 2 | elephant | 3 |
| balloon | 2 | family | 3 |
| basketball | 3 | fence | 1 |
| breakfast | 2 | ladder | 2 |
| block | 1 | open | 2 |
| candy | 2 | puddle | 2 |
| popcorn | 2 | Saturday | 3 |
| yellow | 2 | wind | 1 |
| understand | 3 | butterfly | 3 |

## Page 68

### Syllables

When a double consonant is used in the middle of a word, the word can usually be divided between the consonants.

**Directions:** Look at the words in the word box. Divide each word into two syllables. Leave space between each syllable. One is done for you.

| butter | puppy | kitten | yellow |
| dinner | chatter | ladder | happy |
| pillow | letter | mitten | summer |

| | | | | | |
|---|---|---|---|---|---|
| but | ter | chat | ter | mit | ten |
| din | ner | let | ter | yel | low |
| pil | low | kit | ten | hap | py |
| pup | py | lad | der | sum | mer |

Many words are divided between two consonants that are not alike.
**Directions:** Look at the words in the word box. Divide each word into two syllables. One is done for you.

| window | doctor | number | carpet |
| mister | winter | pencil | candle |
| barber | sister | picture | under |

| | | | | | |
|---|---|---|---|---|---|
| win | dow | win | ter | pic | ture |
| mis | ter | sis | ter | car | pet |
| bar | ber | num | ber | can | dle |
| doc | tor | pen | cil | un | der |

## Page 69

### Syllables

**Directions:** Write 1 or 2 on the line to tell how many syllables are in each word. If the word has 2 syllables, draw a line between the syllables. **Example: sup|per**

| | | | |
|---|---|---|---|
| dog | 1 | timber | 2 |
| bed|room | 2 | cat | 1 |
| slip|per | 2 | street | 1 |
| tree | 1 | chalk | 1 |
| bat|ter | 2 | blan|ket | 2 |
| chair | 1 | mar|ker | 2 |
| fish | 1 | brush | 1 |
| mas|ter | 2 | rab|bit | 2 |

## Page 70

### Haiku

A **haiku** is an Oriental form of poetry. Most haiku are about nature.

    first line - 5 syllables
    second line - 7 syllables
    third line - 5 syllables

**Example:**    The squirrel is brown.
       He lives in a great big tree.
       He eats nuts all day.

**Directions:** Write your own haiku. Draw a picture to go with it.

Results will vary.

## Page 71

### Suffixes

A **suffix** is a syllable that is added at the end of a word to change its meaning.

**Directions:** Add the suffixes to the root words to make new words. Use your new words to complete the sentences.

help + ful = **helpful**
care + less = **careless**
build + er = **builder**
talk + ed = **talked**
love + ly = **lovely**
loud + er = **louder**

1. My mother **talked** to my teacher about my homework.
2. The radio was **louder** than the television.
3. Sally is always **helpful** to her mother.
4. A **builder** put a new garage on our house.
5. The flowers are **lovely** .
6. It is **careless** to cross the street without looking both ways.

## Page 72

### Suffixes

Adding **ing** to a word means that it is happening now. Adding **ed** to a word means it happened in the past.

**Directions:** Look at the words in the word box. Underline the root word in each one. Write a word to complete each sentence.

| | | |
|---|---|---|
| snowing | wished | played | looking | crying |
| talking | walked | eating | going | doing |

1. We like to play. We **played** yesterday.
2. Is that snow? Yes, it is **snowing** .
3. Do you want to go with me? No, I am **going** with my friend.
4. The baby will cry if we leave. The baby is **crying** .
5. We will walk home from school. We **walked** to school this morning.
6. Did you wish for a new bike? Yes, I **wished** for one.
7. Who is going to do it while we are away? I am **doing** it.
8. Did you talk to your friend? Yes, we are **talking** now.
9. Will you look at my book? I am **looking** at it now.
10. I like to eat pizza. We are **eating** it today.

## Page 73

### Suffixes

**Directions:** Write a word from the word box next to its root word.

| | | |
|---|---|---|
| coming | running | sitting |
| lived | rained | swimming |
| visited | carried | racing |
| hurried | | |

run **running**    come **coming**
live **lived**    carry **carried**
hurry **hurried**    race **racing**
swim **swimming**    rain **rained**
visit **visited**    sit **sitting**

**Directions:** Write a word from the word box to finish each sentence.

1. I **visited** my grandmother during vacation.
2. Mary went **swimming** at the lake with her cousin.
3. Jim **carried** the heavy package for his mother.
4. It **rained** and stormed all weekend.
5. Cars go very fast when they are **racing** .

## Page 74

### Suffixes

**Directions:** Read the story. Underline the words that end with **est**, **ed** or **ing**. On the lines below, write the root words for each word you underlined.

The funniest book I ever read was about a girl named Nan. Nan did everything backward. She even spelled her name backward. Nan slept in the day and played at night. She dried her hair before washing it. She turned on the light after she finished her book—which read from the back to the front! When it rained, Nan waited until she was inside before opening her umbrella. She even walked backward. The silliest part: The only thing Nan did forward was back up!

1. **funny**   6. **wash**   11. **open**
2. **name**   7. **turn**   12. **walk**
3. **spell**   8. **finish**   13. **silly**
4. **play**   9. **rain**
5. **dry**   10. **wait**

## Page 75

### Prefixes: The Three R's

**Prefixes** are syllables added to the beginning of words that change their meaning. The prefix **re** means "again."

**Directions:** Read the story. Then follow the instructions.

Kim wants to find ways she can save the Earth. She studies the "three R's"—reduce, reuse and recycle. Reduce means to make less. Both reuse and recycle mean to use again.

Add **re** to the beginning of each word below. Use the new words to complete the sentences.

**re** build    **re** fill
**re** read    **re** tell
**re** write    **re** run

1. The race was a tie, so Dawn and Kathy had to **rerun** it.
2. The block wall fell down, so Simon had to **rebuild** it.
3. The water bottle was empty, so Luna had to **refill** it.
4. Javier wrote a good story, but he wanted to **rewrite** it to make it better.
5. The teacher told a story, and students had to **retell** it.
6. Toni didn't understand the directions, so she had to **reread** them.

## Page 76

### Prefixes

**Directions:** Read the story. Change Unlucky Sam to Lucky Sam by taking the **un** prefix off of the **bold** words.

**Unlucky Sam**

Sam was **unhappy** about a lot of things in his life. His parents were **uncaring**. His teacher was **unfair**. His big sister was **unkind**. His neighbors were **unfriendly**. He was **unhealthy**, too! How could one boy be as **unlucky** as Sam?

**Lucky Sam**

Sam was **happy** about a lot of things in his life. His parents were **caring** . His teacher was **fair** . His big sister was **kind** . His neighbors were **friendly** . He was **healthy** , too! How could one boy be as **lucky** as Sam?

## Page 77

**Prefixes**

**Directions:** Change the meaning of the sentences by adding the prefixes to the **bold** words.

The boy was **lucky** because he guessed the answer **correctly**.

The boy was (un) ___unlucky___ because he guessed the answer (in) ___incorrectly___ .

When Mary **behaved**, she felt **happy**.

When Mary (mis) ___misbehaved___ , she felt (un) ___unhappy___

Mike wore his jacket **buttoned** because the dance was **formal**.

Mike wore his jacket (un) ___unbuttoned___ because the dance was (in) ___informal___ .

Tim **understood** because he was **familiar** with the book.

Tim (mis) ___misunderstood___ because he was (un) ___unfamiliar___ with the book.

## Page 78

**Prefixes**

**Directions:** Read the story. Change the story by removing the prefix **re** from the **bold** words. Write the new words in the new story.

**Repete** is a **rewriter** who has to **redo** every story. He has to **rethink** up the ideas. He has to **rewrite** the sentences. He has to **redraw** the pictures. He even has to **retype** the pages. Who will **repay** **Repete** for all the work he **redoes**?

___Pete___ is a ___writer___ who has to ___do___ every story. He has to ___think___ up the ideas. He has to ___write___ the sentences.

He has to ___draw___ the pictures.

He even has to ___type___ the pages.

Who will ___pay___ ___Pete___ for all the work he ___does___ ?

## Page 79

**Review**

**Directions:** Read each sentence. Look at the words in bold. Circle the prefix and write the root word on the line.

1. The (pre)view of the movie was funny. ___view___
2. We always drink (non)fat milk. ___fat___
3. We will have to (re)schedule the trip. ___schedule___
4. Are you tired of (re)runs on television? ___run___
5. I have (out)grown my new shoes already. ___grow___
6. You must have (mis)placed the papers. ___place___
7. Police (en)force the laws of the city. ___force___
8. I (dis)liked that book. ___like___
9. The boy (dis)trusted the big dog. ___trust___
10. Try to (en)joy yourself at the party. ___joy___
11. Please try to keep the cat (in)side the house. ___side___
12. That song is total (non)sense! ___sense___
13. We will (re)place any parts that we lost. ___place___
14. Can you help me (un)zip this jacket? ___zip___
15. Let's (re)work today's arithmetic problems. ___work___

## Page 80

**Parts of a Book**

A book has many parts. The title is the name of the book. The author is the person who wrote the words. The illustrator is the person who drew the pictures. The table of contents is located at the beginning to list what is in the book. The glossary is a little dictionary in the back to help you with unfamiliar words. Books are often divided into smaller sections of information called chapters.

**Directions:** Look at one of your books. Write the parts you see below.

**Answers will vary.**

The title of my book is _____

The author is _____

The illustrator is _____

My book has a table of contents.        Yes or No

My book has a glossary.        Yes or No

My book is divided into chapters.        Yes or No

## Page 82

**Recalling Details: Nikki's Pets**

**Directions:** Read about Nikki's pets. Then answer the questions.

Nikki has two cats, Tiger and Sniffer, and two dogs, Spot and Wiggles. Tiger is an orange striped cat who likes to sleep under a big tree and pretend she is a real tiger. Sniffer is a gray cat who likes to sniff the flowers in Nikki's garden. Spot is a Dalmatian with many black spots. Wiggles is a big furry brown dog who wiggles all over when he is happy.

1. Which dog is brown and furry? ___Wiggles___
2. What color is Tiger? ___orange with stripes___
3. What kind of dog is Spot? ___Dalmation___
4. Which cat likes to sniff flowers? ___Sniffer___
5. Where does Tiger like to sleep? ___under a big tree___
6. Who wiggles all over when he is happy? ___Wiggles___

## Page 83

**Recalling Details: Pet Pests**

**Directions:** Read the story. Then answer the questions.

Sometimes Marvin and Mugsy scratch and itch. Marcy knows that fleas or ticks are insect pests to her pets. Their bites are painful. Fleas suck the blood of animals. They don't have wings, but they can jump. Ticks are very flat, suck blood and are related to spiders. They like to hide in dogs' ears. That is why Marcy checks Marvin and Mugsy every week for fleas and ticks.

1. What is a pest? ___an insect such as a flea or tick___

2. List three facts about fleas.
   1) ___They suck the blood of animals.___
   2) ___They don't have wings.___
   3) ___They can jump.___

3. List three facts about ticks.
   1) ___They are very flat.___
   2) ___They suck blood.___
   3) ___They are related to spiders.___

## Page 84

### Reading for Details

**Directions:** Read the story about baby animals. Answer the questions with words from the story.

Baby cats are called kittens. They love to play and drink lots of milk. A baby dog is a puppy. Puppies chew on old shoes. They run and bark. A lamb is a baby sheep. Lambs eat grass. A baby duck is called a duckling. Ducklings swim with their wide, webbed feet. Foals are baby horses. A foal can walk the day it is born! A baby goat is a kid. Some people call children kids, too!

1. A baby cat is called a _____kitten_____.

2. A baby dog is a _____puppy_____.

3. A _____lamb_____ is a baby sheep.

4. _____Ducklings_____ swim with their webbed feet.

5. A _____foal_____ can walk the day it is born.

6. A baby goat is a _____kid_____.

## Page 85

### Reading for Details

**Directions:** Read the story about bike safety. Answer the questions below the story.

Mike has a red bike. He likes his bike. Mike wears a helmet. Mike wears knee pads and elbow pads. They keep him safe. Mike stops at signs. Mike looks both ways. Mike is safe on his bike.

1. What color is Mike's bike? _____red_____

2. Which sentence in the story tells why Mike wears pads and a helmet? Write it here.

_____They keep him safe._____

3. What else does Mike do to keep safe?

He _____stops_____ at signs and _____looks_____ both ways.

## Page 86

### Reading for Details

**Directions:** Read the story about different kinds of transportation. Answer the questions with words from the story.

People use many kinds of transportation. Boats float on the water. Some people fish in a boat. Airplanes fly in the sky. Flying in a plane is a fast way to get somewhere. Trains run on a track. The first car is the engine. The last car is the caboose. Some people even sleep in beds on a train! A car has four wheels. Most people have a car. A car rides on roads. A bus can hold many people. A bus rides on roads. Most children ride a bus to school.

1. A boat floats on the _____water_____.

2. If you want to get somewhere fast, which transportation would you use? _____airplane_____.

3. The first car on a train is called an engine and the last car is a _____caboose_____.

4. _____Children_____ ride on a bus.

5. A _____car_____ has four wheels.

## Page 87

### Following Directions

**Directions:** Read the story. Answer the questions. Try the recipe.

#### Cows Give Us Milk

Cows live on a farm. The farmer milks the cow to get milk. Many things are made from milk. We make ice cream, sour cream, cottage cheese and butter from milk. Butter is fun to make! You can learn to make your own butter. First, you need cream. Put the cream in a jar and shake it. Then you need to pour off the liquid. Next, you put the butter in a bowl. Add a little salt and stir! Finally, spread it on crackers and eat!

1. What animal gives us milk? _____COW_____

2. What 4 things are made from milk?
_____ice cream_____ _____sour cream_____ _____cottage cheese_____ _____butter_____

3. What did the story teach you to make? _____butter_____

4. Put the steps in order. Place 1, 2, 3, 4 by the sentence.

___4___ Spread the butter on crackers and eat!

___2___ Shake cream in a jar.

___1___ Start with cream.

___3___ Add salt to the butter.

## Page 88

### Following Directions: Parrot Art

**Directions:** Draw the missing parts on each parrot.

1. Draw the parrot's eye.

2. Draw the parrot's tail.

3. Draw the parrot's beak.

4. Draw the parrot's wings.

## Page 89

### Following Directions: How to Treat a Ladybug

**Directions:** Read about how to treat ladybugs. Then follow the instructions.

Ladybugs are shy. If you see a ladybug, sit very still. Hold out your arm. Maybe the ladybug will fly to you. If it does, talk softly. Do not touch it. It will fly away when it is ready.

1. Complete the directions on how to treat a ladybug.

a. Sit very still.

b. _____Hold out your arm._____

c. Talk softly.

d. _____Do not touch it._____

2. Ladybugs are red. They have black spots. Color the ladybug.

## Page 90

### Following Directions: Insect Art

**Directions:** Read about insects. Then follow the instructions.

All insects have these body parts:

Head at the front

Thorax in the middle

Abdomen at the back

Six legs—three on each side of the thorax

Two eyes on the head

Two antennae attached to the head

Some insects also have wings.

Draw your favorite insect. Include all the body parts listed above.

Drawings will vary.

## Page 91

### Sequencing: Packing Bags

**Directions:** Read about packing bags. Then number the objects in the order they should be packed.

Cans are heavy. Put them in first. Then put in boxes. Now, put in the apple. Put the bread in last.

## Page 92

### Sequencing: 1, 2, 3, 4!

**Directions:** Write numbers by each sentence to show the order of the story.

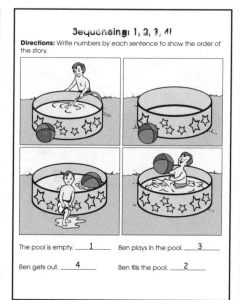

The pool is empty. __1__    Ben plays in the pool. __3__

Ben gets out. __4__    Ben fills the pool. __2__

## Page 93

### Sequencing/Predicting: A Game for Cats

**Directions:** Read about what cats like. Then follow the instructions.

Cats like to play with paper bags. Pull a paper bag open. Take everything out. Now, lay it on its side.

1. Write 1, 2 and 3 to put the pictures in order.

2. In box 4, draw what you think the cat will do.

Drawings will vary.

## Page 94

### Sequencing: Story Events

Spencer likes to make new friends. Today, he made friends with the dog in the picture.

**Directions:** Number the sentences in order to find out what Spencer did today.

__3__ Spencer kissed his mother good-bye.

__5__ Spencer saw the new dog next door.

__4__ Spencer went outside.

__6__ Spencer said hello.

__2__ Spencer got dressed and ate breakfast.

__1__ Spencer woke up.

## Page 95

### Sequencing: Yo-Yo Trick

**Directions:** Read about the yo-yo trick.

Wind up the yo-yo string. Hold the yo-yo in your hand. Now, hold your palm up. Throw the yo-yo downward on the string. Hold your palm down. Now, swing the yo-yo forward. Make it "walk." This yo-yo trick is called "walk the dog."

**Directions:** Number the directions in order.

__3__ Swing the yo-yo forward and make it "walk."

__1__ Hold your palm up and drop the yo-yo.

__2__ Turn your palm down as the yo-yo reaches the ground.

## Page 96

### Sequencing: Make a Hat

Mrs. Posey made a new hat, but she forgot how she did it. When she tried to tell her friend, she got all mixed up.

**Directions:** Read Mrs. Posey's story. Write her story on the lines in the order you think it happened. Then color the picture.

I glued flowers on it. Then I bought this straw hat. Now, I am wearing my hat. Then I added ribbon around the flowers. I tried on many hats at the store.

The real story:

I tried on many hats at the store.

Then I bought this straw hat. I glued flowers on it. Then

I added ribbon around the flowers. Now, I am wearing

my hat.

## Page 97

### Following Directions

Here is a recipe for chocolate peanut butter cookies. When you use a recipe, you must follow the directions carefully. The sentences below are not in the correct order.

**Directions:** Write number 1 to show what you would do first. Then number each step to show the correct sequence.

__1__ Melt the chocolate almond bark in a microsafe bowl.

__6__ Eat!

__2__ While the chocolate is melting, spread peanut butter on a cracker and place another cracker on top.

__4__ Let the melted candy drip off the cracker into the bowl before you place it on wax paper.

__5__ Let it cool!

__3__ Carefully use a fork or spoon to dip the crackers into the melted chocolate.

Try the recipe with an adult.

Do you like to cook? __Answers will vary.__

## Page 98

### Sequencing: Follow a Recipe

Alana and Marcus are hungry for a snack. They want to make nacho chips and cheese. The steps they need to follow are all mixed up.

**Directions:** Read the steps. Number them in 1, 2, 3 order. Then color the picture.

__5__ Bake the chips in the oven for 2 minutes.

__1 or 2__ Get a cookie sheet to bake on.

__1 or 2__ Get out the nacho chips and cheese.

__6__ Eat the nachos and chips.

__3__ Put the chips on the cookie sheet.

__4__ Put grated cheese on the chips.

## Page 99

### Sequencing: Making a Snowman

**Directions:** Read about how to make a snowman. Then follow the instructions.

It is fun to make a snowman. First, find things for the snowman's eyes and nose. Dress warmly. Then go outdoors. Roll a big snowball. Then roll another to put on top of it. Now, roll a small snowball for the head. Put on the snowman's face.

 1   2

 3   4

1. Number the pictures in order.

2. Write two things to do before going outdoors.

1) Find things for the snowman's eyes and nose.

2) Dress warmly.

## Page 100

### Sequencing: Baking a Cake

**Directions:** Read about baking a cake. Then write the missing steps.

Dylan, Dana and Dad are baking a cake. Dad turns on the oven. Dana opens the cake mix. Dylan adds the eggs. Dad pours in the water. Dana stirs the batter. Dylan pours the batter into a cake pan. Dad puts it in the oven.

1. Turn on the oven.

2. Open the cake mix.

3. Add the eggs.

4. Pour in the water.

5. Stir the batter.

6. Pour the batter into a cake pan.

7. Put the pan in the oven.

## Page 101

### Sequencing: Story Events

Mari was sick yesterday.

**Directions:** Number the events in 1, 2, 3 order to tell the story about Mari.

__2__ She went to the doctor's office.

__9__ Mari felt much better.

__1__ Mari felt very hot and tired.

__6__ Mari's mother went to the drugstore.

__4__ The doctor wrote down something.

__3__ The doctor looked in Mari's ears.

__7__ Mari took a pill.

__5__ The doctor gave Mari's mother the piece of paper.

__8__ Mari drank some water with her pill.

## Page 102

### Sequencing: Making a Card

**Directions:** Read about how to make a card. Then follow the instructions.

You will need scissors, glue and colored paper. First, look at all your old cards. Then, cut out what you like. Now, fold the colored paper in half. Glue the cut-outs to the front of your card. Write your name inside.

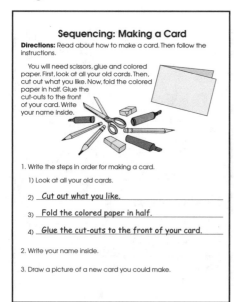

1. Write the steps in order for making a card.

   1) Look at all your old cards.

   2) _Cut out what you like._

   3) _Fold the colored paper in half._

   4) _Glue the cut-outs to the front of your card._

2. Write your name inside.

3. Draw a picture of a new card you could make.

## Page 103

### Sequencing: Making Clay

**Directions:** Read about making clay. Then follow the instructions.

It is fun to work with clay. Here is what you need to make it:

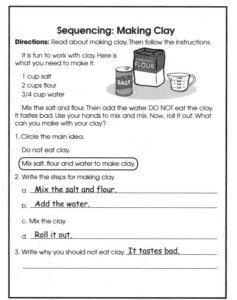

1 cup salt
2 cups flour
3/4 cup water

Mix the salt and flour. Then add the water. DO NOT eat the clay. It tastes bad. Use your hands to mix and mix. Now, roll it out. What can you make with your clay?

1. Circle the main idea:

   Do not eat clay.

   (Mix salt, flour and water to make clay.)

2. Write the steps for making clay.

   a. _Mix the salt and flour._

   b. _Add the water._

   c. Mix the clay.

   d. _Roll it out._

3. Write why you should not eat clay. _It tastes bad._

## Page 104

### Sequencing: Play a Game

Children all around the world like to play games. Think about your favorite game. Maybe you could teach your friends to play it.

**Directions:** Write, in order, how to play your game.

_Answers will vary._

**Directions:** Draw a picture of you playing your favorite game.

_Pictures will vary._

## Page 105

### Sequencing: A Visit to the Zoo

**Directions:** Read the story. Then follow the instructions.

One Saturday morning in May, Gloria and Anna went to the zoo. First, they bought tickets to get into the zoo. Second, they visited the Gorilla Garden and had fun watching the gorillas stare at them. Then they went to Tiger Town and watched the tigers as they slept in the sunshine. Fourth, they went to Hippo Haven and laughed at the hippos cooling off in their pool. Next, they visited Snake Station and learned about poisonous and nonpoisonous snakes. It was noon, and they were hungry, so they ate lunch at the Parrot Patio.

Write **first, second, third, fourth, fifth** and **sixth** to put the events in order.

_Fourth_ They went to Hippo Haven.

_First_ Gloria and Anna bought zoo tickets.

_Third_ They watched the tigers sleep.

_Sixth_ They ate lunch at Parrot Patio.

_Second_ The gorillas stared at them.

_Fifth_ They learned about poisonous and nonpoisonous snakes.

## Page 106

### Sequencing: Why Does It Rain?

**Directions:** Read about rain. Then follow the instructions.

Clouds are made up of little drops of ice and water. They push and bang into each other. Then they join together to make bigger drops and begin to fall. More raindrops cling to them. They become heavy and fall quickly to the ground.

Write **first, second, third, fourth** and **fifth** to put the events in order.

_fourth_ More raindrops cling to them.

_first_ Clouds are made up of little drops of ice and water.

_third_ They join together and make bigger drops that begin to fall.

_second_ The drops of ice and water bang into each other.

_fifth_ The drops become heavy and fall quickly to the ground.

## Page 107

### Sequencing: Make a Pencil Holder

**Directions:** Read how to make a pencil holder. Then follow the instructions.

You can use "junk" to make a pencil holder! First, you need a clean can with one end removed. Make sure there are no sharp edges. Then you need glue, scissors and paper. Find colorful paper such as wrapping paper, wallpaper or construction paper. Cut the paper to fit the can. Glue the paper around the can. Decorate your can with glitter, buttons and stickers. Then put your pencils inside!

1. Write **first, second, third, fourth, fifth, sixth** and **seventh** to put the steps in order.

   _second_ Make sure there are no sharp edges.

   _third_ Get glue, scissors and paper.

   _fourth_ Cut the paper to fit the can.

   _seventh_ Put your pencils in the can!

   _fifth_ Glue colorful paper to the can.

   _first_ Remove one end of a clean can.

   _sixth_ Decorate the can with glitter and stickers.

## Page 108

### Tracking: Where Does She Go?

Every morning when Lisa wakes up, she goes somewhere. Find out where she goes.

**Directions:**
Read the sentences. Follow the instructions.

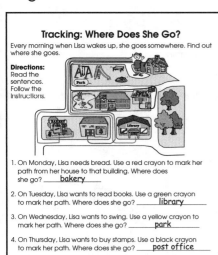

1. On Monday, Lisa needs bread. Use a red crayon to mark her path from her house to that building. Where does she go? __bakery__

2. On Tuesday, Lisa wants to read books. Use a green crayon to mark her path. Where does she go? __library__

3. On Wednesday, Lisa wants to swing. Use a yellow crayon to mark her path. Where does she go? __park__

4. On Thursday, Lisa wants to buy stamps. Use a black crayon to mark her path. Where does she go? __post office__

5. On Friday, Lisa wants to get money. Use a purple crayon to mark her path. Where does she go? __bank__

## Page 109

### Tracking: Sequencing

**Directions:** Look at the paths you drew for Lisa on page 62. Number, in order, the places that Lisa went each day. Draw a line to connect the place with the day of the week.

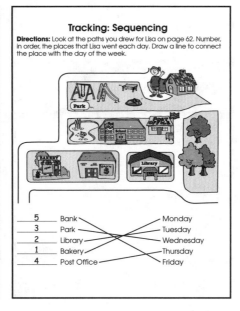

| 5 | Bank | | Monday |
| 3 | Park | | Tuesday |
| 2 | Library | | Wednesday |
| 1 | Bakery | | Thursday |
| 4 | Post Office | | Friday |

## Page 110

### Tracking: With a Map

Greg and Tess walk to and from school together each day. After school, they stop at the park to play. Then they go home.

**Directions:** Read the sentences. Draw Greg's path in red and Tess's path in blue.

Greg starts at his home.
He walks to school.
When he leaves school, he stops at the park.
Then he goes home.
Tess goes the same places that Greg goes.
Some of their paths will be the same.

## Page 111

### Tracking: With a Map

**Directions:** Study the map of the United States. Follow the instructions.
**Answers 1, 2 and 5 will vary.**
1. Draw a star on the state where you live.
2. Draw a line from your state to the Atlantic Ocean.
3. Draw a triangle in the Gulf of Mexico.
4. Draw a circle in the Pacific Ocean.
5. Color each state that borders your state a different color.

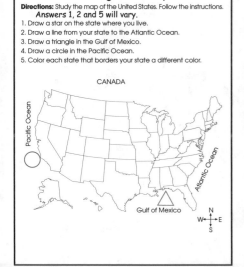

## Page 112

### Tracking: Alternate Paths

Look at Spotty Dog's home. Look at the paths he takes to the oven and the back door. The numbers by each path show how many steps Spotty must take to get there.

**Directions:** Follow the instructions.

1. Spotty Dog's cookies are done. Trace Spotty's path from his chair to the oven.

2. How many steps does Spotty take? __5__

3. While Spotty is looking in his oven, he hears a noise in the backyard. Trace Spotty's path to the door.

4. How many steps has Spotty taken in all? __9__

5. Spotty goes back to his chair. How many steps must he take? __7__

6. How many steps has he taken in all? __16__

7. Spotty's path has made a shape. What shape is it? __triangle__

## Page 113

### Same/Different: Objects

**Directions:** Look at the pictures. Draw an **X** on the picture in each row that is different.

## Page 114

### Same/Different: Stuffed Animals

Kate and Oralia like to collect and trade stuffed animals.

**Directions:** Draw two stuffed animals that are alike and two that are different.

**Alike**

**Different**

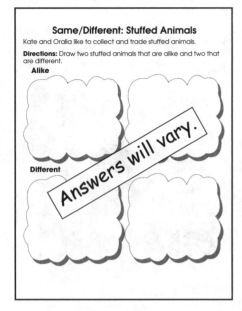

Answers will vary.

## Page 115

### Same/Different: Shell Homes

**Directions:** Read about shells. Then answer the questions.

Shells are the homes of some animals. Snails live in shells on the land. Clams live in shells in the water. Clam shells open. Snail shells stay closed. Both shells keep the animals safe.

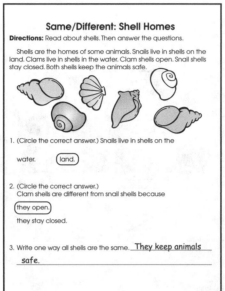

1. (Circle the correct answer.) Snails live in shells on the

    water.  (land.)

2. (Circle the correct answer.)
    Clam shells are different from snail shells because

    (they open.)

    they stay closed.

3. Write one way all shells are the same.  __They keep animals__

    __safe.__

## Page 116

### Same/Different: Venn Diagram

A **Venn diagram** is a diagram that shows how two things are the same and different.

**Directions:** Choose two outdoor sports. Then follow the instructions to complete the Venn diagram.

1. Write the first sport name under the first circle. Write some words that describe the sport. Write them in the first circle.

2. Write the second sport name under the second circle. Write some words that describe the sport. Write them in the circle.

3. Where the 2 circles overlap, write some words that describe both sports.

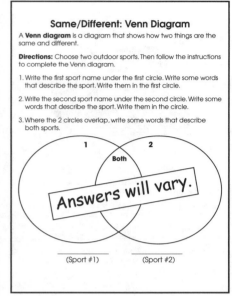

Answers will vary.

_____   _____
(Sport #1)         (Sport #2)

## Page 117

### Same/Different: Dina and Dina

**Directions:** Read the story. Then complete the Venn diagram, telling how Dina, the duck, is the same or different than Dina, the girl.

One day in the library, Dina found a story about a duck named Dina!

My name is Dina. I am a duck, and I like to swim. When I am not swimming, I walk on land or fly. I have two feet and two eyes. My feathers keep me warm. Ducks can be different colors. I am gray, brown and black. I really like being a duck. It is fun.

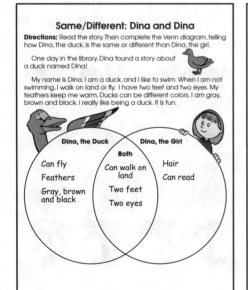

**Dina, the Duck**

Can fly
Feathers
Gray, brown and black

**Both**

Can walk on land
Two feet
Two eyes

**Dina, the Girl**

Hair
Can read

## Page 118

### Same/Different: Ann and Lee Have Fun

**Directions:** Read about Ann and Lee. Then write how they are the same and different in the Venn diagram.

Ann and Lee like to play ball. They like to jump rope. Lee likes to play a card game called "Old Maid." Ann likes to play a card game called "Go Fish." What do you do to have fun?

**Ann**

Play "Go Fish"

**Both**

Jump rope
Play ball

**Lee**

Play "Old Maid"

## Page 119

### Same/Different: Cats and Tigers

**Directions:** Read about cats and tigers. Then complete the Venn diagram, telling how they are the same and different.

Tigers are a kind of cat. Pet cats and tigers both have fur. Pet cats are small and tame. Tigers are large and wild.

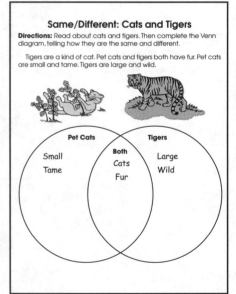

**Pet Cats**

Small
Tame

**Both**

Cats
Fur

**Tigers**

Large
Wild

## Page 120

### Same/Different: Marvin and Mugsy

**Directions:** Read about Marvin and Mugsy. Then complete the Venn diagram, telling how they are the same and different.

Marcy has two dogs, Marvin and Mugsy. Marvin is a black-and-white spotted Dalmatian. Marvin likes to run after balls in the backyard. His favorite food is Canine Crunchy Crunch. Marcy likes to take Marvin for walks, because dogs need exercise. Marvin loves to sleep in his doghouse. Mugsy is a big furry brown dog, who wiggles when she is happy. Since she is big, she needs lots of exercise. So Marcy takes her for walks in the park. Her favorite food is Canine Crunchy Crunch. Mugsy likes to sleep on Marcy's bed.

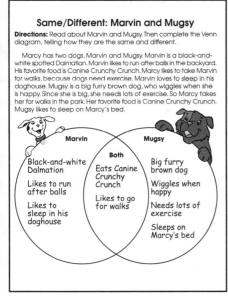

**Marvin**
Black-and-white Dalmation
Likes to run after balls
Likes to sleep in his doghouse

**Both**
Eats Canine Crunchy Crunch
Likes to go for walks

**Mugsy**
Big furry brown dog
Wiggles when happy
Needs lots of exercise
Sleeps on Marcy's bed

## Page 121

### Same/Different: Bluebirds and Parrots

**Directions:** Read about parrots and bluebirds. Then complete the Venn diagram, telling how they are the same and different.

Bluebirds and parrots are both birds. Bluebirds and parrots can fly. They both have beaks. Parrots can live inside a cage. Bluebirds must live outdoors.

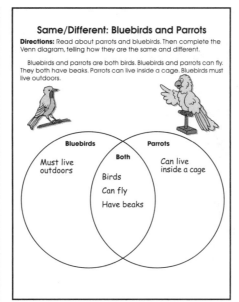

**Bluebirds**
Must live outdoors

**Both**
Birds
Can fly
Have beaks

**Parrots**
Can live inside a cage

## Page 122

### Same/Different: Sleeping Whales

**Directions:** Read more about whales. Then complete the Venn diagram, telling how whales and people are the same and different.

Whales do not sleep like we do. They take many short naps. Like us, whales breathe air. Whales live in very cold water, but they have fat that keeps them warm.

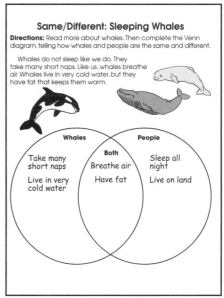

**Whales**
Take many short naps
Live in very cold water

**Both**
Breathe air
Have fat

**People**
Sleep all night
Live on land

## Page 123

### Similes

A **simile** is a figure of speech that compares two different things. The words **like** or **as** are used in similes.

**Directions:** Draw a line to the picture that goes with each set of words.

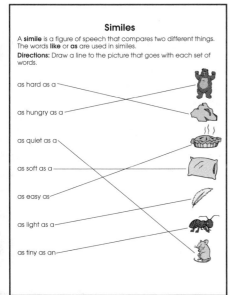

as hard as a
as hungry as a
as quiet as a
as soft as a
as easy as
as light as a
as tiny as an

## Page 124

### Classifying: A Rainy Day

**Directions:** Read the story. Then circle the objects Jonathan needs to stay dry.

It is raining. Jonathan wants to play outdoors. What should he wear to stay dry? What should he carry to stay dry?

## Page 125

### Classifying: Outdoor/Indoor Games

**Classifying** is putting things that are alike into groups.

**Directions:** Read about games. Draw an **X** on the games you can play indoors. Circle the objects used for outdoor games.

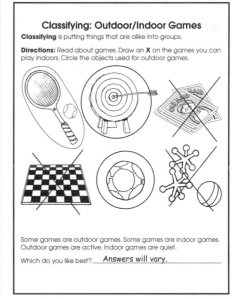

Some games are outdoor games. Some games are indoor games. Outdoor games are active. Indoor games are quiet.

Which do you like best? _Answers will vary._

## Page 126

### Classifying: Art Tools

**Directions:** Read about art tools. Then color only the art tools.

Andrea uses different art tools to help her design her masterpieces. To cut, she needs scissors. To draw, she needs a pencil. To color, she needs crayons. To paint, she needs a brush.

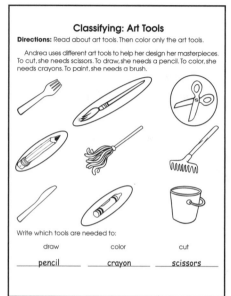

Write which tools are needed to:

| draw | color | cut |
|------|-------|-----|
| pencil | crayon | scissors |

## Page 127

### Classifying

**Classifying** is putting similar things into groups.
**Directions:** Write each word from the word box on the correct line.

| baby | donkey | whale | family | fox |
|------|--------|-------|--------|-----|
| uncle | goose | grandfather | kangaroo | policeman |

| people | animals |
|--------|---------|
| baby | goose |
| family | whale |
| grandfather | fox |
| policeman | kangaroo |
| uncle | donkey |

## Page 128

### Classifying

**Directions:** Read the sentences. Write the words from the word box where they belong.

| bush | rocket | cake | thunder | bicycle | Danger |
|------|--------|------|---------|---------|--------|
| airplane | wind | candy | rain | car | grass |
| Stop | truck | Poison | flower | pie | bird |

1. These things taste sweet.

cake        candy        pie

2. These things come when it storms.

wind        thunder        rain

3. These things have wheels.

car        truck        bicycle

4. These are words you see on signs.

Stop        Poison        Danger

5. These things can fly.

rocket        bird        airplane

6. These things grow in the ground.

flower        grass        bush

## Page 129

### Classifying: Animals

**Directions:** Use a red crayon to circle the names of three animals that would make good pets. Use a blue crayon to circle the names of three wild animals. Use an orange crayon to circle the two animals that live on a farm.

BEAR  CAT  LION  SHEEP  BIRD  DOG  COW  TIGER

## Page 130

### Classifying

**Directions:** The words in each box form a group. Choose the word from the word box that describes each group and write it on the line.

| clothes | family | noises | colors | flowers |
|---------|--------|--------|--------|---------|
| fruits | animals | coins | toys | |

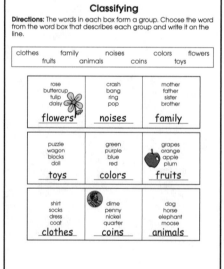

| rose buttercup tulip daisy | crash bang ring pop | mother father sister brother |
|---|---|---|
| **flowers** | **noises** | **family** |

| puzzle wagon blocks doll | green purple blue red | grapes orange apple plum |
|---|---|---|
| **toys** | **colors** | **fruits** |

| shirt socks dress coat | dime penny nickel quarter | dog horse elephant moose |
|---|---|---|
| **clothes** | **coins** | **animals** |

## Page 131

### Classifying

**Living** things need air, food and water to live. **Non-living** things are not alive.
**Directions:** Cut out the words on the bottom. Glue each word in the correct column.

| Living | | Non-living | |
|--------|------|------------|------|
| horse | tree | camera | car |
| flower | ant | shoe | book |
| dog | boy | chair | bread |

cut ✂ - - - - - - - - - - - - - - - - - - - - - - - - - - - - - - - - - -

# ANSWER KEY

## Page 133

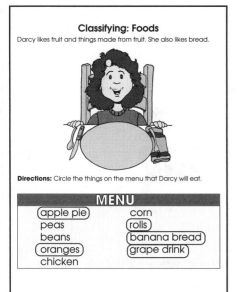

**Classifying: Foods**

Darcy likes fruit and things made from fruit. She also likes bread.

**Directions:** Circle the things on the menu that Darcy will eat.

**MENU**
- (apple pie)
- peas
- beans
- (oranges)
- chicken
- corn
- (rolls)
- (banana bread)
- (grape drink)

## Page 134

**Classifying: Words**

Dapper Dog is going camping.

**Directions:** Draw an **X** on the word in each row that does not belong in that group.

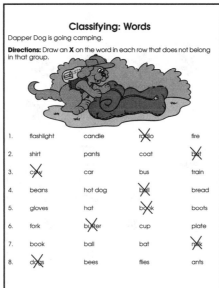

1. flashlight | candle | ~~radio~~ | fire
2. shirt | pants | coat | ~~bat~~
3. ~~cow~~ | car | bus | train
4. beans | hot dog | ~~ball~~ | bread
5. gloves | hat | ~~book~~ | boots
6. fork | ~~butter~~ | cup | plate
7. book | ball | bat | ~~milk~~
8. ~~dogs~~ | bees | flies | ants

## Page 135

**Classifying: Leaves**

**Directions:** Look at each leaf and read its name. Write the name of each leaf on the line. Then color the leaves.

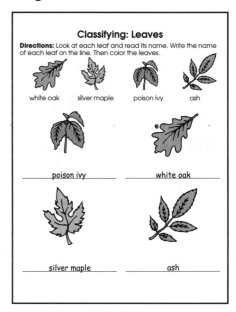

white oak | silver maple | poison ivy | ash

poison ivy | white oak

silver maple | ash

## Page 136

**Classifying: Leaves**

This tricky tree has four different kinds of leaves: ash, poison ivy, silver maple and white oak.

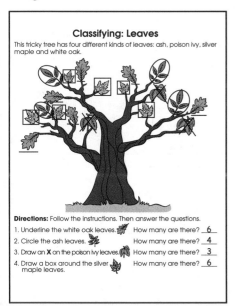

**Directions:** Follow the instructions. Then answer the questions.

1. Underline the white oak leaves. How many are there? __6__
2. Circle the ash leaves. How many are there? __4__
3. Draw an **X** on the poison ivy leaves. How many are there? __3__
4. Draw a box around the silver maple leaves. How many are there? __6__

## Page 137

**Classifying: Watch Out for Poison Ivy!**

Poison ivy is not safe. If you touch it, it can make your skin red and itchy. It can hurt. It grows on the ground. It has three leaves. It can be green or red. Watch out, Jay! There is poison ivy in these woods.

**Directions:** Color the poison ivy leaves red. Then color the "safe" leaves other colors.

## Page 138

**Classifying: Leaves**

**Directions:** Gather some leaves. Put your leaves into groups by type. Then answer the questions.

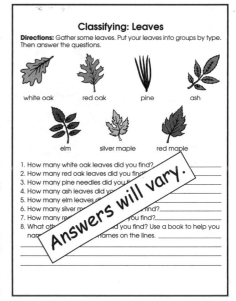

white oak | red oak | pine | ash

elm | silver maple | red maple

1. How many white oak leaves did you find?
2. How many red oak leaves did you find?
3. How many pine needles did you f
4. How many ash leaves did yo
5. How many elm leaves d
6. How many silver m
7. How many re
8. What ot

*Answers will vary.*

## Page 139

**Classifying: Animal Habitats**

**Directions:** Read the story. Then write each animal's name under **Water** or **Land** to tell where it lives.

Animals live in different habitats. A habitat is the place of an animal's natural home. Many animals live on land and others live in water. Most animals that live in water breathe with gills. Animals that live on land breathe with lungs.

| fish | shrimp | giraffe | dog |
| cat | eel | whale | horse |
| bear | deer | shark | jellyfish |

**WATER**
1. fish          4. whale
2. shrimp          5. shark
3. eel          6. jellyfish

**LAND**
1. cat          4. giraffe
2. bear          5. dog
3. deer          6. horse

## Page 140

**Review**

**Directions:** Compare the leaves on the left to the pictures of the other leaves. Write the missing names under the leaves.

ash          red oak          poison ivy          ash

silver maple          silver maple          elm          white oak

**Directions:** Color the pictures that are fruits.

apple          carrot          peach          corn

**Directions:** Draw an **X** on the word in each group that does not belong.

night          black          dark          sun

rose          ash          oak          elm

muffin          banana          rolls          bread

## Page 141

**Comprehension: Ladybugs**

**Directions:** Read about ladybugs. Then answer the questions.

Have you ever seen a ladybug? Ladybugs are red. They have black spots. They have six legs. Ladybugs are pretty!

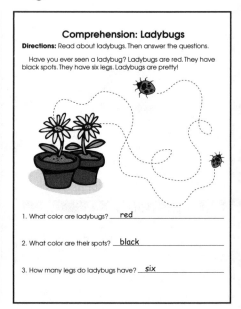

1. What color are ladybugs? _red_

2. What color are their spots? _black_

3. How many legs do ladybugs have? _six_

## Page 142

**Comprehension: Playful Cats**

**Directions:** Read about cats. Then follow the instructions.

Cats make good pets. They like to play. They like to jump. They like to run. Do you?

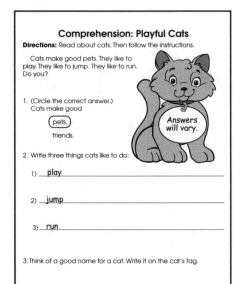

1. (Circle the correct answer.) Cats make good
   (pets.)
   friends.

   Answers will vary.

2. Write three things cats like to do:
   1) _play_
   2) _jump_
   3) _run_

3. Think of a good name for a cat. Write it on the cat's tag.

## Page 143

**Comprehension: Types of Tops**

The **main idea** is the most important point or idea in a story.

**Directions:** Read about tops. Then answer the questions.

Tops come in all sizes. Some tops are made of wood. Some tops are made of tin. All tops do the same thing. They spin! Do you have a top?

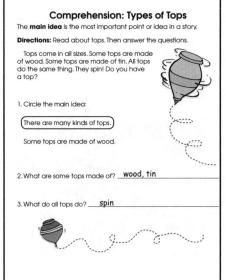

1. Circle the main idea:
   (There are many kinds of tops.)
   Some tops are made of wood.

2. What are some tops made of? _wood, tin_

3. What do all tops do? _spin_

## Page 144

**Comprehension: Playing Store**

**Directions:** Read about playing store. Then answer the questions.

Tyson and his friends like to play store. They use boxes and cans. They line them up. Then they put them in bags.

1. Circle the main idea:
   (Tyson and his friends use boxes, cans and bags to play store.)
   You need bags to play store.

2. (Circle your answer.) Who likes to play store?
   all kids          (some kids)

3. Do you like to play store? **Answers will vary.**

# ANSWER KEY

## Page 145

### Comprehension: Singing Whales

**Directions:** Read about singing whales. Then follow the instructions.

Some whales can sing! We cannot understand the words. But we can hear the tune of the humpback whale. Each season, humpback whales sing a different song.

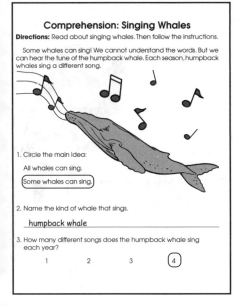

1. Circle the main idea:

   All whales can sing.

   (Some whales can sing.)

2. Name the kind of whale that sings.

   humpback whale

3. How many different songs does the humpback whale sing each year?

   1        2        3        (4)

## Page 146

### Comprehension: Paper-Bag Puppets

**Directions:** Read about paper-bag puppets. Then follow the instructions.

It is easy to make a hand puppet. You need a small paper bag. You need colored paper. You need glue. You need scissors. Are you ready?

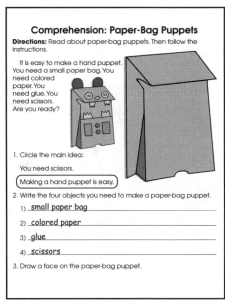

1. Circle the main idea:

   You need scissors.

   (Making a hand puppet is easy.)

2. Write the four objects you need to make a paper-bag puppet.

   1) small paper bag

   2) colored paper

   3) glue

   4) scissors

3. Draw a face on the paper-bag puppet.

## Page 147

### Comprehension: Sea Horses Look Strange!

**Directions:** Read about sea horses. Then answer the questions.

Sea horses are fish, not horses. A sea horse's head looks like a horse's head. It has a tail like a monkey's tail. A sea horse looks very strange!

1. (Circle the correct answer.) A sea horse is a kind of

   horse.

   monkey.

   (fish.)

2. What does a sea horse's head look like?

   a horse's head

3. What makes a sea horse look strange?

   a. It's head looks like a horse's head.

   b. It has a tail like a monkey's tail.

## Page 148

### Comprehension: Carla and Tony Jump Rope

**Directions:** Read about jumping rope. Then follow the instructions.

Carla and Tony like to jump rope. Carla likes to jump rope alone. Tony likes to have two people turn the rope for him. Carla and Tony can jump slowly. They can also jump fast.

1. Name another way to jump rope.

   a. Have two people turn the rope.

   b. One person jumps alone.

2. Name two speeds for jumping rope.

   1) slow        2) fast

3. Do you like to jump rope? Answers will vary.

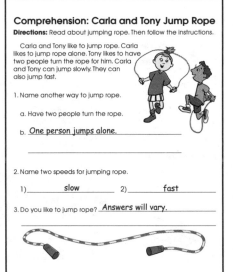

## Page 149

### Comprehension: How to Stop a Dog Fight

**Directions:** Read about how to stop a dog fight. Then answer the questions.

Sometimes dogs fight. They bark loudly. They may bite. Do not try to pull apart fighting dogs. Turn on a hose and spray them with water. This will stop the fight.

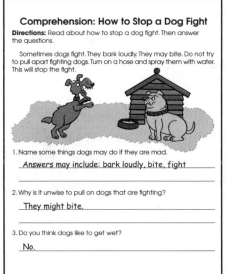

1. Name some things dogs may do if they are mad.

   Answers may include: bark loudly, bite, fight

2. Why is it unwise to pull on dogs that are fighting?

   They might bite.

3. Do you think dogs like to get wet?

   No.

## Page 150

### Comprehension: Training a Dog

**Directions:** Read about how to train dogs. Then answer the questions.

A dog has a ball in his mouth. You want the ball. What should you do? Do not pull on the ball. Hold out something else for the dog. The dog will drop the ball to take it!

1. Circle the main idea:

   Always get a ball away from a dog.

   (Offer the dog something else to get him to drop the ball.)

2. What should you **not** do if you want the dog's ball?

   Do not pull on the ball.

3. What could you hold out for the dog to take?

   Answers may include: a bone, another toy

# ANSWER KEY

## Page 151

### Comprehension: How to Meet a Dog

**Directions:** Read about how to meet a dog. Then follow the instructions.

Do not try to pet a dog right away. First, let the dog sniff your hand. Do not move quickly. Do not talk loudly. Just let the dog sniff.

1. Predict what the dog will let you do if it likes you.
   Pet it.

2. What should you let the dog do? Sniff your hand.

3. Name three things you should not do when you meet a dog.
   1) try to pet it
   2) move quickly
   3) talk loudly

## Page 152

### Comprehension: Dirty Dogs

**Directions:** Read about dogs. Then answer the questions.

Like people, dogs get dirty. Some dogs get a bath once a month. Baby soap is a good soap for cleaning dogs. Fill a tub with warm water. Get someone to hold the dog still in the tub. Then wash the dog fast.

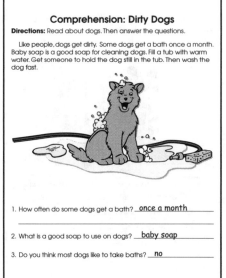

1. How often do some dogs get a bath? once a month

2. What is a good soap to use on dogs? baby soap

3. Do you think most dogs like to take baths? no

## Page 153

### Comprehension: Pretty Parrots

**Directions:** Read about parrots. Then follow the instructions.

Big parrots are pretty. Their feet have four toes each. Two toes are in front. Two toes are in back. Parrots use their feet to climb. They use them to hold food.

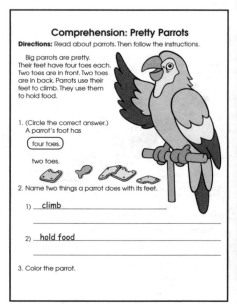

1. (Circle the correct answer.)
   A parrot's foot has
   (four toes.)
   two toes.

2. Name two things a parrot does with its feet.
   1) climb
   2) hold food

3. Color the parrot.

## Page 154

### Comprehension: A Winter Story

**Directions:** Read about winter. Then follow the instructions.

It is cold in winter. Snow falls. Water freezes. Most kids like to play outdoors. Some kids make a snowman. Some kids skate. What do you do in winter?

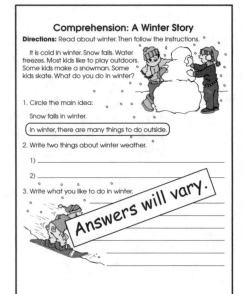

1. Circle the main idea:
   Snow falls in winter.
   (In winter, there are many things to do outside.)

2. Write two things about winter weather.
   1) _____
   2) _____

3. Write what you like to do in winter.

*Answers will vary.*

## Page 155

### Comprehension: The Puppet Play

**Directions:** Read the play out loud with a friend. Then answer the questions.

**Pip:** Hey, Pep. What kind of turkey eats very fast?

**Pep:** Uh, I don't know.

**Pip:** A gobbler!

**Pep:** I have a good joke for you, Pip. What kind of burger does a polar bear eat?

**Pip:** Uh, a cold burger?

**Pep:** No, an iceberg-er!

**Pip:** Hey, that was a great joke!

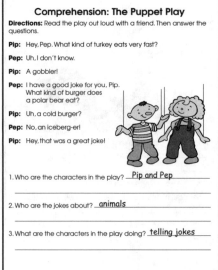

1. Who are the characters in the play? Pip and Pep

2. Who are the jokes about? animals

3. What are the characters in the play doing? telling jokes

## Page 156

### Comprehension: Just Junk?

**Directions:** Read about saving things. Then follow the instructions.

Do you save old crayons? Do you save old buttons or cards? Some people call these things junk. They throw them out. Leah saves these things. She likes to use them for art projects. She puts them in a box. What do you do?

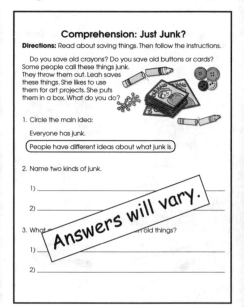

1. Circle the main idea:
   Everyone has junk.
   (People have different ideas about what junk is.)

2. Name two kinds of junk.
   1) _____
   2) _____

3. What _____ old things?
   1) _____
   2) _____

*Answers will vary.*

# ANSWER KEY

## Page 157

### Comprehension: Snakes!

**Directions:** Read about snakes. Then answer the questions.

There are many facts about snakes that might surprise someone. A snake's skin is dry. Most snakes are shy. They will hide from people. Snakes eat mice and rats. They do not chew them up. Snakes' jaws drop open to swallow their food whole.

1. How does a snake's skin feel? __dry__

2. Most snakes are __shy__ .

3. What do snakes eat?

   a. __mice__

   b. __rats__

## Page 158

### Comprehension: More About Snakes!

**Directions:** Read more about snakes. Then follow the instructions.

Unlike people, snakes have cold blood. They like to be warm. They hunt for food when it is warm. They lie in the sun. When it is cold, snakes curl up into a ball.

1. What do snakes do when it is warm?

   a. __hunt for food__

   b. __lie in the sun__

2. Why do you think snakes curl up when it is cold? _____
   __Answers will vary.__

3. (Circle the correct answer.)
   People have:

   cold blood.    (warm blood.)

## Page 159

### Comprehension: Sean's Basketball Game

**Directions:** Read about Sean's basketball game. Then answer the questions.

Sean really likes to play basketball. One sunny day, he decided to ask his friends to play basketball at the park, but there were six people—Sean, Aki, Lance, Kate, Zac and Oralia. A basketball team only allows five to play at a time. So, Sean decided to be the coach. Sean and his friends had fun.

1. How many kids wanted to play basketball? __six__

2. Write their names in ABC order:

   __Aki__        __Lance__       __Sean__

   __Kate__       __Oralia__      __Zac__

3. How many players can play on a basketball team

   at a time? __five__

4. Where did they play basketball? __at the park__

5. Who decided to be the coach? __Sean__

## Page 160

### Comprehension: Outdoor/Indoor Games

**Directions:** Read the story. Then answer the questions.

Derrick likes to play outdoor and indoor games. His favorite outdoor game is baseball because he likes to hit the ball with the bat and run around the bases. He plays this game in the park with the neighborhood kids.

When it rains, he plays checkers with Lorenzo on the dining-room table in his apartment. He likes the game, because he has to use his brain to think about his next move, and the rules are easy to follow.

1. What is your favorite outdoor game? _____

2. Why do you like this game? _____

3. Where is this game ~~_____~~

4. What is ~~_____~~ game?

5. Why do you ~~_____~~ this game? _____

   _____

6. Where is this game played? _____

*Answers will vary.*

## Page 161

### Reading Comprehension

**Directions:** Read the story. Then complete the sentences with words from the story.

Mike lives on a farm. There are many animals on the farm: birds, cows, pigs, goats and chickens. But Mike likes his horse the best. His horse's name is Stormy. Stormy stays in a barn. For fun, Mike rides Stormy to the lake. Stormy helps Mike, too. Stormy pulls a cart to carry weeds from the garden. After a hard day, Mike feeds Stormy corn and hay. For a treat, Stormy gets a pear.

1. Mike lives on a __farm__ .
2. His favorite animal is a __horse__ .
3. The horse's name is __Stormy__ .
4. Stormy stays in a __barn__ .
5. It is fun to ride to the __lake__ .
6. Stormy eats __corn__ and __hay__.
7. Stormy's treat is a __pear__ .

Write 5 words from the story that have an **r-controlled vowel.** *Answers include:*

   __farm__      __horse__      __Stormy__
          __birds__      __barn__

Now, write 5 words from the story that have a **long vowel sound.**
*Answers include:*

   __Mike__      __goats__      __likes__
          __name__      __stays__

## Page 162

### Comprehension: Ant Farms

**Directions:** Read about ant farms. Then answer the questions.

Ant farms are sold at toy stores and pet stores. Ant farms come in a flat frame. The frame has glass on each side. Inside the glass is sand. The ants live in the sand.

1. Where are ant farms sold? __at toy stores and pet stores__

2. The frame has __glass__ on each side.

Circle the correct answer.

3. The ants live in

   water.    (sand.)

4. The ant farm frame is

   (flat.)    round.

**Grade 2 - Comprehensive Curriculum**

## Page 163

### Comprehension: Amazing Ants

**Directions:** Read about ants. Then answer the questions.

Ants are insects. Ants live in many parts of the world and make their homes in soil, sand, wood and leaves. Most ants live for about 6 to 10 weeks. But the queen ant, who lays the eggs, can live for up to 15 years!

The largest ant is the bulldog ant. This ant can grow to be 5 inches long, and it eats meat! The bulldog ant can be found in Australia.

1. Where do ants make their homes? __in soil, sand, wood__ __and leaves__

2. How long can a queen ant live? __up to 15 years__

3. What is the largest ant? __bulldog ant__

4. What does it eat? __meat__

## Page 164

### Comprehension: Sharks Are Fish, Too!

**Directions:** Read the story. Then follow the instructions.

Angela learned a lot about sharks when her class visited the city aquarium. She learned that sharks are fish. Some sharks are as big as an elephant, and some can fit into a small paper bag. Sharks have no bones. They have hundreds of teeth, and when they lose them, they grow new ones. They eat animals of any kind. Whale sharks are the largest of all fish.

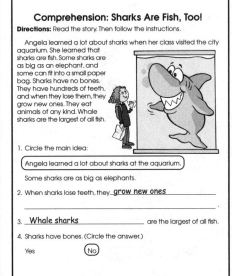

1. Circle the main idea:

   (Angela learned a lot about sharks at the aquarium.)

   Some sharks are as big as elephants.

2. When sharks lose teeth, they __grow new ones__

3. __Whale sharks__ are the largest of all fish.

4. Sharks have bones. (Circle the answer.)

   Yes     (No)

## Page 165

### Comprehension: Fish

**Directions:** Read about fish. Then follow the instructions.

Some fish live in warm water. Some live in cold water. Some fish live in lakes. Some fish live in oceans. There are 20,000 kinds of fish!

1. Name two types of water in which fish live.

   a. __warm water__

   b. __cold water__

2. Name another place fish live __Answers may include: fish tank, ponds__

   Some fish live in lakes and some live in __oceans__ .

3. There are __20,000__ kinds of fish.

## Page 166

### Comprehension: Fish Come in Many Colors

**Directions:** Read about the color of fish. Then follow the instructions.

All fish live in water. Fish that live at the top are blue, green or black. Fish that live down deep are silver or red. The colors make it hard to see the fish.

1. List the colors of fish at the top.

   __blue__     __green__     __black__

2. List the two colors of fish that live down deep.

   __silver__     __red__

3. Color the top fish and the bottom fish the correct colors.

## Page 167

### Comprehension: Fish Can Protect Themselves

**Directions:** Read about two fish. Then follow the instructions.

Most fish have ways to protect themselves from danger. Two of these fish are the trigger fish and the porcupine fish. The trigger fish lives on the ocean reef. When it sees danger, it swims into its private hole and puts its top fin up and squeezes itself in tight. Then it cannot be taken from its hiding place. The porcupine fish also lives on the ocean reef. When danger comes, it puffs up like a balloon by swallowing air or water. When it puffs up, poisonous spikes stand out on its body. When danger is past, it deflates its body.

1. Circle the main idea:

   Trigger fish and procupine fish can be dangerous.

   (Some fish have ways to protect themselves from danger.)

2. Trigger fish and porcupine fish live on the __ocean reef__

3. The porcupine fish puffs up by swallowing __air__ or __water__

## Page 168

### Comprehension: Ideas Come From Books

**Directions:** Read the story. Then follow the instructions.

Tonda has many books. She gets different ideas from these books. Some of her books are about fish. Some are about cardboard and paper crafts. Some are about nature. Others are about reusing junk. Tonda wants to make a paper airplane. She reads about it in one of her books. Then she asks an adult to help her.

1. Circle the main idea:

   (Tonda learns about different ideas from books.)

   Tonda likes crafts.

2. (Circle the correct answer.) Tonda is:

   (a person who likes to read.)

   a person who doesn't like books.

3. What does Tonda want to make from paper? __an airplane__

4. Write two ways to learn how to do something.

   1) __Read about it.__

   2) __Ask an adult for help.__

# ANSWER KEY

## Page 169

### Predicting: A Rainy Game

**Predicting** is telling what is likely to happen based on the facts.

**Directions:** Read the story. Then check each sentence below that tells how the story could end.

One cloudy day, Juan and his baseball team, the Bears, played the Crocodiles. It was the last half of the fifth inning, and it started to rain. The coaches and umpires had to decide what to do.

✓ They kept playing until nine innings were finished.

✓ They ran for cover and waited until the rain stopped.

_____ Each player grabbed an umbrella and returned to the field to finish the game.

✓ They canceled the game and played it another day.

_____ They acted like crocodiles and slid around the wet bases.

_____ The coaches played the game while the players sat in the dugout.

## Page 170

### Predicting: Oops!

**Directions:** Look at the pictures on the left. On the right, draw and write what you predict will happen next.

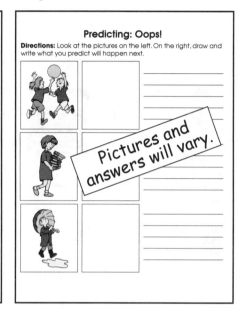

*Pictures and answers will vary.*

## Page 171

### Predicting: Dog Derby

**Directions:** Read the story. Then answer the questions.

Marcy had a great idea for a game to play with her dogs, Marvin and Mugsy. The game was called "Dog Derby." Marcy would stand at one end of the driveway and hold on to the dogs by their collars. Her friend Mitch would stand at the other end of the driveway. When he said, "Go!" Marcy would let go of the dogs and they would race to Mitch. The first one there would get a dog biscuit. If there was a tie, both dogs would get a biscuit.

1. Who do you think will win the race?

Why? _____

*Answers will vary.*

2. What _____ happen when they race again?

## Page 172

### Predicting: What Will Bobby Do?

**Directions:** Read about Bobby the cat. Then write what you think will happen.

One sunny spring day, Bobby was sleeping under her favorite tree. She was dreaming about her favorite food—tuna. Suddenly she became hungry for a treat. Bobby woke up and listened when she heard someone call her name.

1. Why do you think Bobby was being called? _____

2. What do yo _____

*Answers will vary.*

## Page 173

### Predicting: Dog-Gone!

**Directions:** Read the story. Then follow the instructions.

Scotty and Simone were washing their dog, Willis. His fur was wet. Their hands were wet. Willis did NOT like to be wet. Scotty dropped the soap. Simone picked it up and let go of Willis. Uh-oh!

1. Write what happened next.

_____

2. Draw

*Answers and drawings will vary.*

## Page 174

### Predicting Outcome

**Directions:** Read the story. Complete the story in the last box.

1. A cat is playing with a ball of yarn.

3. The mouse tiptoes past the playful cat.

2. A mouse peeks around the corner.

4. _Answers will vary._

_____

*Drawings will vary.*

# ANSWER KEY

## Page 175

### Predicting Outcome

**Directions:** Read the story. Complete the story in the last box.

1. "Look at that elephant! He sure is big!"

3. "Stop, Amy! Look at that sign!"

2. "I'm hungry." "I bet that elephant is, too."

4. Answers will vary.

Drawings will vary.

## Page 176

### Predicting Outcome

**Directions:** Read the story. In the last box, draw what you think will happen next. Then write the words for the end of the story.

1. Do you want to go to the library with me?"
"Yes, I want a book about seashells."

3. "Excuse me. Where can I find a book about seashells?"

2. "Have you found your book?"
"No. I can't find it."
"Why don't you ask someone?"

4.

Drawings will vary

## Page 177

### Predicting Outcomes

**Directions:** Complete the story. Then draw pictures to match the four parts.

1. Sylvia and Marge are flying a kite.

3. Answers will vary.

Drawings will vary.

Middle

2. 

4. Answers will vary.

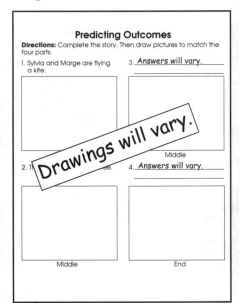

Middle          End

## Page 178

### Predicting Outcome

**Directions:** Create your own story in the squares. Show the beginning in box 1, the middle in boxes 2 and 3 and the end in box 4.

Beginning (Setting)     Middle (Problem)

1.     3.

Drawings will vary.

2.     4.

Middle (Problem)     End (Solution)

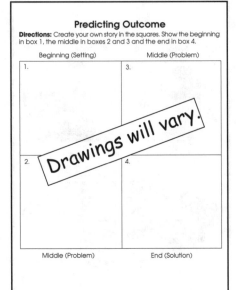

## Page 179

### Predicting Outcome

Kelly and Gina always have fun at the fair.

**Directions:** Read the sentences. Write what you think will happen next.

1. Kelly and Gina are riding the Ferris wheel. It stops when they are at the top.

2. As they walk into the anim... ...rds them.

3. Snow c... ...their favorite way to cool off. The ones they bought are made from real snow.

4. They play a "toss the ring over the bottle" game, but when the ring goes around the bottle, it disappears.

Answers will vary.

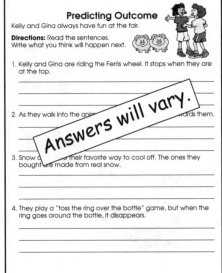

## Page 180

### Predicting: Puff and Trigg

**Directions:** Read about Puff and Trigg. Then write what happens next in the story.

It was a sunny, warm day in the Pacific Ocean. Puff, the happy porcupine fish, and Trigg, the jolly trigger fish, were having fun playing fish tag. They were good friends. Suddenly, they saw the shadow of a giant fish! It was coming right at them! They knew the giant fish might like eating smaller fish! What did they do?

What did Puff and Trigg do to get away from the giant fish?

Answers will vary.

# ANSWER KEY

## Page 181

### Fact and Opinion: Games!

A **fact** is something that can be proven. An **opinion** is a feeling or belief about something and cannot be proven.

**Directions:** Read these sentences about different games. Then write **F** next to each fact and **O** next to each opinion.

- O   1. Tennis is cool!
- F   2. There are red and black markers in a Checkers game.
- F   3. In football, a touchdown is worth six points.
- O   4. Being a goalie in soccer is easy.
- F   5. A yo-yo moves on a string.
- O   6. June's sister looks like the queen on the card.
- F   7. The six kids need three more players for a baseball team.
- O   8. Table tennis is more fun than court tennis.
- F   9. Hide-and-Seek is a game that can be played outdoors or indoors.
- F   10. Play money is used in many board games.

## Page 182

### Fact and Opinion: Recycling

**Directions:** Read about recycling. Then follow the instructions.

What do you throw away every day? What could you do with these things? You could change an old greeting card into a new card. You could make a puppet with an old paper bag. Old buttons make great refrigerator magnets. You can plant seeds in plastic cups. Cardboard tubes make perfect rockets. So, use your imagination!

1. Write **F** next to each fact and **O** next to each opinion.

- O   Cardboard tubes are ugly.
- F   Buttons can be made into refrigerator magnets.
- F   An old greeting card can be changed into a new card.
- O   Paper-bag puppets are cute.
- F   Seeds can be planted in plastic cups.
- F   Rockets can be made from cardboard tubes.

2. What could you do with a cardboard tube? __Make a rocket.__

## Page 183

### Fact and Opinion: An Owl Story

**Directions:** Read the story. Then follow the instructions.

My name is Owen Owl, and I am a bird. I go to Nocturnal School. Our teacher is Mr. Screech Owl. In his class I learned that owls are birds and can sleep all day and hunt at night. Some of us live in nests in trees. In North America, it is against the law to harm owls. I like being an owl!

Write **F** next to each fact and **O** next to each opinion.

- F   1. No one can harm owls in North America.
- O   2. It would be great if owls could talk.
- F   3. Owls sleep all day.
- F   4. Some owls sleep in nests.
- O   5. Mr. Screech Owl is a good teacher.
- F   6. Owls are birds.
- O   7. Owen Owl would be a good friend.
- F   8. Owls hunt at night.
- O   9. Nocturnal School is a good school for smart owls.
- O   10. This story is for the birds.

## Page 184

### Fact and Opinion: A Bounty of Birds

**Directions:** Read the story. Then follow the instructions.

Tashi's family likes to go to the zoo. Her favorite animals are all the different kinds of birds. Tashi likes birds because they can fly, they have colorful feathers and they make funny noises.

Write **F** next to each fact and **O** next to each opinion.

- F   1. Birds have two feet.
- F   2. All birds lay eggs.
- O   3. Parrots are too noisy.
- F   4. All birds have feathers and wings.
- O   5. It would be great to be a bird and fly south for the winter.
- F   6. Birds have hard beaks or bills instead of teeth.
- O   7. Pigeons are fun to watch.
- F   8. Some birds cannot fly.
- O   9. Parakeets make good pets.
- F   10. A penguin is a bird.

## Page 185

### Fact and Opinion: Henrietta the Humpback

**Directions:** Read the story. Then follow the instructions.

My name is Henrietta, and I am a humpback whale. I live in cold seas in the summer and warm seas in the winter. My long flippers are used to move forward and backward. I like to eat fish. Sometimes, I show off by leaping out of the water. Would you like to be a humpback whale?

Write **F** next to each fact and **O** next to each opinion.

- O   1. Being a humpback whale is fun.
- F   2. Humpback whales live in cold seas during the summer.
- O   3. Whales are fun to watch.
- F   4. Humpback whales use their flippers to move forward and backward.
- O   5. Henrietta is a great name for a whale.
- O   6. Leaping out of water would be hard.
- F   7. Humpback whales like to eat fish.
- F   8. Humpback whales show off by leaping out of the water.

## Page 186

### Making Inferences: Ryan's Top

**Directions:** Read about Ryan's top. Then follow the instructions.

Ryan got a new top. He wanted to place it where it would be safe. He asked his dad to put it up high. Where can his dad put the top?

1. Write where Ryan's dad can put the top. __Answers may include:__ __on top of the refrigerator, on a closet shelf__

Draw a place Ryan's dad can put the top.

Drawings will vary.

**Grade 2 - Comprehensive Curriculum**

# ANSWER KEY

## Page 187

### Making Inferences: Down on the Ant Farm

**Directions:** Read about ant farms. Then answer the questions.

Ants are busy on the farm. They dig in the sand. They make roads in the sand. They look for food in the sand. When an ant dies, other ants bury it.

1. Where do you think ants are buried? __in the sand__

2. Is it fair to say ants are lazy? __no__

3. Write a word that tells about ants. __Answers may include:__
__busy, hard-working__

## Page 188

### Inferences: Monty's Trip

**Directions:** Read Monty's answer. Then circle the answer to each question. Color the pictures.

Monty says, "I want to learn more about big cats. Someday, I would like to be an animal trainer or a zoo director. Where can we learn about big cats?"

1. What cat does Monty want to learn about?

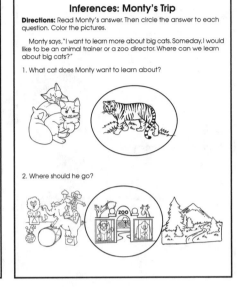

2. Where should he go?

## Page 189

### Making Inferences

**Directions:** Read the story. Then answer the questions.

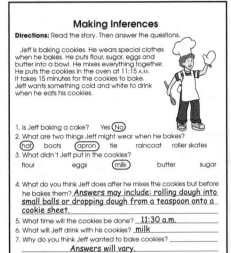

Jeff is baking cookies. He wears special clothes when he bakes. He puts flour, sugar, eggs and butter into a bowl. He mixes everything together. He puts the cookies in the oven at 11:15 A.M. It takes 15 minutes for the cookies to bake. Jeff wants something cold and white to drink when he eats his cookies.

1. Is Jeff baking a cake?    Yes  (No)
2. What are two things Jeff might wear when he bakes?
(hat)  boots  (apron)  tie  raincoat  roller skates
3. What didn't Jeff put in the cookies?
flour    eggs    (milk)    butter    sugar
4. What do you think Jeff does after he mixes the cookies but before he bakes them? __Answers may include: rolling dough into small balls or dropping dough from a teaspoon onto a cookie sheet.__
5. What time will the cookies be done? __11:30 a.m.__
6. What will Jeff drink with his cookies? __milk__
7. Why do you think Jeff wanted to bake cookies? _____
__Answers will vary.__

## Page 190

### Making Inferences

**Directions:** Read the story. Then answer the questions.

Shawn and his family are on a trip. It is very sunny. Shawn loves to swim. He also likes the waves. There is something else he likes even more. Shawn builds drip castles. He makes drips by using very wet sand. He lets it drip out of his hand into a tall pile. He makes the drip piles as high as he can.

1. Where is Shawn? __at the beach__
2. What does Shawn wear on his trip? __swimming suit__
3. Is Shawn hot or cold? __hot__
4. What does Shawn like to do best? __build drip castles__
5. What are drip castles made from? __very wet sand__
6. What do you think happens when drip castles get too big?
__They fall over.__
7. If Shawn gets too hot, what do you think he will do?
__He will swim.__

## Page 191

### Making Inferences

**Directions:** Read the story. Then answer the questions.

Mrs. Sweet looked forward to a visit from her niece, Candy. In the morning, she cleaned her house. She also baked a cherry pie. An hour before Candy was to arrive, the phone rang. Mrs. Sweet said, "I understand." When she hung up the phone, she looked very sad.

**Answers may include:**
1. Who do you think called Mrs. Sweet?
__Candy called Mrs. Sweet.__

2. How do you know that?
__Mrs. Sweet probably said, "I understand," when Candy said she wouldn't visit today.__

3. Why is Mrs. Sweet sad?
__Her niece, Candy, probably can't come visit today.__

## Page 192

### Making Inferences: More About Sea Horses

**Directions:** Read more about sea horses. Then answer the questions.

A father sea horse helps the mother. He has a small sack, or pouch, on the front of his body. The mother sea horse lays the eggs. She does not keep them. She gives the eggs to the father.

1. What does the mother sea horse do with her eggs?
__She gives them to the father.__

2. Where does the father sea horse put the eggs?
__in his pouch__

3. Sea horses can change color. Color the sea horses.

## Page 193

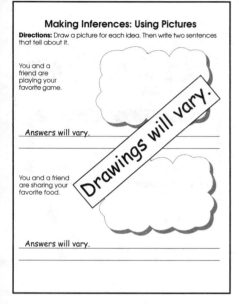

**Making Inferences: Using Pictures**

**Directions:** Draw a picture for each idea. Then write two sentences that tell about it.

You and a friend are playing your favorite game.

Answers will vary.

You and a friend are sharing your favorite food.

Answers will vary.

Drawings will vary.

## Page 194

**Making Inferences: Visualizing**

**Directions:** Read this story about Ling and Bradley. Draw pictures for the beginning and middle to describe each part of the story.

**Beginning:** One sunny day, Ling and Bradley, wearing their empty backpacks, rode their bikes down the street to the park.

**Middle:** They stopped by an oak tree with many acorns under it. They picked up some and stuffed them into their backpacks.

**Directions:** Draw an ending that tells what you think they did with the acorns.

**End:** With the heavy backpacks strapped on their backs, they pedaled home.

Drawings will vary.

## Page 195

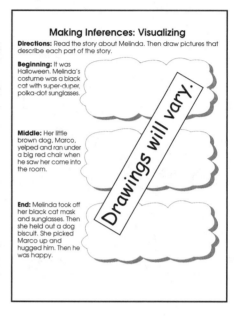

**Making Inferences: Visualizing**

**Directions:** Read the story about Melinda. Then draw pictures that describe each part of the story.

**Beginning:** It was Halloween. Melinda's costume was a black cat with super-duper, polka-dot sunglasses.

**Middle:** Her little brown dog, Marco, yelped and ran under a big red chair when he saw her come into the room.

**End:** Melinda took off her black cat mask and sunglasses. Then she held out a dog biscuit. She picked Marco up and hugged him. Then he was happy.

Drawings will vary.

## Page 196

**Making Inferences: Visualizing**

**Directions:** Read the story about Chad and Leon. Then draw pictures that describe each part of the story.

**Beginning:** One chilly morning, Chad and Leon rolled two big snowballs to make a snowman in Chad's front yard.

**Middle:** Chad put his big snowball on top of the bigger one. Leon added a carrot nose, two charcoal eyes, a stick mouth and a cowboy hat. Then they went into the house.

**End:** Later, when they looked out the window, they saw the snowman dancing around. "Thank you!" he shouted to the boys.

Drawings will vary.

## Page 197

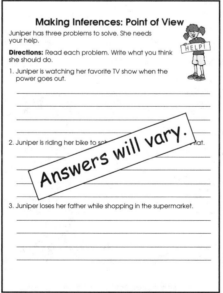

**Making Inferences: Point of View**

Juniper has three problems to solve. She needs your help.

**Directions:** Read each problem. Write what you think she should do.

1. Juniper is watching her favorite TV show when the power goes out.

2. Juniper is riding her bike to school when she gets a flat.

3. Juniper loses her father while shopping in the supermarket.

Answers will vary.

## Page 198

**Making Inferences: Point of View**

Toran also has three problems. Now that you have helped Juniper, he would like you to help him, too.

**Directions:** Read each problem. Write what you think he should do.

1. The class is having a picnic, and Toran left his lunch at home.

2. Toran wants to buy a special toy, but he needs three more dollars.

3. Toran's best friend, Felix, made the third out, and their team lost the kickball game.

Answers will vary.

## Page 199

### Making Inferences: Sequencing

**Directions:** Draw three pictures to tell a story about each topic.

1. Feeding a pet

| Beginning | Middle | End |

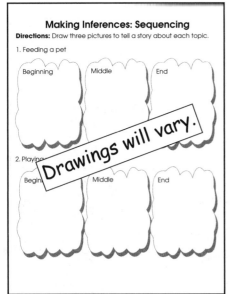

*Drawings will vary.*

2. Playing...

| Begin... | Middle | End |

## Page 200

### Making Inferences: Sequencing

Help make a "doggie pizza" for Spotty Dog. The steps to follow are all mixed-up. Three of the steps are not needed.

**Directions:** Number the steps in order from 1 to 7. Draw a dog bone by the 3 steps that are not needed.

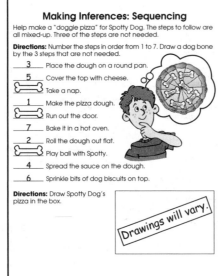

- 3 — Place the dough on a round pan.
- 5 — Cover the top with cheese.
- 🦴 — Take a nap.
- 1 — Make the pizza dough.
- 🦴 — Run out the door.
- 7 — Bake it in a hot oven.
- 2 — Roll the dough out flat.
- 🦴 — Play ball with Spotty.
- 4 — Spread the sauce on the dough.
- 6 — Sprinkle bits of dog biscuits on top.

**Directions:** Draw Spotty Dog's pizza in the box.

*Drawings will vary.*

## Page 201

### Making Deductions: Find the Books

**Directions:** Use the clues to help the children find their books. Draw a line from each child's name to the correct book.

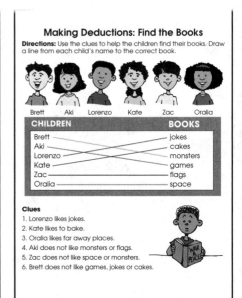

Brett   Aki   Lorenzo   Kate   Zac   Oralia

| CHILDREN | BOOKS |
| --- | --- |
| Brett | jokes |
| Aki | cakes |
| Lorenzo | monsters |
| Kate | games |
| Zac | flags |
| Oralia | space |

(Brett—games, Aki—cakes, Lorenzo—jokes, Kate—monsters, Zac—flags, Oralia—space)

**Clues**
1. Lorenzo likes jokes.
2. Kate likes to bake.
3. Oralia likes far away places.
4. Aki does not like monsters or flags.
5. Zac does not like space or monsters.
6. Brett does not like games, jokes or cakes.

## Page 202

### Making Deductions: Travel

Six children from the same neighborhood each travel to school in a different way. Can you find out how each one gets to school?

**Directions:** Read the clues. Draw a dot to show how each child travels to school. Draw X's on the remaining boxes.

| | Brian | Gina | Lawrence | Luna | Taylor | Marianna |
| --- | --- | --- | --- | --- | --- | --- |
| car | X | X | X | X | ● | X |
| bus | ● | X | X | X | X | X |
| walk | X | X | ● | X | X | X |
| bicycle | X | X | X | ● | X | X |
| truck | X | ● | X | X | X | X |
| van | X | X | X | X | X | ● |

**Clues:**
1. Lawrence likes to walk to school.
2. Taylor hates to walk, so his mother takes him in a car.
3. Luna lives next door to Lawrence and waves to Gina as Gina goes by in a pickup truck.
4. Brian joins his pals on the bus.
5. Gina's friend, who lives next door to Lawrence, rides a bike to school.
6. Marianna likes to sit in the middle seat while riding to school.

## Page 203

### Making Deductions: Sports

Children all over the world like to play sports. They like many different kinds of sports: football, soccer, basketball, softball, in-line skating, swimming and more.

**Directions:** Read the clues. Draw dots and X's on the chart to match the children with their sports.

| | swimming | football | soccer | basketball | baseball | in-line skating |
| --- | --- | --- | --- | --- | --- | --- |
| J.J. | X | ● | X | X | X | X |
| Zoe | X | X | X | X | X | ● |
| Andy | X | X | X | ● | X | X |
| Amber | X | X | ● | X | X | X |
| Raul | X | X | X | X | ● | X |
| Sierra | ● | X | X | X | X | X |

**Clues**
1. Zoe hates football.
2. Andy likes basketball.
3. Raul likes to pitch in his favorite sport.
4. J.J. likes to play what Zoe hates.
5. Amber is good at kicking the ball to her teammates.
6. Sierra needs a pool for her favorite sport.

## Page 204

### Making Deductions: What Day Is It?

Dad is cooking dinner tonight. You can find out what day of the week it is.

**Directions:** Read the clues. Complete the menu. Answer the question.

**Menu**
Monday — pizza
Tuesday — chicken
Wednesday — corn-on-the-cob
Thursday — meat pie
Friday — hot dogs
Saturday — fish
Sunday — cheese rolls

1. Mom fixed pizza on Monday.
2. Dad fixed cheese rolls the day before that.
3. Tess made meat pie three days after Mom fixed pizza.
4. Tom fixed corn-on-the-cob the day before Tess made meat pie.
5. Mom fixed hot dogs the day after Tess made meat pie.
6. Tess cooked fish the day before Dad fixed cheese rolls.
7. Dad is making chicken today. What day is it? <u>Tuesday</u>

## Page 205

### Review

**Directions:** Read the story. Then answer the questions.

Randa, Emily, Ali, Dave, Liesl and Deana all love to read. Every Tuesday, they all go to the library together and pick out their favorite books. Randa likes books about fish. Emily likes books about sports and athletes. Ali likes books about art. Dave likes books about wild animals. Liesl likes books with riddles and puzzles. Deanna likes books about cats and dogs.

1. Circle the main idea:

Randa, Emily, Ali, Dave, Liesl and Deana are good friends.

(Randa, Emily, Ali, Dave, Liesl and Deana all like books.)

2. Who do you think might grow up to be an artist? __Ali__

3. Who do you think might grow up to be an oceanographer (someone who studies the ocean)? __Randa__

4. Who do you think might grow up to be a veterinarian (an animal doctor)? __Deanna__

5. Who do you think might grow up to be a zookeeper (someone who cares for zoo animals)? __Dave__

## Page 206

### Fiction/Nonfiction: Heavy Hitters

**Fiction** is a make-believe story. **Nonfiction** is a true story.

**Directions:** Read the stories about two famous baseball players. Then write **fiction** or **nonfiction** in the baseball bats.

In 1998, Mark McGwire played for the St. Louis Cardinals. He liked to hit home runs. On September 27, 1998, he hit home run number 70, to set a new record for the most home runs hit in one season. The old record was set in 1961 by Roger Maris, who later played for the St. Louis Cardinals (1967 to 1968), when he hit 61 home runs.

nonfiction

The Mighty Casey played baseball for the Mudville Nine and was the greatest of all baseball players. He could hit the cover off the ball with the power of a hurricane. But, when the Mudville Nine was behind 4 to 2 in the championship game, Mighty Casey struck out with the bases loaded. There was no joy in Mudville that day, because the Mudville Nine had lost the game.

fiction

## Page 207

### Nonfiction: Tornado Tips

**Directions:** Read about tornadoes. Then follow the instructions.

A tornado begins over land with strong winds and thunderstorms. The spinning air becomes a funnel. It can cause damage. If you are inside, go to the lowest floor of the building. A basement is a safe place. A bathroom or closet in the middle of a building can be a safe place, too. If you are outside, lie in a ditch. Remember, tornadoes are dangerous.

**Answers may include:**

Write five facts about tornadoes.

1. __A tornado begins over land.__

2. __Spinning air becomes a funnel.__

3. __Tornadoes can cause damage.__

4. __A basement is a safe place to be in a tornado.__

5. __If you are outside during a tornado, you should lie in a ditch.__

## Page 208

### Fiction: Hercules

The setting is where a story takes place. The characters are the people in a story or play.

**Directions:** Read about Hercules. Then answer the questions.

Hercules was born in the warm Atlantic Ocean. He was a very small and weak baby. He wanted to be the strongest hurricane in the world. But he had one problem. He couldn't blow 75-mile-per-hour winds. Hercules blew and blew in the ocean, until one day, his sister, Hola, told him it would be more fun to be a breeze than a hurricane. Hercules agreed. It was a breeze to be a breeze!

1. What is the setting of the story? __Atlantic Ocean__

2. Who are the characters? __Hercules, Hola__

3. What is the problem? __Hercules couldn't blow 75 mile-per-hour winds.__

4. How does Hercules solve his problem? __He decides that it is more fun to be a breeze than a hurricane.__

## Page 209

### Fiction/Nonfiction: The Fourth of July

**Directions:** Read each story. Then write whether it is fiction or nonfiction.

One sunny day in July, a dog named Stan ran away from home. He went up one street and down the other looking for fun, but all the yards were empty. Where was everybody? Stan kept walking until he heard the sound of band music and happy people. Stan walked faster until he got to Central Street. There he saw men, women, children and dogs getting ready to walk in a parade. It was the Fourth of July!

Fiction or Nonfiction? __Fiction__

Americans celebrate the Fourth of July every year, because it is the birthday of the United States of America. On July 4, 1776, the United States got its independence from Great Britain. Today, Americans celebrate this holiday with parades, picnics and fireworks as they proudly wave the red, white and blue American flag.

Fiction or Nonfiction? __Nonfiction__

## Page 210

### Fiction and Nonfiction: Which Is It?

**Directions:** Read about fiction and nonfiction books. Then follow the instructions.

There are many kinds of books. Some books have make-believe stories about princesses and dragons. Some books contain poetry and rhymes, like Mother Goose. These are fiction.

Some books contain facts about space and plants. And still other books have stories about famous people in history like Abraham Lincoln. These are nonfiction.

Write **F** for fiction and **NF** for nonfiction.

__F__ 1. nursery rhyme

__F__ 2. fairy tale

__NF__ 3. true life story of a famous athlete

__F__ 4. Aesop's fables

__NF__ 5. dictionary entry about foxes

__NF__ 6. weather report

__F__ 7. story about a talking tree

__NF__ 8. story about how a tadpole becomes a frog

__NF__ 9. story about animal habitats

__F__ 10. riddles and jokes

# ANSWER KEY

## Page 211

### Writing: My Snake Story

**Directions:** Write a fictional (make-believe) story about a snake. Make sure to include details and a title.

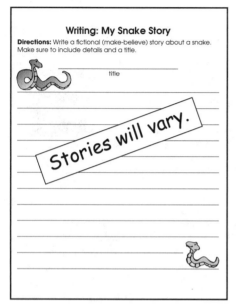

_____ title

Stories will vary.

## Page 212

### Review: All About You!

In this book you learned about many children and what they like to do. You have many interests, too!

**Directions:** Write a story telling what you like to do. Then draw a picture to go with your story on the next page.

Stories will vary.

## Page 214

### ABC Order

**Directions:** Put the words in ABC order on the bags.

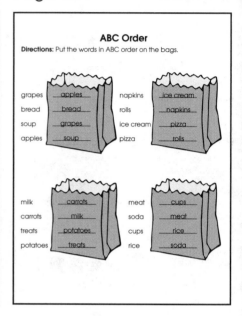

| | | | |
|---|---|---|---|
| grapes | apples | napkins | ice cream |
| bread | bread | rolls | napkins |
| soup | grapes | ice cream | pizza |
| apples | soup | pizza | rolls |

| | | | |
|---|---|---|---|
| milk | carrots | meat | cups |
| carrots | milk | soda | meat |
| treats | potatoes | cups | rice |
| potatoes | treats | rice | soda |

## Page 215

### Alphabetical Order

**Directions:** Cut out the scoops of ice cream on the bottom. Place them on the correct cone in the correct alphabetical order.

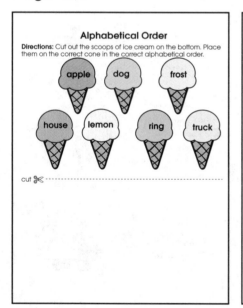

apple    dog    frost

house    lemon    ring    truck

cut ✂ - - - - - - - - - - - - - - - - - - - - - - -

## Page 217

### ABC Order

**Directions:** Write these words in order. If two words start with the same letter, look at the second letter in each word.

**Example: lamb light** — Lamb comes first because **a** comes before **i** in the alphabet.

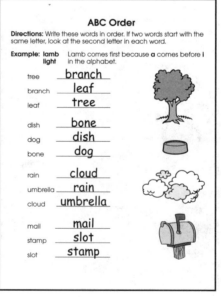

| | |
|---|---|
| tree | branch |
| branch | leaf |
| leaf | tree |
| dish | bone |
| dog | dish |
| bone | dog |
| rain | cloud |
| umbrella | rain |
| cloud | umbrella |
| mail | mail |
| stamp | slot |
| slot | stamp |

## Page 218

### Sequencing: ABC Order

**Directions:** Write 1, 2, 3 or 4 on the lines in each row to put the words in ABC order.

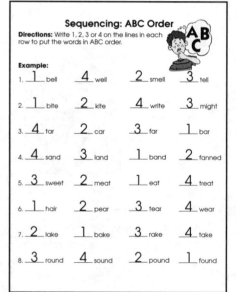

**Example:**
1. 1 bell    4 well    2 smell    3 tell
2. 1 bite    2 kite    4 write    3 might
3. 4 tar    2 car    3 far    1 bar
4. 4 sand    3 land    1 band    2 fanned
5. 3 sweet    2 meat    1 eat    4 treat
6. 1 hair    2 pear    3 tear    4 wear
7. 2 lake    1 bake    3 rake    4 take
8. 3 round    4 sound    2 pound    1 found

## Page 219

### Sequencing: ABC Order

If the first letters of two words are the same, look at the second letters in both words. If the second letters are the same, look at the third letters.

**Directions:** Write 1, 2, 3 or 4 on the lines in each row to put the words in ABC order.

**Example:**

1. **1** candy **2** carrot **4** duck **3** dance
2. **2** cold **4** hot **1** carry **3** hit
3. **2** flash **1** fan **3** fun **4** garden
4. **2** seat **4** sun **1** saw **3** sit
5. **3** row **1** ring **2** rock **4** run
6. **2** truck **3** turn **4** twin **1** talk
7. **1** seven **2** shoe **4** soup **3** smell

## Page 220

### Sequencing: ABC Order

**Directions:** Write the following names in ABC order: Oscar, Ali, Lance, Kim, Zane and Bonita.

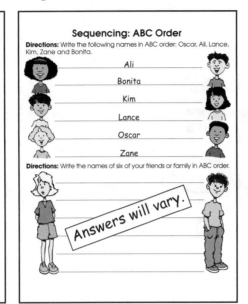

Ali

Bonita

Kim

Lance

Oscar

Zane

**Directions:** Write the names of six of your friends or family in ABC order.

*Answers will vary.*

## Page 221

### Sequencing: ABC Order

Kwan likes to make rhymes. Help Kwan think of rhyming words.

**Directions:** Write three words in ABC order that rhyme with each word Kwan wrote.

Sample answers:

| cap | bet | bill |
|-----|-----|------|
| map | get | drill |
| sap | set | mill |
| tap | yet | pill |
| dog | man | hat |
| bog | fan | bat |
| hog | pan | cat |
| jog | tan | rat |

**Directions:** Write a short poem using some of the rhyming words you wrote.

*Poem will vary.*

## Page 222

### Synonyms

Words that mean the same or nearly the same are called **synonyms**.

**Directions:** Read the sentence that tells about the picture. Draw a circle around the word that means the same as the **bold** word.

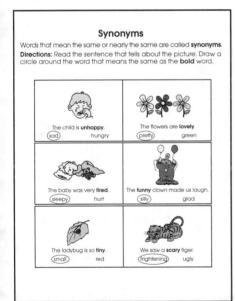

The child is **unhappy**.
(sad)   hungry

The flowers are **lovely**.
(pretty)   green

The baby was very **tired**.
(sleepy)   hurt

The **funny** clown made us laugh.
(silly)   glad

The ladybug is so **tiny**.
(small)   red

We saw a **scary** tiger.
(frightening)   ugly

## Page 223

### Synonyms

**Synonyms** are words that have almost the same meaning.

**Directions:** Read the story. Then fill in the blanks with the synonyms.

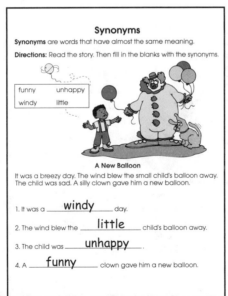

| funny | unhappy |
|-------|---------|
| windy | little |

**A New Balloon**

It was a breezy day. The wind blew the small child's balloon away. The child was sad. A silly clown gave him a new balloon.

1. It was a **windy** day.

2. The wind blew the **little** child's balloon away.

3. The child was **unhappy**.

4. A **funny** clown gave him a new balloon.

## Page 224

### Synonyms

**Directions:** Read each sentence. Fill in the blanks with the synonyms.

| friend | tired | story |
|--------|-------|-------|
| presents | little | |

I want to go to bed because I am very <u>sleepy</u>.
**tired**

On my birthday I like to open my <u>gifts</u>.
**presents**

My <u>pal</u> and I like to play together.
**friend**

My favorite <u>tale</u> is *Cinderella*.
**story**

The mouse was so <u>tiny</u> that it was hard to catch him.
**little**

# ANSWER KEY

## Page 225

### Antonyms

**Antonyms** are words that mean the opposite of another word.

**Examples:**
**hot** and **cold**
**short** and **tall**

**Directions:** Draw a line from each word on the left to its antonym on the right.

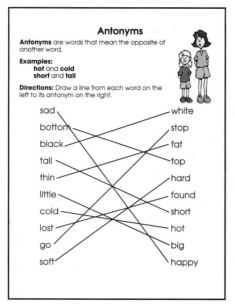

sad — happy
bottom — top
black — white
tall — short
thin — fat
little — big
cold — hot
lost — found
go — stop
soft — hard

## Page 226

### Antonyms

**Antonyms** are words that are opposites.

**Directions:** Read the words next to the pictures. Draw a line to the antonyms.

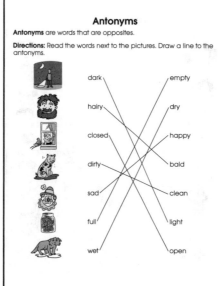

dark — light
hairy — bald
closed — open
dirty — clean
sad — happy
full — empty
wet — dry

## Page 227

### Antonyms: Words

**Directions:** Read the sentences. Complete each sentence with the correct antonym. Use the clues in the picture and below each sentence. Then color the picture.

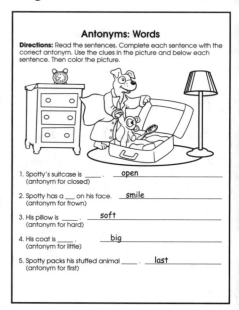

1. Spotty's suitcase is ____. **open**
(antonym for closed)
2. Spotty has a __ on his face. **smile**
(antonym for frown)
3. His pillow is ____. **soft**
(antonym for hard)
4. His coat is ____. **big**
(antonym for little)
5. Spotty packs his stuffed animal ____. **last**
(antonym for first)

## Page 228

### Antonyms: Words and Pictures

Anna and Luke often like to do opposite things. Help them design their new white tee-shirts—using opposites, of course.

**Directions:** Think of a pair of antonyms. Write one on each shirt. Draw pictures on their shirts to match the antonyms.

Answers will vary.

## Page 229

### Antonyms

Words that mean the opposite are called **antonyms**.

**Directions:** Read the sentence. Write the word from the word box that means the opposite of the **bold** word.

| bottom | outside | black | summer | after |
| light | sister | clean | last | evening |

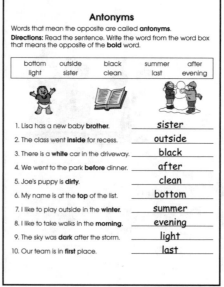

1. Lisa has a new baby **brother**. — sister
2. The class went **inside** for recess. — outside
3. There is a **white** car in the driveway. — black
4. We went to the park **before** dinner. — after
5. Joe's puppy is **dirty**. — clean
6. My name is at the **top** of the list. — bottom
7. I like to play outside in the **winter**. — summer
8. I like to take walks in the **morning**. — evening
9. The sky was **dark** after the storm. — light
10. Our team is in **first** place. — last

## Page 230

### Antonyms

**Directions:** Look at each picture and read the sentence. Cross out the incorrect word and write its antonym in the blank.

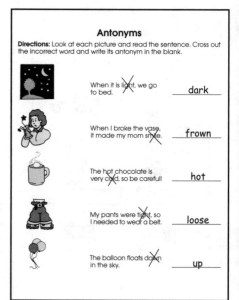

When it is ~~light~~, we go to bed. — dark
When I broke the vase, it made my mom ~~smile~~. — frown
The hot chocolate is very ~~cold~~, so be careful! — hot
My pants were ~~tight~~, so I needed to wear a belt. — loose
The balloon floats ~~down~~ in the sky. — up

## Page 231

### Homophones

**Directions:** Look at each picture. Circle the correct homophone.

(deer) dear

blue (blew)

**2** (two) to

hi (high)

by (bye)

(new) knew

**8** ate (eight)

(red) read

## Page 232

### Homophones

**Homophones** are words that sound the same but are spelled differently and have different meanings. Sometimes homophones can be more than two words.

**Examples:**
Pear and pair are homophones.
To, too and two are three homophones.

**Directions:** Draw a line from each word on the left to its homophone on the right.

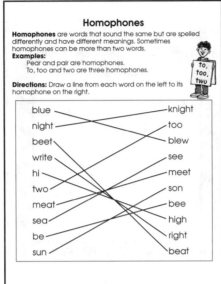

| | |
|---|---|
| blue | knight |
| night | too |
| beet | blew |
| write | see |
| hi | meet |
| two | son |
| meat | bee |
| sea | high |
| be | right |
| sun | beat |

## Page 233

### Homophones

**Homophones** are words that sound the same but are spelled differently and mean different things.

**Directions:** Write the homophone from the box next to each picture.

| so | see | blew | pear |
|---|---|---|---|

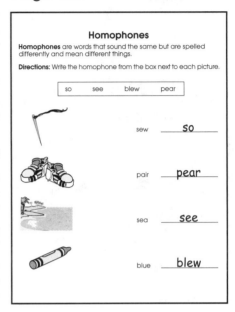

sew __so__

pair __pear__

sea __see__

blue __blew__

## Page 234

### Homophones

**Directions:** Read each word. Circle the picture that goes with the word.

1. sun
2. ate
3. buy
4. hi
5. four
6. hear

## Page 235

### Homophones

**Directions:** Match each word with its homophone.

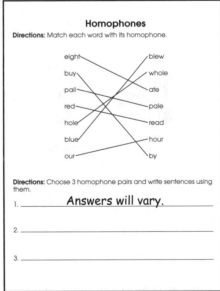

| | |
|---|---|
| eight | blew |
| buy | whole |
| pail | ate |
| red | pale |
| hole | read |
| blue | hour |
| our | by |

**Directions:** Choose 3 homophone pairs and write sentences using them.

1. _____ Answers will vary. _____

2. _____

3. _____

## Page 236

### Homophones: Doggy Birthday Cake

**Homophones** are words that sound alike but have different spellings and meanings.

**Directions:** Read the sentences. The bold words are homophones. Then follow the directions for a doggy birthday cake.

1. The baker **read** a recipe to bake a doggy cake. Color the plate he put it on **red**.

2. Draw a **hole** in the middle of the doggy cake. Then color the **whole** cake yellow.

3. Look **for** the top of the doggy cake. Draw **four** candles there.

4. In the hole draw what you think the doggy would really like.

*Answers will vary.*

5. Write a sentence using the words **hole** and **whole**.
   _Answers will vary._

6. Write a sentence using the words **read** and **red**.
   _Answers will vary._

## Page 237

### Nouns

A **noun** is the name of a person, place or thing.

**Directions:** Read the story and circle all the nouns. Then write the nouns next to the pictures below.

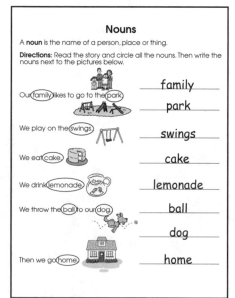

Our family likes to go to the park.

family

park

We play on the swings.

swings

We eat cake.

cake

We drink lemonade.

lemonade

We throw the ball to our dog.

ball

dog

Then we go home.

home

## Page 238

### Nouns

**Directions:** Look through a magazine. Cut out pictures of nouns and glue them below. Write the name of the noun next to the picture.

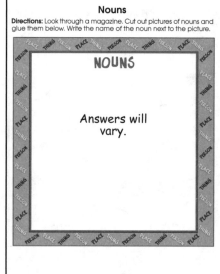

NOUNS

Answers will vary.

## Page 239

### Proper Nouns

**Proper nouns** are the names of specific people, places and pets. Proper nouns begin with a capital letter.

**Directions:** Write the proper nouns on the lines below. Use capital letters at the beginning of each word.

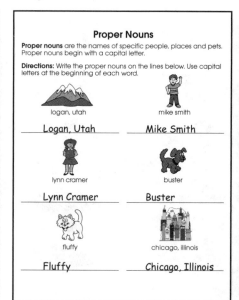

logan, utah

Logan, Utah

mike smith

Mike Smith

lynn cramer

Lynn Cramer

buster

Buster

fluffy

Fluffy

chicago, illinois

Chicago, Illinois

## Page 240

### Proper Nouns

The days of the week and the months of the year are always capitalized.

**Directions:** Circle the words that are written correctly. Write the words that need capital letters on the lines below.

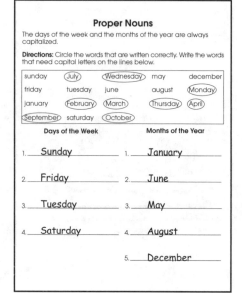

| sunday | July | Wednesday | may | december |
| friday | tuesday | june | august | Monday |
| january | February | March | Thursday | April |
| September | saturday | October | | |

**Days of the Week**

1. Sunday
2. Friday
3. Tuesday
4. Saturday

**Months of the Year**

1. January
2. June
3. May
4. August
5. December

## Page 241

### Capitalization

The first word and all of the important words in a title begin with a capital letter.

**Directions:** Write the book titles on the lines below. Use capital letters.

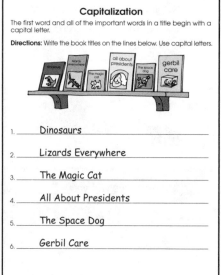

1. Dinosaurs
2. Lizards Everywhere
3. The Magic Cat
4. All About Presidents
5. The Space Dog
6. Gerbil Care

## Page 242

### Review

**Directions:** Write capital letters where they should appear in the sentences below.

**Example:** joe can play in january.

Joe can play in January.

1. we celebrate thanksgiving on the fourth thursday in november.

We celebrate Thanksgiving on the fourth Thursday in November.

2. in june, michelle and mark will go camping every friday.

In June, Michelle and Mark will go camping every Friday.

3. on mondays in october, i will take piano lessons.

On Mondays in October, I will take piano lessons.

## Page 243

### Plural Nouns

**Plural nouns** name more than one person, place or thing.

**Directions:** Read the words in the box. Write the words in the correct column.

| hats | girl | cows | kittens | cake |
| spoons | glass | book | horse | trees |

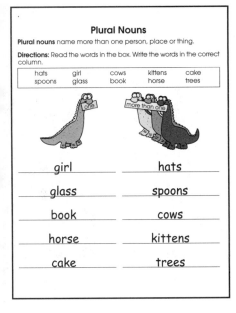

**one**

**more than one**

| girl | hats |
| glass | spoons |
| book | cows |
| horse | kittens |
| cake | trees |

## Page 244

### Plurals

**Plurals** are words that mean more than one. You usually add an **s** or **es** to the word. In some words ending in **y**, the **y** changes to an **i** before adding **es**. For example, **baby** changes to **babies**.

**Directions:** Look at the following lists of plural words. Write the word that means one next to it. The first one has been done for you.

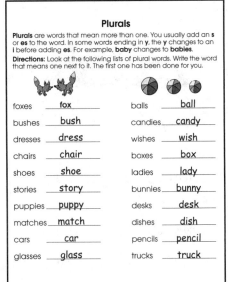

| foxes | fox | balls | ball |
| bushes | bush | candies | candy |
| dresses | dress | wishes | wish |
| chairs | chair | boxes | box |
| shoes | shoe | ladies | lady |
| stories | story | bunnies | bunny |
| puppies | puppy | desks | desk |
| matches | match | dishes | dish |
| cars | car | pencils | pencil |
| glasses | glass | trucks | truck |

## Page 245

### Pronouns

**Pronouns** are words that can be used instead of nouns. **She**, **he**, **it** and **they** are pronouns.

**Directions:** Read the sentence. Then write the sentence again, using **she**, **he**, **it** or **they** in the blank.

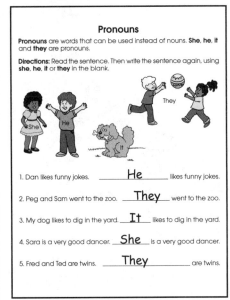

1. Dan likes funny jokes. **He** likes funny jokes.

2. Peg and Sam went to the zoo. **They** went to the zoo.

3. My dog likes to dig in the yard. **It** likes to dig in the yard.

4. Sara is a very good dancer. **She** is a very good dancer.

5. Fred and Ted are twins. **They** are twins.

## Page 246

### Subjects

The **subject** of a sentence is the person, place or thing the sentence is about.

**Directions:** Underline the subject in each sentence.

**Example:** Mom read a book.
(Think: Who is the sentence about? Mom)

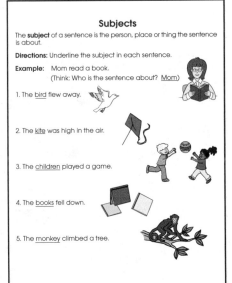

1. The bird flew away.

2. The kite was high in the air.

3. The children played a game.

4. The books fell down.

5. The monkey climbed a tree.

## Page 247

### Compound Subjects

Two similar sentences can be joined into one sentence if the predicate is the same. A **compound subject** is made up of two subjects joined together by the word **and**.

**Example:** Jamie can sing.
Sandy can sing.
Jamie **and** Sandy can sing.

**Directions:** Combine the sentences. Write the new sentence on the line.

1. The cats are my pets.
The dogs are my pets.

The cats and dogs are my pets.

2. Chairs are in the store.
Tables are in the store.

Chairs and tables are in the store.

3. Tom can ride a bike.
Jack can ride a bike.

Tom and Jack can ride a bike.

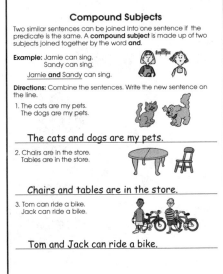

## Page 248

### Verbs

A **verb** is the action word in a sentence. Verbs tell what something does or that something exists.

**Example: Run**, **sleep** and **jump** are verbs.

**Directions:** Circle the verbs in the sentences below.

1. We play baseball everyday.

2. Susan pitches the ball very well.

3. Mike swings the bat harder than anyone.

4. Chris slides into home base.

5. Laura hit a home run.

# ANSWER KEY

## Page 249

### Verbs

We use verbs to tell when something happens. Sometimes we add an **ed** to verbs that tell us if something has already happened.

**Example:** Today, we will **play**. Yesterday, we **played**.

**Directions:** Write the correct verb in the blank.

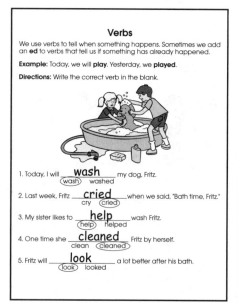

1. Today, I will **wash** my dog, Fritz. (wash / washed)
2. Last week, Fritz **cried** when we said, "Bath time, Fritz." (cry / cried)
3. My sister likes to **help** wash Fritz. (help / helped)
4. One time she **cleaned** Fritz by herself. (clean / cleaned)
5. Fritz will **look** a lot better after his bath. (look / looked)

## Page 250

### Verbs

**Directions:** Write each verb in the correct column.

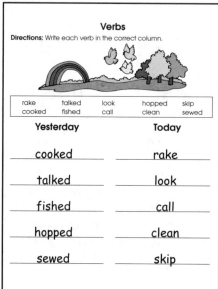

rake   talked   look   hopped   skip
cooked   fished   call   clean   sewed

| Yesterday | Today |
|-----------|-------|
| cooked | rake |
| talked | look |
| fished | call |
| hopped | clean |
| sewed | skip |

## Page 251

### Predicates

The **predicate** is the part of the sentence that tells about the action.

**Directions:** Circle the predicate in each sentence.

**Example:** The boys ran on the playground.
(Think: The boys did what? (Ran))

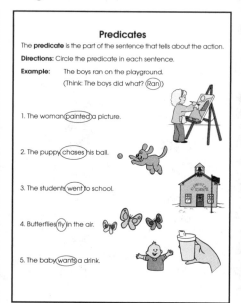

1. The woman (painted) a picture.
2. The puppy (chases) his ball.
3. The students (went) to school.
4. Butterflies (fly) in the air.
5. The baby (wants) a drink.

## Page 252

### Compound Predicates

A **compound predicate** is made by joining two sentences that have the same subject. The predicates are joined together by the word **and**.

**Example:** Tom can jump.
Tom can run.
Tom can run **and** jump.

**Directions:** Combine the sentences. Write the new sentence on the line.

1. The dog can roll over.
The dog can bark.
**The dog can roll over and bark.**

2. My mom plays with me.
My mom reads with me.
**My mom plays and reads with me.**

3. Tara is tall.
Tara is smart.
**Tara is tall and smart.**

## Page 253

### Subjects and Predicates

The **subject** part of the sentence is the person, place or thing the sentence is about. The **predicate** is the part of the sentence that tells what the subject does.

**Directions:** Draw a line between the subject and the predicate. Underline the noun in the subject and circle the verb.

**Example:** The furry cat | (ate) food.

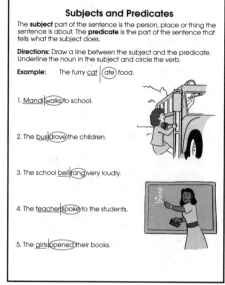

1. Mandi | (walks) to school.
2. The bus | (drove) the children.
3. The school bell | (rang) very loudly.
4. The teacher | (spoke) to the students.
5. The girls | (opened) their books.

## Page 254

### Compound Subjects and Predicates

The following sentences have either a compound subject or a compound predicate.

**Directions:** If the sentence has a compound subject (more than one thing doing the action), **underline** the subject. If it has a compound predicate (more than one action), **circle** the predicate.

**Example:** Bats and owls like the night.
The fox (slinks and spies).

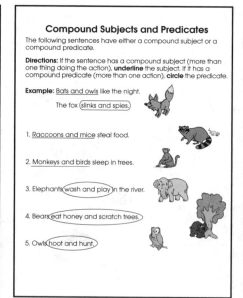

1. Raccoons and mice steal food.
2. Monkeys and birds sleep in trees.
3. Elephants (wash and play) in the river.
4. Bears (eat honey and scratch trees).
5. Owls (hoot and hunt).

## Page 255

### Compound Subjects and Predicates

**Directions:** Write one new sentence using a compound subject or predicate.

**Example:** The boy will jump. The girl will jump.
The <u>boy and girl</u> will jump.

1. The clowns run. The clowns play.

   The clowns run and play.

2. The dogs dance. The bears dance.

   The dogs and bears dance.

3. Seals bark. Seals clap.

   Seals bark and clap.

4. The girls play. The girls laugh.

   The girls play and laugh.

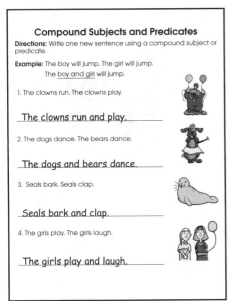

## Page 256

### Parts of a Sentence

**Directions:** Draw a circle around the noun, the naming part of the sentence. Draw a line under the verb, the action part of the sentence.

**Example:** (John) <u>drinks</u> juice every morning.

1. Our (class) skates at the roller-skating rink.
2. (Mike) and (Jan) go very fast.
3. (Fred) eats hot dogs.
4. (Sue) dances to the music.
5. (Everyone) likes the skating rink.

## Page 257

### Parts of a Sentence

**Directions:** Look at the pictures. Draw a line from the naming part of the sentence to the action part to complete the sentence.

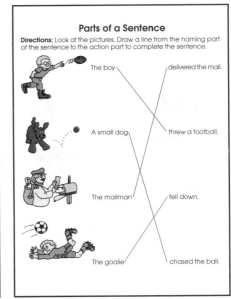

The boy — threw a football.
A small dog — delivered the mail.
The mailman — chased the ball.
The goalie — fell down.

## Page 258

### Adjectives

**Adjectives** are words that tell more about a person, place or thing.

**Examples:** cold, fuzzy, dark

**Directions:** Circle the adjectives in the sentences.

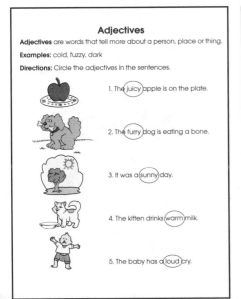

1. The (juicy) apple is on the plate.
2. The (furry) dog is eating a bone.
3. It was a (sunny) day.
4. The kitten drinks (warm) milk.
5. The baby has a (loud) cry.

## Page 259

### Adjectives

**Directions:** Choose an adjective from the box to fill in the blanks.

| hungry | sunny | busy | funny |
|--------|-------|------|-------|
| fresh | deep | pretty | cloudy |

1. It is a __sunny__ day on Farmer Brown's farm.
2. Farmer Brown is a very __busy__ man.
3. Mrs. Brown likes to feed the __hungry__ chickens.
4. Every day she collects the __fresh__ eggs.
5. The ducks swim in the __deep__ pond.

## Page 260

### Adjectives

**Directions:** Think of your own adjectives. Write a story about Fluffy the cat.

Answers will vary.

1. Fluffy is a _____ cat.
2. The color of his fur is _____ .
3. He likes to chew on my _____ shoes.
4. He likes to eat _____ cat food.
5. I like Fluffy because he is so _____ .

## Page 261

### Articles

**Articles** are small words that help us to better understand nouns. **A** and **an** are articles. We use **an** before a word that begins with a vowel. We use **a** before a word that begins with a consonant.

**Example:** We looked in **a** nest. It had **an** eagle in it.

**Directions:** Read the sentences. Write **a** or **an** in the blank.

1. I found ___a___ book.

2. It had a story about ___an___ ant in it.

3. In the story, ___a___ lion gave three wishes to ___an___ ant.

4. The ant's first wish was to ride ___an___ elephant.

5. The second wish was to ride ___an___ alligator.

6. The last wish was ___a___ wish for three more wishes.

## Page 262

### Sentences and Non-Sentences

A **sentence** tells a complete idea. It has a noun and a verb. It begins with a capital letter and has punctuation at the end.

**Directions:** Circle the group of words if it is a sentence.

1. (Grass is a green plant.)

2. Mowing the lawn.

3. (Grass grows in fields and lawns.)

4. Tickle the feet.

5. (Sheep, cows and horses eat grass.)

6. We like to play in.

7. (My sister likes to mow the lawn.)

8. A picnic on the grass.

9. (My dog likes to roll in the grass.)

10. Plant flowers around.

## Page 263

### Sentences and Non-Sentences

**Directions:** Circle the group of words if it tells a complete idea.

1. (A secret is something you know.)

2. (My mom's birthday gift is a secret.)

3. No one else.

4. If you promise not to.

5. (I'll tell you a secret.)

6. Something nobody knows.

## Page 264

### Statements

**Statements** are sentences that tell us something. They begin with a capital letter and end with a period.

**Directions:** Write the sentences on the lines below. Begin each sentence with a capital letter and end it with a period.

1. we like to ride our bikes

   We like to ride our bikes.

2. we go down the hill very fast

   We go down the hill very fast.

3. we keep our bikes shiny and clean

   We keep our bikes shiny and clean.

4. we know how to change the tires

   We know how to change the tires.

## Page 265

### Surprising Sentences

**Surprising sentences** tell a strong feeling and end with an exclamation point. A surprising sentence may be only one or two words showing fear, surprise or pain. **Example: Oh, no!**

**Directions:** Put a period at the end of the sentences that tell something. Put an exclamation point at the end of the sentences that tell a strong feeling. Put a question mark at the end of the sentences that ask a question.

1. The cheetah can run very fast .

2. Wow !

3. Look at that cheetah go !

4. Can you run fast ?

5. Oh, my !

6. You're faster than I am .

7. Let's run together .

8. We can run as fast as a cheetah .

9. What fun !

10. Do you think cheetahs get tired ?

## Page 266

### Commands

**Commands** tell someone to do something. **Example: "Be careful."** It can also be written as "Be careful!" if it tells a strong feeling.

**Directions:** Put a period at the end of the command sentences. Use an exclamation point if the sentence tells a strong feeling. Write your own commands on the lines below.

1. Clean your room .

2. Now !

3. Be careful with your goldfish .

4. Watch out !

5. Be a little more careful .

   Answers will vary.

## Page 267

### Questions

**Questions** are sentences that ask something. They begin with a capital letter and end with a question mark.

**Directions:** Write the questions on the lines below. Begin each sentence with a capital letter and end it with a question mark.

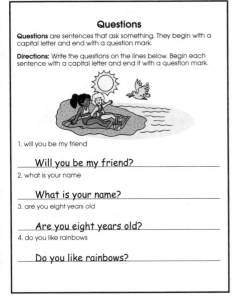

1. will you be my friend

   Will you be my friend?

2. what is your name

   What is your name?

3. are you eight years old

   Are you eight years old?

4. do you like rainbows

   Do you like rainbows?

## Page 268

### Making Inferences: Writing Questions

Tommy likes to answer questions. He knows the answers, but you need to write the questions.

**Directions:** Write two questions for each answer.

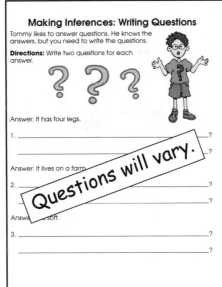

Answer: It has four legs.

1. _____?

Answer: It lives on a farm.

2. _____?
   _____?

Answer: It is soft.

3. _____?
   _____?

*Questions will vary.*

## Page 269

### Making Inferences: Writing Questions

Toban and Sean use many colors when they paint.

**Directions:** Write two questions for each answer.

Answer: It is red.

1. _____?
   _____?

Answer: It is purple.

2. _____?
   _____?

Answer: _____.

3. _____?
   _____?

*Questions will vary.*

## Page 270

### Making Inferences: Writing Questions

Ron likes sports. He enjoys meeting athletes. He would like to be a sports reporter someday.

**Directions:** Write a question Ron could ask each of these athletes.

1. An Olympic champion skier _____

2. An All-Star basketball player _____

3. The Quarterback of the Year _____

4. The winner of the _____

5. The _____

6. An Olympic champion runner _____

7. A first place winner in diving _____

*Questions will vary.*

## Page 271

### Making Inferences: Writing Questions

Erin found many solid shapes in her house.

**Directions:** Write two questions for each answer.

Answer: It is a cube.

1. _____?
   _____?

Answer: It is a cylinder.

2. _____?
   _____?

Answer: It is a sphere.

3. _____?
   _____?

*Questions will vary.*

## Page 272

### Making Inferences: Point of View

Chelsea likes to pretend she will meet famous people someday. She would like to ask them many questions.

**Directions:** Write a question you think Chelsea would ask if she met these people.

1. an actor in a popular, new film _____?

2. an Olympic gold medal _____?

3. an alien from space _____?

*Questions will vary.*

**Directions:** Now, write the answers these people might have given to Chelsea's questions.

4. an actor in a popular, new film _____

5. an Olympic Gold _____

6. an alien from outer space _____

*Answers will vary.*

# ANSWER KEY

## Page 273

### Making Inferences: Point of View

Ellen likes animals. Someday she might want to be an animal doctor.

**Directions:** Write one question you think Ellen would ask each of these animals if she could speak their language.

1. a giraffe _____?
2. a mouse _____?
3. a shark _____?
4. a hippopotamus _____?
5. a penguin _____?
6. a gorilla _____?
7. an eagle _____?

*Questions will vary.*

**Directions:** Now, write the answers you think these animals might have given Ellen.

9. a giraffe _____
10. a mouse _____
11. a shark _____
12. a hippopotamus _____
13. a penguin _____
14. a gorilla _____
15. an eagle _____

*Answers will vary.*

## Page 274

### Creative Writing

**Directions:** Look at the picture below. Write a story about the picture.

Results will vary.

## Page 275

### Ownership

We add **'s** to nouns (people, places or things) to tell who or what owns something.

**Directions:** Read the sentences. Fill in the blanks to show ownership.

**Example:** The doll belongs to **Sara**.
It is **Sara's** doll.

1. Sparky has a red collar.

   **Sparky's** collar is red.

2. Jimmy has a blue coat.

   **Jimmy's** coat is blue.

3. The tail of the cat is short.

   The **cat's** tail is short.

4. The name of my mother is Karen.

   My **mother's** name is Karen.

## Page 276

### Ownership

**Directions:** Read the sentences. Choose the correct word and write it in the sentences below.

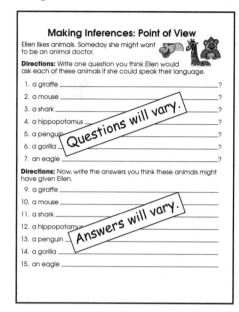

1. The **boy's** lunchbox is broken.  boys ⟨boy's⟩
2. The **gerbils** played in the cage.  gerbil's ⟨gerbils⟩
3. **Ann's** hair is brown.  Anns ⟨Ann's⟩
4. The **horses** ran in the field.  horse's ⟨horses⟩
5. My **sister's** coat is torn.  ⟨sister's⟩ sisters
6. The **cat's** fur is brown.  cats ⟨cat's⟩
7. Three **birds** flew past our window.  ⟨birds⟩ bird's
8. The **dog's** paws are muddy.  dogs ⟨dog's⟩
9. The **giraffe's** neck is long.  giraffes ⟨giraffe's⟩
10. The **lions** are big and powerful.  lion's ⟨lions⟩

## Page 277

### Is, Are and Am

**is**, **are** and **am** are special action words that tell us something is happening now.
Use **am** with **I**. **Example: I am.**
Use **is** to tell about one person or thing. **Example: He is.**
Use **are** to tell about more than one. **Example: We are.**
Use **are** with **you**. **Example: You are.**

**Directions:** Write **is**, **are** or **am** in the sentences below.

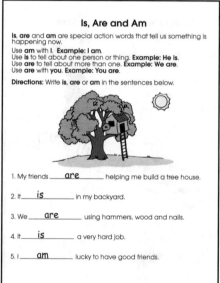

1. My friends **are** helping me build a tree house.
2. It **is** in my backyard.
3. We **are** using hammers, wood and nails.
4. It **is** a very hard job.
5. I **am** lucky to have good friends.

## Page 278

### Was and Were

**Was** and **were** tell us about something that already happened.
Use **was** to tell about one person or thing. **Example: I was**, he **was**.
Use **were** to tell about more than one person or thing or when using the word **you**. **Example: We were**, you **were**.

**Directions:** Write **was** or **were** in each sentence.

1. Lily **was** eight years old on her birthday.
2. Tim and Steve **were** happy to be at the party.
3. Megan **was** too shy to sing "Happy Birthday."
4. Ben **was** sorry he dropped his cake.
5. All of the children **were** happy to be invited.

## Page 279

### Go, Going and Went

We use **go** or **going** to tell about now or later. Sometimes we use **going** with the words **am** or **are**. We use **went** to tell about something that already happened.

**Directions:** Write **go**, **going** or **went** in the sentences below.

1. Today, I will **go** to the store.

2. Yesterday, we **went** shopping.

3. I am **going** to take Muffy to the vet.

4. Jan and Steve **went** to the party.

5. They are **going** to have a good day.

## Page 280

### Have, Has and Had

We use **have** and **has** to tell about now. We use **had** to tell about something that already happened.

**Directions:** Write **has**, **have** or **had** in the sentences below.

1. We **have** three cats at home.

2. Ginger **has** brown fur.

3. Bucky and Charlie **have** gray fur.

4. My friend Tom **had** one cat, but he died.

5. Tom **has** a new cat now.

## Page 281

### See, Saw and Sees

We use **see** or **sees** to tell about now. We use **saw** to tell about something that already happened.

**Directions:** Write **see**, **sees** or **saw** in the sentences below.

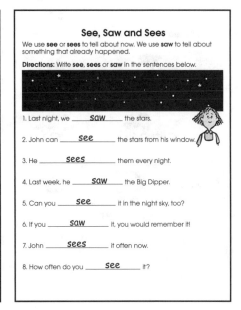

1. Last night, we **saw** the stars.

2. John can **see** the stars from his window.

3. He **sees** them every night.

4. Last week, he **saw** the Big Dipper.

5. Can you **see** it in the night sky, too?

6. If you **saw** it, you would remember it!

7. John **sees** it often now.

8. How often do you **see** it?

## Page 282

### Eat, Eats and Ate

We use **eat** or **eats** to tell about now. We use **ate** to tell about what already happened.

**Directions:** Write **eat**, **eats** or **ate** in the sentences below.

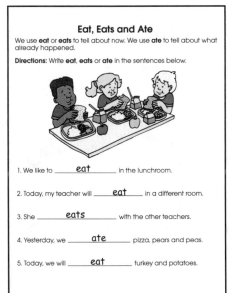

1. We like to **eat** in the lunchroom.

2. Today, my teacher will **eat** in a different room.

3. She **eats** with the other teachers.

4. Yesterday, we **ate** pizza, pears and peas.

5. Today, we will **eat** turkey and potatoes.

## Page 283

### Leave, Leaves and Left

We use **leave** and **leaves** to tell about now. We use **left** to tell about what already happened.

**Directions:** Write **leave**, **leaves** or **left** in the sentences below.

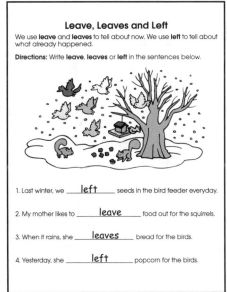

1. Last winter, we **left** seeds in the bird feeder everyday.

2. My mother likes to **leave** food out for the squirrels.

3. When it rains, she **leaves** bread for the birds.

4. Yesterday, she **left** popcorn for the birds.

## Page 284

### Learning Dictionary Skills

A dictionary is a book that gives the meaning of words. It also tells how words sound. Words in a dictionary are in ABC order. That makes them easier to find. A picture dictionary lists a word, a picture of the word and its meaning.

**Directions:** Look at this page from a picture dictionary. Then answer the questions.

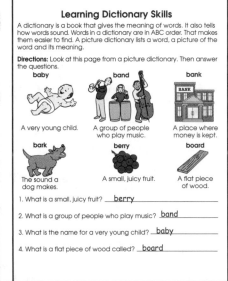

**baby** — A very young child.

**band** — A group of people who play music.

**bank** — A place where money is kept.

**bark** — The sound a dog makes.

**berry** — A small, juicy fruit.

**board** — A flat piece of wood.

1. What is a small, juicy fruit? **berry**

2. What is a group of people who play music? **band**

3. What is the name for a very young child? **baby**

4. What is a flat piece of wood called? **board**

## Page 285

### Learning Dictionary Skills

**Directions:** Look at this page from a picture dictionary. Then answer the questions.

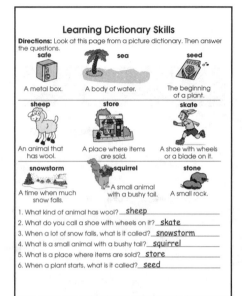

**safe** A metal box.
**sea** A body of water.
**seed** The beginning of a plant.
**sheep** An animal that has wool.
**store** A place where items are sold.
**skate** A shoe with wheels or a blade on it.
**snowstorm** A time when much snow falls.
**squirrel** A small animal with a bushy tail.
**stone** A small rock.

1. What kind of animal has wool? __sheep__
2. What do you call a shoe with wheels on it? __skate__
3. When a lot of snow falls, what is it called? __snowstorm__
4. What is a small animal with a bushy tail? __squirrel__
5. What is a place where items are sold? __store__
6. When a plant starts, what is it called? __seed__

## Page 286

### Learning Dictionary Skills

**Directions:** Look at this page from a picture dictionary. Then answer the questions.

**table** Furniture with legs and a flat top.
**tail** A slender part that is on the back of an animal.
**teacher** A person who teaches lessons.
**telephone** A machine that sends and receives sounds.
**ticket** A paper slip or card.
**tiger** An animal with stripes.

1. Who is a person who teaches lessons? __teacher__
2. What is the name of an animal with stripes? __tiger__
3. What is a piece of furniture with legs and a flat top? __table__
4. What is the definition of a ticket?
   __a paper slip or card__
5. What is a machine that sends and receives sounds?
   __telephone__

## Page 287

### Learning Dictionary Skills

The guide words at the top of a page in a dictionary tell you what the first and last words on the page will be. Only words that come in ABC order between those two words will be on that page. Guide words help you find the page you need to look up a word.

**Directions:** Write each word from the box in ABC order between each pair of guide words.

| faint | far | fence | feed | farmer |
|-------|-----|-------|------|--------|
| fan | feet | farm | family | face |

**face**        **fence**

| face | farm |
|------|------|
| faint | farmer |
| family | feed |
| fan | feet |
| far | fence |

## Page 288

### Learning Dictionary Skills

**Directions:** Write each word from the box in ABC order between each pair of guide words.

| fierce | fix | fight | first | few |
|--------|-----|-------|-------|-----|
| fish | fill | flush | flat | finish |

**few**        **flush**

| few | first |
|-----|-------|
| fierce | fish |
| fight | fix |
| fill | flat |
| finish | flush |

## Page 289

### Learning Dictionary Skills

**Directions:** Create your own dictionary page. Include guide words at the top. Write the words with their meanings in ABC order.

guide word     word     guide word     word

1. ___
2. ___
3. ___
4. ___

**Answers will vary.**

## Page 290

### Learning Dictionary Skills

When words have more than one meaning, the meanings are numbered in a dictionary.

**Directions:** Read the meanings of **tag**. Write the number of the correct definition after each sentence.

**tag**
1. A small strip or tab attached to something else.
2. To label.
3. To follow closely and constantly.
4. A game of chase.

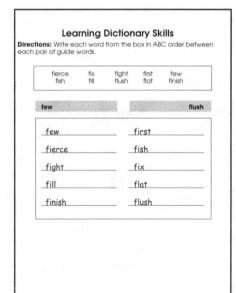

1. We will play a game of tag after we study. __4__
2. I will tag this coat with its price. __2__
3. My little brother will tag along with us. __3__
4. My mother already took off the price tag. __1__
5. The tag on the puppy said, "For Sale." __1__
6. Do not tag that tree. __2__

## Page 291

### Silly Sentences!

**Directions:** Cut out the binoculars. Cut out the beginning and ending sentence strips on the next page. Thread the strips through the lenses to make sentences. Write each sentence on a piece of paper. Draw a picture to illustrate your silly sentences. Staple your sentences and illustrations into a book to share.

cut ✂ - - - - - - - - - - - - - - - - - - - - - - - - - - - - - - - - - -

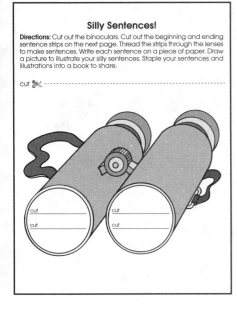

cut
cut

cut
cut

## Page 293

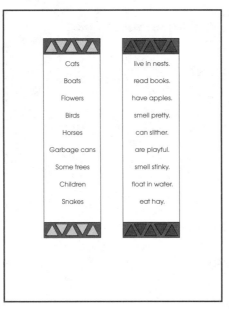

| Cats | live in nests. |
| Boats | read books. |
| Flowers | have apples. |
| Birds | smell pretty. |
| Horses | can slither. |
| Garbage cans | are playful. |
| Some trees | smell stinky. |
| Children | float in water. |
| Snakes | eat hay. |

## Page 296

### Number Words

**Directions:** Write each number word beside the correct picture. Then write it again.

**Example:** 〰〰〰 six six

one two three four five six seven eight nine ten

one one
three three
two two
nine nine
four four
seven seven
five five
ten ten
eight eight

## Page 297

### Number Words

**Directions:** Write the correct number words in the blanks.

one two three four five six seven eight nine ten

Add a letter to each of these words to make a number word.

**Example:**

| even | on | tree |
| seven | one | three |

Change a letter to make these words into number words.

**Example:**

| live | fix | line |
| five | six | nine |

Write the number words that sound the same as these:

**Example:**

| ate | to | for |
| eight | two | four |

Write the number word you did not use: ten

## Page 298

### Number Words: Asking Sentences

**Directions:** Write an asking sentence about each picture. Begin each sentence with **How many**. Then answer your question. Begin each sentence with a capital letter and end it with a period or a question mark.

one two three four five six seven eight nine ten

**Example:**

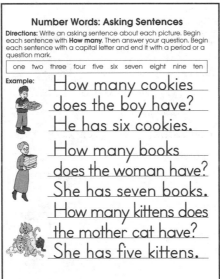

How many cookies does the boy have?
He has six cookies.

How many books does the woman have?
She has seven books.

How many kittens does the mother cat have?
She has five kittens.

## Page 299

### Number Words: Sentences

**Directions:** Change the telling sentences into asking sentences. Change the asking sentences into telling sentences. Begin each one with a capital letter and end it with a period or a question mark.

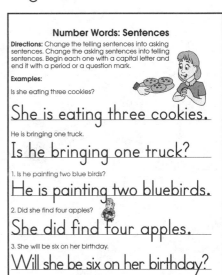

**Examples:**

Is she eating three cookies?

She is eating three cookies.

He is bringing one truck.

Is he bringing one truck?

1. Is he painting two blue birds?

He is painting two bluebirds.

2. Did she find four apples?

She did find four apples.

3. She will be six on her birthday.

Will she be six on her birthday?

## Page 300

### Short a Words: Rhyming Words

**Short a** is the sound you hear in the word **math**.

**Directions:** Use the **short a** words in the box to write rhyming words.

| lamp | fat | bat | van |
| path | can | cat | Dan |
| math | stamp | fan | sat |

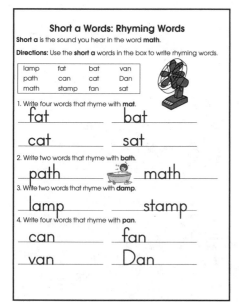

1. Write four words that rhyme with **mat**.

fat  bat
cat  sat

2. Write two words that rhyme with **bath**.

path  math

3. Write two words that rhyme with **damp**.

lamp  stamp

4. Write four words that rhyme with **pan**.

can  fan
van  Dan

## Page 301

### Short a Words: Sentences

**Directions:** Use a word from the box to complete each sentence.

| fat | path | lamp | can |
| van | stamp | Dan | math |
| sat | cat | fan | bat |

**Example:**

1. The **lamp** had a pink shade.
2. The bike **path** led us to the park.
3. I like to add in **math** class.
4. The cat is very **fat**.
5. The **can** of beans was hard to open.
6. The envelope needed a **stamp**.
7. He swung the **bat** and hit the ball.
8. The **fan** blew air around.
9. My mom drives a blue **van**.
10. I **sat** in the backseat.

## Page 302

### Long a Words

**Long a** is the vowel sound which says its own name. **Long a** can be spelled **ai** as in the word **mail**, **ay** as in the word **say** and **a** with a **silent e** at the end of a word as in the word **same**.

**Directions:** Say each word and listen for the **long a** sound. Then write each word and underline the letters that make the **long a** vowel sound.

| mail | bake | train |
| game | day | sale |
| paint | play | name |
| made | gray | tray |

1. mail
2. paint
3. game
4. made
5. bake
6. play
7. day
8. gray
9. train
10. name
11. sale
12. tray

## Page 303

### Long a Words: Rhyming Words

**Long a** is the vowel sound you hear in the word **cake**.

**Directions:** Use the **long a** words in the box to write rhyming words.

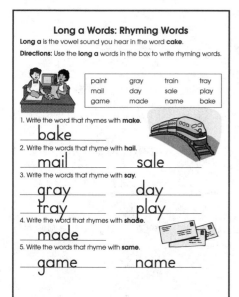

| paint | gray | train | tray |
| mail | day | sale | play |
| game | made | name | bake |

1. Write the word that rhymes with **make**.

bake

2. Write the words that rhyme with **hail**.

mail  sale

3. Write the words that rhyme with **say**.

gray  day
tray  play

4. Write the word that rhymes with **shade**.

made

5. Write the words that rhyme with **same**.

game  name

## Page 304

### Long a Words: Sentence Order

**Directions:** Write the words in order so that each sentence tells a complete idea. Begin each Sentence with a capital letter and end it with a period or a question mark.

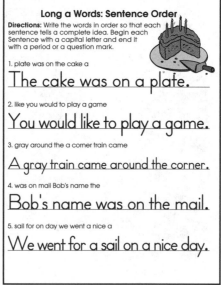

1. plate was on the cake a

The cake was on a plate.

2. like you would to play a game

You would like to play a game.

3. gray around the a corner train came

A gray train came around the corner.

4. was on mail Bob's name the

Bob's name was on the mail.

5. sail for on day we went a nice a

We went for a sail on a nice day.

## Page 305

### Short o Words

**Short o** is the vowel sound you hear in the word **pot**.

**Directions:** Say each word and listen for the **short o** sound. Then write each word and underline the letter that makes the **short o** sound.

| hot | box | sock | mop |
| stop | not | fox | cot |
| Bob | rock | clock | lock |

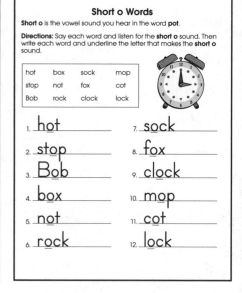

1. hot
2. stop
3. Bob
4. box
5. not
6. rock
7. sock
8. fox
9. clock
10. mop
11. cot
12. lock

## Page 306

### Short o Words: Rhyming Words

**Short o** is the vowel sound you hear in the word **got**.

**Directions:** Use the **short o** words in the box to write rhyming words.

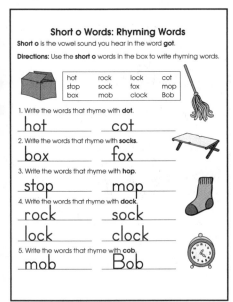

| hot | rock | lock | cot |
|-----|------|------|-----|
| stop | sock | fox | mop |
| box | mob | clock | Bob |

1. Write the words that rhyme with **dot**.

hot     cot

2. Write the words that rhyme with **socks**.

box     fox

3. Write the words that rhyme with **hop**.

stop     mop

4. Write the words that rhyme with **dock**.

rock     sock

lock     clock

5. Write the words that rhyme with **cob**.

mob     Bob

## Page 307

### Long o Words

**Long o** is the vowel sound which says its own name. **Long o** can be spelled **oa** as in the word **float** or **o** with a **silent e** at the end as in **cone**.

**Directions:** Say each word and listen for the **long o** sound. Then write each word and underline the letters that make the **long o** sound.

| rope | coat | soap | wrote |
|------|------|------|-------|
| note | hope | boat | cone |
| bone | pole | phone | hole |

1. rope
2. note
3. bone
4. coat
5. hope
6. pole
7. soap
8. boat
9. phone
10. wrote
11. cone
12. hole

## Page 308

### Long o Words: Rhyming Words

**Long o** is the vowel sound you hear in the word **home**.

**Directions:** Use the **long o** words in the box to write rhyming words.

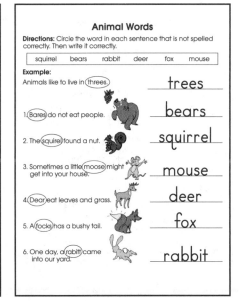

| rope | soap | coat | wrote |
|------|------|------|-------|
| note | boat | hope | cone |
| bone | phone | pole | hole |

1. Write the words that rhyme with **mope**.

rope     soap     hope

2. Write the words that rhyme with **tote**.

note     boat

coat     wrote

3. Write the words that rhyme with **lone**.

bone     phone     cone

4. Write the words that rhyme with **goal**.

pole     hole

## Page 309

### Long o Words: Sentences

**Directions:** Draw a line from the first part of the sentence to the part which completes the sentence.

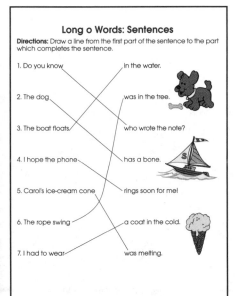

1. Do you know — who wrote the note?
2. The dog — has a bone.
3. The boat floats — in the water.
4. I hope the phone — rings soon for me!
5. Carol's ice-cream cone — was melting.
6. The rope swing — was in the tree.
7. I had to wear — a coat in the cold.

## Page 310

### Animal Words

**Directions:** Write the animal names twice beside each picture.

| fox | rabbit | bear | squirrel | mouse | deer |
|-----|--------|------|----------|-------|------|

**Example:**

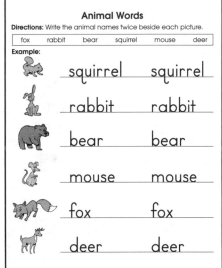

squirrel     squirrel

rabbit     rabbit

bear     bear

mouse     mouse

fox     fox

deer     deer

## Page 311

### Animal Words

**Directions:** Circle the word in each sentence that is not spelled correctly. Then write it correctly.

| squirrel | bears | rabbit | deer | fox | mouse |
|----------|-------|--------|------|-----|-------|

**Example:**

Animals like to live in (threes).     trees

1. (Bares) do not eat people.     bears

2. The (squirel) found a nut.     squirrel

3. Sometimes a little (moose) might get into your house.     mouse

4. (Dear) eat leaves and grass.     deer

5. A (focks) has a bushy tail.     fox

6. One day, a (rabitt) came into our yard.     rabbit

## Page 312

**Animal Words: More Than One**

To show more than one of something, we add **s** to most words.

**Example:** one dog – **two dogs**    one book – **two books**

But some words are different. For words that end with **x**, use **es** to show two.

**Example:** one fox – **two foxes**    one box – **two boxes**

The spelling of some words changes a lot when there are two.

**Example:** one mouse – **two mice**

Some words stay the same, even when you mean two of something.

**Example:** one deer – **two deer**    one fish – **two fish**

**Directions:** Complete the sentences below with the correct word.

1. The ___ run fast. — rabbits

2. The ___ are eating. — deer

3. Have you seen any ___ today? — bears

4. Where do the ___ live? — foxes

5. Did you ever have ___ for pets? — mice

## Page 313

**Animal Words: More Than One**

**Directions:** Write the two sentences below as one sentence. Remember the special spelling of **fox**, **mouse** and **deer** when there are more than one.

**Example:**

I saw a mouse. You saw a mouse.

We saw two mice.

1. Julie petted a deer.
   Matt petted a deer.

Julie and Matt petted a deer.

2. Mike colored a fox.
   Kim colored a fox.

Mike and Kim colored two foxes.

## Page 314

**Animal Words: Kinds of Sentences**

Another name for an asking sentence is a **question**.

**Directions:** Use the words in the box to write a telling sentence. Then use the words to write a question.

**Example:**

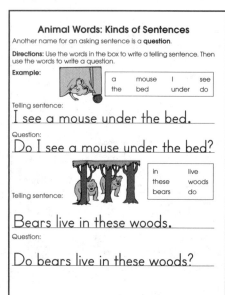

| a | mouse | I | see |
| the | bed | under | do |

Telling sentence:

I see a mouse under the bed.

Question:

Do I see a mouse under the bed?

| in | live |
| these | woods |
| bears | do |

Telling sentence:

Bears live in these woods.

Question:

Do bears live in these woods?

## Page 315

**Animal Words: Sentences**

**Directions:** Read the sentences on each line and draw a line between them. Then write each sentence again on the lines below. Begin each one with a capital letter and put a period or question mark at the end.

**Example:**

why do squirrels hide nuts | they eat them in the winter

Why do squirrels hide nuts?
They eat them in the winter.

1. bears sleep in the winter | they don't need food then

Bears sleep in the winter.
They don't need food then.

2. he said he saw a fox | do you think he did

He said he saw a fox.
Do you think he did?

## Page 316

**Review**

**Directions:** Complete each line of the poem below with a word from the box. Make sure each line rhymes.

| deer | fox | house | here | mouse | box |

A little gray — mouse

Once ran through my — house

Then a bushy-tailed — fox

Ran into a — box

Last came a — deer

What was he doing — here ?

Answers will vary, but may include:

Now make your own poem using the words **bear** and **there**.

Do you see the big brown bear sitting over there?

## Page 317

**Family Words**

**Directions:** This is Andy's **family tree**. It shows all the people in his family. Use the words in the box to finish writing the names in Andy's family tree.

| grandmother | mother |
| grandfather | father |
| aunt | uncle |
| brother | sister |

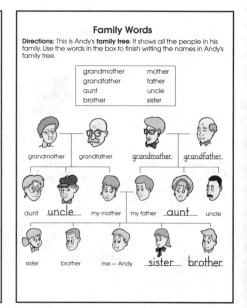

grandmother    grandfather    grandmother    grandfather

aunt    uncle    my mother    my father    aunt    uncle

sister    brother    me — Andy    sister    brother

## Page 318

**Family Words**

Some words tell how a person looks or feels. These are called **describing** words or **adjectives**.

**Directions:** Help Andy write about the people in his family. Cross out the **describing** word that does not tell about each picture. Write a sentence that uses the other two describing words.

Example:

~~asleep~~
funny
tall

My aunt is tall and funny.

~~fast~~
happy
smiling

1. My grandmother is happy and smiling.

hot
~~broken~~
tired

2. My uncle is hot and tired.

thirsty
hungry
~~hard~~

3. My little brother is thirsty and hungry.

## Page 319

**Family Words: Joining Words**

**Joining words** join two ideas to make one long sentence. Three words help do this:

**and** — if both sentences are much the same.
**Example:** I took my dog for a walk, **and** I played with my cat.
**but** — if the second sentence says something different than the first sentence. Sometimes the second sentence tells why you can't do the first sentence.
**Example:** I want to play outside, **but** it is raining.
**or** — if each sentence names a different thing you could do.
**Example:** You could eat your cookie, **or** you could give it to me.

**Directions:** Use the word given to join the two short sentences into one longer sentence.

**(but)**
My aunt lives far away. She calls me often.

My aunt lives far away, but she calls me often.

1. **(and)**
My sister had a birthday. She got a new bike.

My sister had a birthday, and she got a new bike.

2. **(or)**
We can play outside. We can play inside.

We can play outside, or we can play inside.

## Page 320

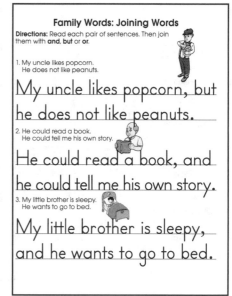

**Family Words: Joining Words**

**Directions:** Read each pair of sentences. Then join them with **and**, **but** or **or**.

1. My uncle likes popcorn.
He does not like peanuts.

My uncle likes popcorn, but he does not like peanuts.

2. He could read a book.
He could tell me his own story.

He could read a book, and he could tell me his own story.

3. My little brother is sleepy.
He wants to go to bed.

My little brother is sleepy, and he wants to go to bed.

## Page 321

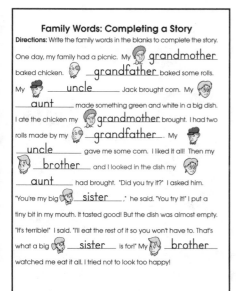

**Family Words: Completing a Story**

**Directions:** Write the family words in the blanks to complete the story.

One day, my family had a picnic. My grandmother baked chicken. My grandfather baked some rolls. My uncle Jack brought corn. My aunt made something green and white in a big dish. I ate the chicken my grandmother brought. I had two rolls made by my grandfather. My uncle gave me some corn. I liked it all! Then my brother and I looked in the dish my aunt had brought. "Did you try it?" I asked him. "You're my big sister," he said. "You try it!" I put a tiny bit in my mouth. It tasted good! But the dish was almost empty.

"It's terrible!" I said. "I'll eat the rest of it so you won't have to. That's what a big sister is for!" My brother watched me eat it all. I tried not to look too happy!

## Page 322

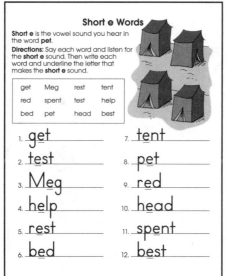

**Short e Words**

**Short e** is the vowel sound you hear in the word **pet**.

**Directions:** Say each word and listen for the **short e** sound. Then write each word and underline the letter that makes the **short e** sound.

| get | Meg | rest | tent |
| red | spent | test | help |
| bed | pet | head | best |

1. g<u>e</u>t
2. t<u>e</u>st
3. M<u>e</u>g
4. h<u>e</u>lp
5. r<u>e</u>st
6. b<u>e</u>d
7. t<u>e</u>nt
8. p<u>e</u>t
9. r<u>e</u>d
10. h<u>e</u>ad
11. sp<u>e</u>nt
12. b<u>e</u>st

## Page 323

**Short e Words: Rhyming Words**

**Short e** is the vowel sound you hear in the word **egg**.

**Directions:** Use the **short e** words in the box to write rhyming words.

| get | test | pet | help |
| let | head | spent | red |
| best | tent | rest | bed |

1. Write the words that rhyme with **fed**.

head     red     bed

2. Write the words that rhyme with **bent**.

tent     spent

3. Write the words that rhyme with **west**.

best     test     rest

4. Write the words that rhyme with **bet**.

get     let     pet

## Page 324

**Short e Words: Sentences**

**Directions:** Write the correct **short e** word in each sentence.

| | | | | | |
|---|---|---|---|---|---|
| get | Meg | rest | bed | spent | best |
| test | help | head | pet | red | tent |

1. Of all my crayons, I like the color **red**

the **best** !

2. I always make my **bed** when I **get** up.

3. My new hat keeps my **head** warm.

4. **Meg** wanted a dog for a **pet** .

5. When we go camping, my job is to **help** put up

the **tent** .

6. I have a **test** in math tomorrow, so I want to get

a good night's **rest** .

## Page 325

**Long e Words**

**Long e** is the vowel sound which says its own name. **Long e** can be spelled **ee** as in the word **teeth**, **ea** as in the word **meat** or **e** as in the word **me**.

**Directions:** Say each word and listen for the **long e** sound. Then write the words and underline the letters that make the **long e** sound.

| | | | |
|---|---|---|---|
| street | neat | treat | feet |
| sleep | keep | deal | meal |
| mean | clean | beast | feast |

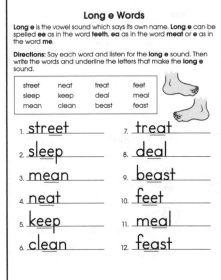

1. street
2. sleep
3. mean
4. neat
5. keep
6. clean
7. treat
8. deal
9. beast
10. feet
11. meal
12. feast

## Page 326

**Long e Words: Rhyming Words**

**Long e** is the vowel sound you hear in the word **meet**.

**Directions:** Use the **long e** words in the box to write rhyming words.

| | | | |
|---|---|---|---|
| street | feet | neat | treat |
| keep | deal | sleep | meal |
| mean | beast | clean | feast |

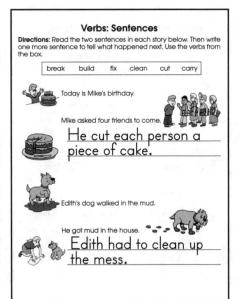

1. Write the words that rhyme with **beat**.

street    feet

neat    treat

2. Write the words that rhyme with **deep**.

keep    sleep

3. Write the words that rhyme with **feel**.

deal    meal

4. Write the words that rhyme with **bean**.

mean    clean

5. Write the words that rhyme with **least**.

beast    feast

## Page 327

**Long e Words: Sentences**

**Directions:** Write a word from the box to complete each sentence.

| | | | |
|---|---|---|---|
| street | feet | neat | treat |
| keep | deal | sleep | meal |
| mean | beast | clean | feast |

1. I went to **sleep** late last night.

2. One of my favorite stories is "Beauty and
the **beast** ."

3. Look both ways when you cross the **street** .

4. It would be **mean** to kick someone.

5. I wear socks and shoes on my **feet** .

6. The most important **meal** of the day
is breakfast.

## Page 328

**Verbs**

**Verbs** are words that tell the action in the sentence.

**Directions:** Draw a line from each sentence to its picture. Then finish the sentence with the verb or action word that is under each picture.

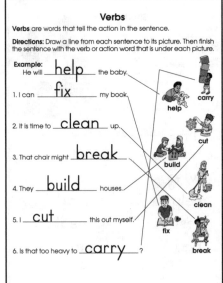

**Example:**
He will **help** the baby.

1. I can **fix** my book.

2. It is time to **clean** up.

3. That chair might **break** .

4. They **build** houses.

5. I **cut** this out myself.

6. Is that too heavy to **carry** ?

## Page 329

**Verbs: Sentences**

**Directions:** Read the two sentences in each story below. Then write one more sentence to tell what happened next. Use the verbs from the box.

| | | | | | |
|---|---|---|---|---|---|
| break | build | fix | clean | cut | carry |

Today is Mike's birthday.

Mike asked four friends to come.

**He cut each person a piece of cake.**

Edith's dog walked in the mud.

He got mud in the house.

**Edith had to clean up the mess.**

## Page 330

### Verbs: Sentences

**Directions:** Join each pair of sentences to make one longer sentence. Use one of the **joining** words: **and, but** or **or**. In the second part of the sentence, use **he, she** or **they** in place of the person's name.

**Example:** I asked Tim to help me. Tim wanted to play.

I asked Tim to help me, but he wanted to play.

1. Kelly dropped a glass.
   Kelly cut her finger.

Kelly dropped a glass, and she cut her finger.

2. Linda and Allen got a new dog.
   Linda and Allen named it Baby.

Linda and Allen got a new dog, and they named it Baby.

## Page 331

### Verbs: Word Endings

Most **verbs** end with **s** when the sentence tells about one thing. The **s** is taken away when the sentence tells about more than one thing.

**Example:**

One dog walks.          One boy runs.
Two **dogs** walk.          Three **boys** run.

The spelling of some **verbs** changes when the sentence tells about only one thing.

**Example:**

One girl carries her lunch.          The boy fixes his car.
Two girls **carry** their lunches.          Two boys **fix** their cars.

**Directions:** Write the missing verbs in the sentences.

**Example:**

Pam works hard. She and Peter __work__ all day.

1. The father bird builds a nest.
   The mother and father __build__ it together.

2. The girls clean their room. Jenny __cleans__ under her bed.

3. The children cut out their pictures. Henry __cuts__ his slowly.

4. These workers fix things. This man __fixes__ televisions.

5. Two trucks carry horses. One truck __carries__ pigs.

## Page 332

### Verbs: Completing a Story

**Directions:** Write a sentence that tells what happens in each picture. Use the **verb** under the picture.

**Example:**

fall          break          clean

A glass falls off the table.

Answers will vary, but may include:

She saw it hit the floor and break.

She used a mop to clean up the mess.

fix          cut          carry

Dad will fix the lawn mower.

She can cut the grass.

He has to carry the bag of grass clippings.

## Page 333

### Verbs

**Directions:** Circle the words in each sentence which are not spelled correctly. Then write the sentence correctly.

**Example:**

I need to (klean) the cage my (mouses) live in.

I need to clean the cage my mice live in.

2. The chair will (brake) if (free) of us sit on it.

The chair will break if three of us sit on it.

3. A (muther) (bare) carries her baby in (hir) mouth.

A mother bear carries her baby in her mouth.

## Page 334

### Short i Words

**Short i** is the vowel sound you hear in the word **pig**.

**Directions:** Say each word and listen for the **short i** sound. Then write each word and underline the letter that makes the **short i** sound.

| | | | |
|---|---|---|---|
| pin | fin | dip | dish |
| kick | rich | ship | wish |
| win | fish | sick | pitch |

1. p**i**n                7. d**i**sh
2. sh**i**p              8. f**i**sh
3. f**i**n                9. k**i**ck
4. w**i**sh            10. s**i**ck
5. d**i**p              11. r**i**ch
6. w**i**n              12. p**i**tch

## Page 335

### Short i Words: Rhyming Words

**Short i** is the sound you hear in the word **pin**.

**Directions:** Use the **short i** words in the box to write rhyming words.

| | | | |
|---|---|---|---|
| pin | fin | win | fish |
| pitch | wish | rich | kick |
| ship | dip | dish | sick |

1. Write the words that rhyme with **spin**.

pin          fin          win

2. Write the words that rhyme with **ditch**.

pitch          rich

3. Write the words that rhyme with **rip**.

ship          dip

4. Write the words that rhyme with **squish**.

wish          dish          fish

5. Write the words that rhyme with **lick**.

kick          sick

## Page 336

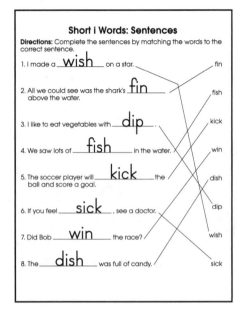

**Short i Words: Sentences**

**Directions:** Complete the sentences by matching the words to the correct sentence.

1. I made a **wish** on a star. — fin

2. All we could see was the shark's **fin** above the water. — fish

3. I like to eat vegetables with **dip**. — kick

4. We saw lots of **fish** in the water. — win

5. The soccer player will **kick** the ball and score a goal. — dish

6. If you feel **sick**, see a doctor. — dip

7. Did Bob **win** the race? — wish

8. The **dish** was full of candy. — sick

## Page 337

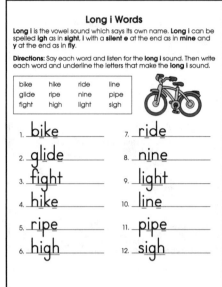

**Long i Words**

**Long i** is the vowel sound which says its own name. **Long i** can be spelled **igh** as in **sight**, **i** with a **silent e** at the end as in **mine** and **y** at the end as in **fly**.

**Directions:** Say each word and listen for the **long i** sound. Then write each word and underline the letters that make the **long i** sound.

| bike | hike | ride | line |
| glide | ripe | nine | pipe |
| fight | high | light | sigh |

1. bike
2. glide
3. fight
4. hike
5. ripe
6. high
7. ride
8. nine
9. light
10. line
11. pipe
12. sigh

## Page 338

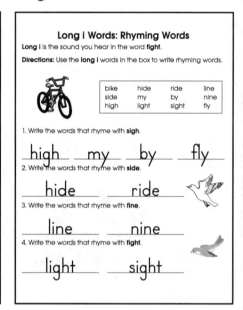

**Long i Words: Rhyming Words**

**Long i** is the sound you hear in the word **fight**.

**Directions:** Use the **long i** words in the box to write rhyming words.

| bike | hide | ride | line |
| side | my | by | nine |
| high | light | sight | fly |

1. Write the words that rhyme with **sigh**.

high    my    by    fly

2. Write the words that rhyme with **side**.

hide    ride

3. Write the words that rhyme with **fine**.

line    nine

4. Write the words that rhyme with **fight**.

light    sight

## Page 339

**Review**

**Directions:** Write **igh** in each blank below. Then read the words.

**Example:**

sight      fight      tight

might      light      bright

night      right      flight

Choose two of the **igh** words above. Draw, label and color a picture for each word.

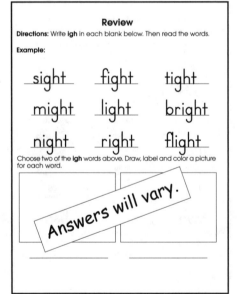

Answers will vary.

## Page 340

**Location Words**

**Directions:** Use one of the location words from the box to complete each sentence.

| between | around | inside | outside | beside | across |

**Example:**

She will hide **under** the basket.

1. In the summer, we like to play **outside**.

2. She can swim **across** the lake.

3. Put the bird **inside** its cage so it won't fly away.

4. Sit **between** Bill and me so we can all work together.

5. Your picture is right **beside** mine on the wall.

6. The fence goes **around** the house.

## Page 341

**Location Words**

**Directions:** Draw a line from each sentence to its picture. Then complete each sentence with the word under the picture.

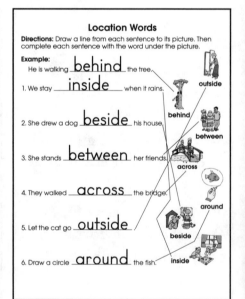

**Example:**

He is walking **behind** the tree.

1. We stay **inside** when it rains.

2. She drew a dog **beside** his house.

3. She stands **between** her friends.

4. They walked **across** the bridge.

5. Let the cat go **outside**.

6. Draw a circle **around** the fish.

outside

behind

between

across

around

beside

inside

## Page 342

**Location Words**

**Directions:** Write the location words that answer the questions.

| between | around | inside | outside | beside | across |

1. Write all the smaller words you find in the location words.

be, bet, we, a, round, in, out, cross

2. Which two words begin with the same sound as 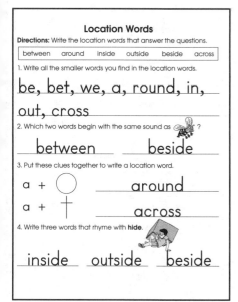 ?

between        beside

3. Put these clues together to write a location word.

a + ○        around

a + †        across

4. Write three words that rhyme with **hide**.

inside    outside    beside

## Page 343

**Location Words: Sentences**

**Directions:** Use a location word from the first box and other words from the second box to complete each sentence.

| between | around | inside | outside | beside | across |

| the yard | the house | the table | the school | the box |
| the hill | the picture | the field | the puddle | the park |

**Example:**

Our garden grows outside in the yard.
Answers will vary, but may include:

1. We like to play inside the house.

2. The street goes beside the school.

3. Can you run across the field?

4. Let's ride bikes around the park.

## Page 344

**Location Words: Sentences**

**Directions:** Join each pair of sentences to make a longer sentence. Use one of the **joining** words **and**, **but** or **or**.

**Example:** We play outside when it is sunny.
Today it is raining.

We play outside when it is sunny, but today it is raining.

1. We could walk between the buildings. We could walk around them.

We could walk between the buildings, or we could walk around them.

2. I drew a tree beside the house. I drew flowers beside the house.

I drew a tree and flowers beside the house.

## Page 345

**Location Words: Sentences**

**Directions:** Use a location word to tell where the cat is in each sentence.

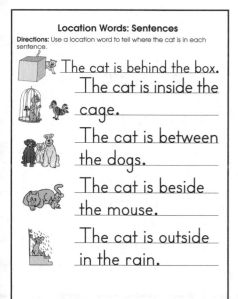

The cat is behind the box.
The cat is inside the cage.
The cat is between the dogs.
The cat is beside the mouse.
The cat is outside in the rain.

## Page 346

**Short u Words**

Short **u** is the sound you hear in the word **bug**.

**Directions:** Say each word and listen for the **short u** sound. Then write each word and underline the letter that makes the **short u** sound.

| dust | must | nut | bug |
| bump | pump | tub | jump |
| cut | hug | rug | cub |

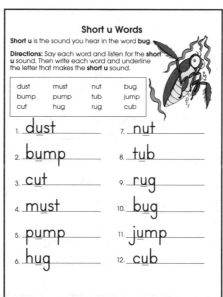

1. d<u>u</u>st
2. b<u>u</u>mp
3. c<u>u</u>t
4. m<u>u</u>st
5. p<u>u</u>mp
6. h<u>u</u>g
7. n<u>u</u>t
8. t<u>u</u>b
9. r<u>u</u>g
10. b<u>u</u>g
11. j<u>u</u>mp
12. c<u>u</u>b

## Page 347

**Short u Words: Sentences**

**Directions:** Circle the words in each sentence which are not correct. Then write the correct **short u** words from the box on the lines.

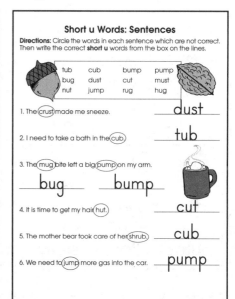

| tub | cub | bump | pump |
| bug | dust | cut | must |
| nut | jump | rug | hug |

1. The crust made me sneeze.          dust

2. I need to take a bath in the cub.          tub

3. The mug bite left a big pump on my arm.

bug          bump

4. It is time to get my hair hut.          cut

5. The mother bear took care of her shrub.          cub

6. We need to jump more gas into the car.          pump

## Page 348

### Long u Words

**Long u** is the vowel sound which says its own name. **Long u** is spelled **u** with a silent **e** at the end as in **cute**. The letters **oo** make a sound very much like **long u**. They make the sound you hear in the word **zoo**. The letters **ew** also make the **oo** sound as in the word **grew**.

**Directions:** Say the words and listen for the **u** and **oo** sounds. Then write each word and underline the letters that make the **long u** and **oo** sounds.

| choose | blew | moon | fuse |
| cube | Ruth | tooth | use |
| flew | loose | goose | noon |

1. ch<u>oo</u>se
2. c<u>u</u>be
3. fl<u>ew</u>
4. bl<u>ew</u>
5. R<u>u</u>th
6. l<u>oo</u>se
7. m<u>oo</u>n
8. t<u>oo</u>th
9. g<u>oo</u>se
10. f<u>u</u>se
11. <u>u</u>se
12. n<u>oo</u>n

## Page 349

### Long u Words: Rhyming Words

**Long u** is the vowel sound you hear in the word **cube**. Another vowel sound which is very much like the **long u** sound is the **oo** sound you hear in the word **boot**.

**Directions:** Use the **long u** and **oo** words in the box to write rhyming words.

| moon | tooth | use | blew |
| flew | loose | Ruth | choose |
| fuse | noon | goose | |

1. Write the words that rhyme with **soon**.
moon    noon

2. Write the words that rhyme with **lose**.
fuse    use    choose

3. Write the words that rhyme with **grew**.
flew    blew

4. Write the words that rhyme with **moose**.
loose    goose

5. Write the words that rhyme with **booth**.
tooth    Ruth

## Page 350

### Long u Words: Sentences

**Directions:** Write the words in the sentences below in the correct order. Begin each sentence with a capital letter and end it with a period or a question mark.

1. the pulled dentist tooth my loose
The dentist pulled my loose tooth.

2. ice cubes I choose in my drink to put
I choose to put ice cubes in my drink.

3. a Ruth fuse blew yesterday
Ruth blew a fuse yesterday.

4. loose the got in garden goose the
The goose got loose in the garden.

5. flew the goose winter for the south
The goose flew south for the winter.

6. is full there a moon tonight
Answer may vary.

## Page 351

### Spelling Concentration Game

Play this game with a friend. Cut out each word card below and on pages 85 and 87. Lay the cards facedown on a flat surface. Take turns turning over two cards at a time. If the cards match, give the pair to your friend. Then spell the word from memory. If you spelled it correctly, you can keep the pair. If not, put the cards back facedown. When all of the word cards have been matched and spelled correctly, the players count their pairs. Whoever has the most pairs, wins.

You can also play this by yourself—or with more than one friend!

| | dust |
|---|---|---|
| light | clean | bump |
| dust | sleep | clean |
| bump | light | sleep |

## Page 353

| note | head | write |
|---|---|---|
| soap | made | nine |
| stop | play | grew |
| clock | stamp | cute |
| tent | math | choose |

## Page 355

| note | head | write |
|---|---|---|
| soap | made | nine |
| stop | play | grew |
| clock | stamp | cute |
| tent | math | choose |

## Page 357

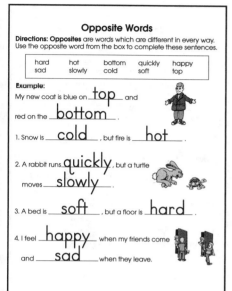

**Opposite Words**

**Directions:** Opposites are words which are different in every way. Use the opposite word from the box to complete these sentences.

| hard | hot | bottom | quickly | happy |
|------|-----|--------|---------|-------|
| sad | slowly | cold | soft | top |

**Example:**

My new coat is blue on **top** and

red on the **bottom**.

1. Snow is **cold**, but fire is **hot**.

2. A rabbit runs **quickly**, but a turtle

moves **slowly**.

3. A bed is **soft**, but a floor is **hard**.

4. I feel **happy** when my friends come

and **sad** when they leave.

## Page 358

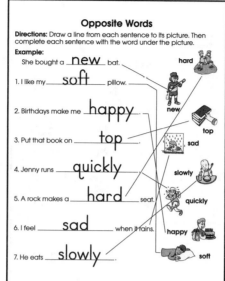

**Opposite Words**

**Directions:** Draw a line from each sentence to its picture. Then complete each sentence with the word under the picture.

**Example:**

She bought a **new** bat.

1. I like my **soft** pillow.

2. Birthdays make me **happy**.

3. Put that book on **top**.

4. Jenny runs **quickly**.

5. A rock makes a **hard** seat.

6. I feel **sad** when it rains.

7. He eats **slowly**.

hard
new
top
sad
slowly
quickly
happy
soft

## Page 359

**Opposite Words: Sentences**

**Directions:** Cross out the word in each box that does not tell about the picture. Write a sentence about the picture using the other two words.

**Example:**

| ~~teeth~~ | garden | digs |

**She digs in her garden.**

Answers will vary, but may include:

| swims | quickly | ~~live~~ |

**The little fish swims quickly.**

| soft | ~~fly~~ | happy |

**The baby is happy to hug his soft bear.**

| popcorn | bottom | sad |

**The boy is sad that he bumped the bottom block.**

## Page 360

**Opposite Words: Sentences**

**Directions:** Look at each picture. Then write a sentence that uses the word under the picture and tells how something is the same as the picture.

**Example:**

cold — **My hands are as cold as ice.**

Answers will vary, but may include:

hard — **This cookie is as hard as a rock.**

slow — **When he walked to school, he was as slow as a turtle.**

soft — **The chair was as soft as a pillow.**

happy — **The girl was as happy as a lark.**

## Page 361

**Opposite Words: Completing a Story**

**Directions:** Write opposite words in the blanks to complete the story.

| hot | hard | top | cold | bottom |
|-----|------|-----|------|--------|
| soft | quickly | happy | slowly | sad |

One day, Grandma came for a visit. She gave my sister Jenny and me a box of chocolate candy. We said, "Thank you!" Then Jenny **quickly** took the **top** off the box. The pieces all looked the same! I couldn't tell which pieces were **soft** inside and which were **hard**. I only liked the **soft** ones. Jenny didn't care. She was **happy** to get any kind of candy! I **slowly** looked at all the pieces. I didn't know which one to pick. Just then Dad called us. Grandma was going home. He wanted us to say good-bye to her. I hurried to the front door where they were standing. Jenny came a minute later.

I told Grandma I hoped I would see her soon. I always feel **sad** when she leaves. Jenny stood behind me and didn't say anything. After Grandma went home, I found out why. Jenny had most of our candy in her mouth! Only a few pieces were left in the **bottom** of the box! Then I was **sad**! That Jenny!

## Page 362

**Review**

**Directions:** Tell a story about the picture by following the directions. Write one or two sentences for each answer.

Answers will vary, but may include:

1. Write about something that is happening **quickly** or **slowly** in the picture.

**The fish swam quickly away from the net.**

2. Use **top** or **bottom** in a sentence about the picture.

**The parrot sat on top of its cage.**

3. Tell about something **hard** and something **soft** in the picture. Use the word **but** in your sentence.

**The rabbit's fur is soft, but the turtle's shell is hard.**

## Page 363

### Learning Words

**Directions:** Write a learning word to complete each sentence. Use each word only once.

| start | watch | listen | teach | finish | write |

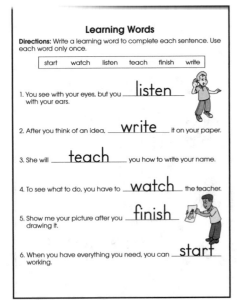

1. You see with your eyes, but you **listen** with your ears.

2. After you think of an idea, **write** it on your paper.

3. She will **teach** you how to write your name.

4. To see what to do, you have to **watch** the teacher.

5. Show me your picture after you **finish** drawing it.

6. When you have everything you need, you can **start** working.

## Page 364

### Learning Words

**Directions:** Circle the words in each sentence which are not spelled correctly. Then write each word correctly on the line.

| start | watch | listen | teach | finish | write |

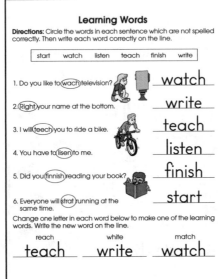

1. Do you like to (wach) television? **watch**

2. (Right) your name at the bottom. **write**

3. I will (teech) you to ride a bike. **teach**

4. You have to (lisen) to me. **listen**

5. Did you (finnish) reading your book? **finish**

6. Everyone will (strat) running at the same time. **start**

Change one letter in each word below to make one of the learning words. Write the new word on the line.

| reach | white | match |
| **teach** | **write** | **watch** |

## Page 365

### Learning Words: Verb Endings

Remember: Verbs end with **s** when the sentence tells about only one thing.

**Example:** One girl **reads**.  Two girls **read**.
But when an action word ends with **ch** or **sh**, add **es**.

**Example:** We **watch** the baby.  She **watches** the baby.
Jane and Sue **finish** their work.  Peter **finishes** his work.

| start | watch | listen | teach | finish | write |

**Directions:** Write the verb from the box which completes each sentence. Add **s** or **es** to the end of the verb if you need to.
**Example:**
Carrie reads the book. She and Chris **read** it together.

1. Todd listens to the teacher. We all **listen** to her.

2. Joy finishes the race first. We **finish** after her.

3. They write letters to our class. Tony **writes** back to them.

4. We watch the puppet show. She **watches** with us.

5. He starts at the top of the page. We **start** in the middle.

## Page 366

### Learning Words: Completing a Story

**Directions:** Write learning words to complete this story.

"How can I **teach** you anything if you don't **listen**?" James asked his little sister Wendy. He was trying to show her how to **write** her name. Wendy smiled up at James. "I'll **listen** now," she said. "Okay. Let's **start** again. **Watch** what I do," he said. "First, you make a big **W**." "Up and down," Wendy said. She tried to **write** a **W** like James, but it looked like a row of upside-down mountains. "That's better," James said. "But you have to know when to stop." He showed her how to **write** the **e**, **n** and **d**. "Now, I'll **teach** you how to **write** your name," he said. He wrote a **y** for her. Wendy made the tail on her **y** go down to the bottom of the page. "I can do it!" she said. "I can **write** my name from **start** to **finish**!" She smiled at her brother again. "Would you **teach** me how to read now, James?" He smiled back at her. "Maybe later, okay?"

## Page 367

### Time Words

The time between breakfast and lunch is **morning**.
The time between lunch and dinner is **afternoon**.
The time between dinner and bedtime is **evening**.

**Directions:** Write a time word from the box to complete each sentence. Use each word only once.

| evening | morning | today | tomorrow | afternoon |

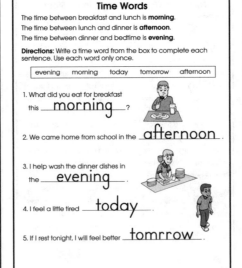

1. What did you eat for breakfast this **morning**?

2. We came home from school in the **afternoon**.

3. I help wash the dinner dishes in the **evening**.

4. I feel a little tired **today**.

5. If I rest tonight, I will feel better **tomrrow**.

## Page 368

### Time Words: Sentences

**Directions:** Make each pair of short sentences into one long sentence. Use the joining words **and**, **or**, **but** or **because**.

**Example:**
This morning, I am sleepy. I stayed up late last night.

**This morning I am sleepy because I stayed up late last night.**

1. Do you want to go in the morning?
Do you want to go in the afternoon?

**Do you want to go in the morning or the afternoon?**

2. Mom asked me to clean my room today. I forgot.

**Mom asked me to clean my room today, but I forgot.**

## Page 369

**Time Words: Sentences**

**Directions:** Write a sentence for these time words. Tell something you do at that time.

**Example:**

day

Every day I walk to school.

morning    Answers will vary, but may include:

I wake up early in the morning.

afternoon

I play outside in the afternoon.

evening

In the evening I watch T.V.

## Page 370

**Review**

**Directions:** Write the story below again and correct all the mistakes. Watch for words that are not spelled correctly, missing periods and question marks, question marks at the end of telling sentences and sentences with the wrong joining words.

One mourning, my granmother said I could have a pet mouse. That evenning, we got my mouse at the pet store, or the next afernoon my mouse had babies! Now, I had nyne mouses! I really liked to wach them? I wanted to pick the babies up, and they were too little. When they get bigger, I have to give too mouses to my sisster.

One morning, my grandmother said I could have a pet mouse. That evening, we got my mouse at the pet store, and the next afternoon my mouse had babies! Now, I had nine mice! I really liked to watch them. I wanted to pick the babies up, but they were too little. When they get bigger, I have to give two mice to my sister.

## Page 372

**Less Than, Greater Than**

**Directions:** The open mouth points to the larger number. The small point goes to the smaller number. Draw the symbol < or > to the correct number.

**Example:**  5 ( > ) 3    This means that 5 is greater than 3, and 3 is less than 5.

12 ( > ) 2          16 ( > ) 6

16 ( > ) 15         1 ( < ) 2

7 ( > ) 1           19 ( > ) 5

9 ( > ) 6           11 ( < ) 13

## Page 373

**Counting**

**Directions:** Write the numbers that are:

| next in order | one less | one greater |
|---|---|---|
| 22, 23, **24**, **25** | **15**, 16 | 6, **7** |
| 674, **675**, **676** | **246**, 247 | 125, **126** |
| 227, **228**, **229** | **549**, 550 | 499, **500** |
| 199, **200**, **201** | **332**, 333 | 750, **751** |
| 329, **330**, **331** | **861**, 862 | 933, **934** |

**Directions:** Write the missing numbers.

## Page 374

**Counting by 2's**

**Directions:** Each basket the players make is worth 2 points. Help your team win by counting by 2's to beat the other team's score.

2
4
6
8
10
12
14
16
18
20
22
24
26
28
30
32

*Winner!*  34

**Final Score**
Home **34**   Visitor **30**

## Page 375

**Counting: 2's, 5's, 10's**

**Directions:** Write the missing numbers.

Count by 2's:

2  4  6  8  10  12  14  16  18  20

Count by 5's:

5  10  15  20  25  30  35  40  45  50

Count by 10's:

10  20  30  40  50  60  70  80  90  100

## Page 376

### Patterns

**Directions:** Write or draw what comes next in the pattern.

Example: 1, 2, 3, 4, __5__

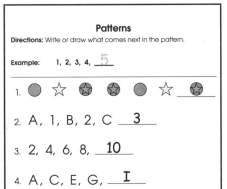

1. ● ☆ ⊛ ⊛ ● ☆ __⊛__

2. A, 1, B, 2, C __3__

3. 2, 4, 6, 8, __10__

4. A, C, E, G, __I__

5. 5, 10, 15, 20, __25__

## Page 377

### Finding Patterns: Numbers

Mia likes to count by twos, threes, fours, fives, tens and hundreds.

**Directions:** Complete the number patterns.

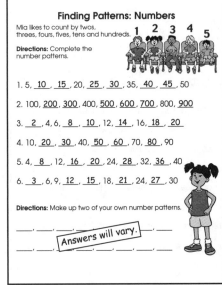

1. 5, __10__, __15__, 20, __25__, __30__, 35, __40__, __45__, 50

2. 100, __200__, __300__, 400, __500__, __600__, __700__, 800, __900__

3. __2__, 4, 6, __8__, __10__, 12, __14__, 16, __18__, __20__

4. 10, __20__, __30__, 40, __50__, __60__, 70, __80__, 90

5. 4, __8__, 12, __16__, __20__, 24, __28__, 32, __36__, 40

6. __3__, 6, 9, __12__, __15__, 18, __21__, 24, __27__, 30

**Directions:** Make up two of your own number patterns.

___, ___, ___, ___ Answers will vary. ___, ___, ___

## Page 378

### Finding Patterns: Shapes

**Directions:** Complete each row by drawing the correct shape.

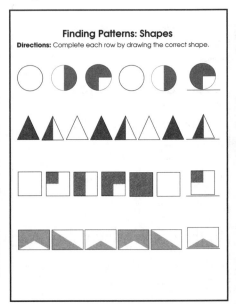

## Page 379

### Ordinal Numbers

Ordinal numbers indicate order in a series, such as **first**, **second** or **third**.

**Directions:** Follow the instructions to color the train cars. The first car is the engine.

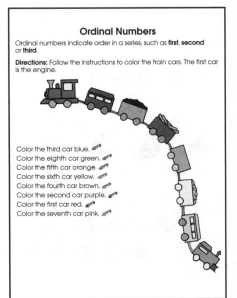

Color the third car blue.
Color the eighth car green.
Color the fifth car orange.
Color the sixth car yellow.
Color the fourth car brown.
Color the second car purple.
Color the first car red.
Color the seventh car pink.

## Page 380

### Ordinal Numbers

**Directions:** Follow the instructions.

Draw glasses on the second one.
Put a hat on the fourth one.
Color blonde hair on the third one.
Draw a tie on the first one.
Draw ears on the fifth one.
Draw black hair on the seventh one.
Put a bow on the head of the sixth one.

## Page 381

### Addition

Addition is "putting together" or adding two or more numbers to find the sum.

**Directions:** Add.

**Example:**

```
 2
+5
 7
```

| 3 | 6 | 7 | 8 | 5 | 3 |
|---|---|---|---|---|---|
| +4 | +2 | +1 | +2 | +4 | +1 |
| 7 | 8 | 8 | 10 | 9 | 4 |

| 8 | 9 | 10 | 6 | 4 | 7 |
|---|---|---|---|---|---|
| +2 | +5 | +3 | +6 | +9 | +7 |
| 10 | 14 | 13 | 12 | 13 | 14 |

| 9 | 8 | 6 | 7 | 7 | 9 |
|---|---|---|---|---|---|
| +3 | +7 | +5 | +9 | +6 | +9 |
| 12 | 15 | 11 | 16 | 13 | 18 |

## Page 382

### Addition: Commutative Property

The commutative property of addition states that even if the order of the numbers is changed in an addition sentence, the sum will stay the same.

**Example:** 2 + 3 = 5
3 + 2 = 5

**Directions:** Look at the addition sentences below. Complete the addition sentences by writing the missing numerals.

5 + 4 = 9          3 + 1 = 4          2 + 6 = 8
4 + <u>5</u> = 9          1 + <u>3</u> = 4          6 + <u>2</u> = 8

6 + 1 = 7          4 + 3 = 7          1 + 9 = 10
1 + <u>6</u> = 7          3 + <u>4</u> = 7          9 + <u>1</u> = 10

**Now try these:**

6 + 3 = 9          10 + 2 = 12          8 + 3 = 11
<u>3</u> + <u>6</u> = 9          <u>2</u> + <u>10</u> = 12          <u>3</u> + <u>8</u> = 11

Look at these sums. Can you think of two number sentences that would show the commutative property of addition?

__ + __ = 7          __ + __ = 11          __ + __ = 9

__ + __ = 7          __ + __ = 11          __ + __ = 9

**Answers will vary.**

## Page 383

### Adding 3 or More Numbers

**Directions:** Add all the numbers to find the sum. Draw pictures to help or break up the problem into two smaller problems.

Example:
1 ○
2 ○○
+3 ○○○
6

+2 > 7
5
+2 > +6
4     13

3
6 > 9
+2
11

8
5 > 9
+4
17

3
1 > 4
+5
9

8
2 > 10
+9
19

2
8 > 10
4
+3 > +7
17

3
6 > 9
5
+2 > +7
16

4
1 > 5
2
+5 > +7
12

6
3 > 13
3
+1 > +4
17

## Page 384

### Subtraction

Subtraction is "taking away" or subtracting one number from another to find the difference.

**Directions:** Subtract.

**Example:**

4
-3
1

5          6          4          3          2          1
-3         -1         -3         -1         -0         -1
2          5          1          2          2          0

9          7          10         14         15         12
-2         -4         -5         -6         -9         -3
7          3          5          8          6          9

18         13         14         11         17         16
-8         -5         -7         -4         -9         -8
10         8          7          7          8          8

## Page 385

### Addition and Subtraction

Addition is "putting together" or adding two or more numbers to find the sum. Subtraction is "taking away" or subtracting one number from another to find the difference.

**Directions:** Add or subtract. Circle the answers that are less than 10.

**Examples:**

3          3
+1         -1
4          2

9          6          12         18         15
+3         -2         - 1        +1         -6
12         4          11         19         9

7          16         10         14         16
+ 6        - 9        - 3        + 5        - 8
13         7          7          19         8

8          12         13         17         9
+7         + 2        - 4        + 2        +9
15         14         9          19         18

## Page 386

### Place Value: Ones, Tens

The place value of a digit or numeral is shown by where it is in the number. For example, in the number **23**, **2** has the place value of **tens**, and **3** is **ones**.

**Directions:** Add the tens and ones and write your answers in the blanks.

Example:

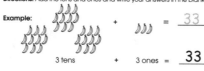

+ )))  = 33

3 tens          +          3 ones  =  **33**

| | tens ones | | tens ones |
|---|---|---|---|
| 7 tens + 5 ones = | 7  5 | 4 tens + 0 ones = | 4  0 |
| 2 tens + 3 ones = | 2  3 | 8 tens + 1 one = | 8  1 |
| 5 tens + 2 ones = | 5  2 | 1 ten + 1 one = | 1  1 |
| 5 tens + 4 ones = | 5  4 | 6 tens + 3 ones = | 6  3 |
| 9 tens + 5 ones = | 9  5 | | |

**Directions:** Draw a line to the correct number.

6 tens + 7 ones — 73
4 tens + 2 ones — 67
8 tens + 0 ones — 51
7 tens + 3 ones — 80
5 tens + 1 one — 42

## Page 387

### Place Value: Ones, Tens

**Directions:** Write the numbers for the tens and ones. Then add.

**Example:**

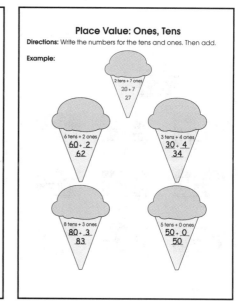

2 tens + 7 ones
20 + 7
27

6 tens + 2 ones
60 + 2
62

3 tens + 4 ones
30 + 4
34

8 tens + 3 ones
80 + 3
83

5 tens + 0 ones
50 + 0
50

## Page 388

### 2-Digit Addition

**Directions:** Study the example. Follow the steps to add.

**Example:**
```
  33
 +41
```

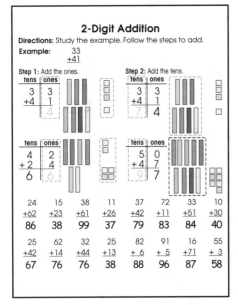

**Step 1:** Add the ones.

| tens | ones |
|------|------|
| 3 | 3 |
| +4 | 1 |
|  | 4 |

**Step 2:** Add the tens.

| tens | ones |
|------|------|
| 3 | 3 |
| +4 | 1 |
| 7 | 4 |

| tens | ones |
|------|------|
| 4 | 2 |
| +2 | 4 |
| 6 | 6 |

| tens | ones |
|------|------|
| 5 | 0 |
| +4 | 7 |
| 9 | 7 |

| | | | | | | | |
|--|--|--|--|--|--|--|--|
| 24 | 15 | 38 | 11 | 37 | 72 | 33 | 10 |
| +62 | +23 | +61 | +26 | +42 | +11 | +51 | +30 |
| 86 | 38 | 99 | 37 | 79 | 83 | 84 | 40 |

| | | | | | | | |
|--|--|--|--|--|--|--|--|
| 25 | 62 | 32 | 25 | 82 | 91 | 16 | 55 |
| +42 | +14 | +44 | +13 | + 6 | + 5 | +71 | + 3 |
| 67 | 76 | 76 | 38 | 88 | 96 | 87 | 58 |

## Page 389

### 2-Digit Addition

**Directions:** Add the total points scored in each game. Remember to add **ones** first and **tens** second.

**Example:**

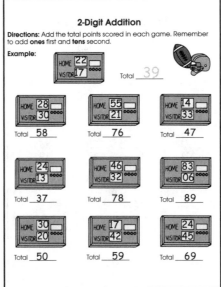

HOME 22 VISITOR 17   Total __39__

| HOME 28 VISITOR 30 | HOME 55 VISITOR 21 | HOME 14 VISITOR 33 |
|---|---|---|
| Total __58__ | Total __76__ | Total __47__ |

| HOME 24 VISITOR 13 | HOME 46 VISITOR 32 | HOME 83 VISITOR 06 |
|---|---|---|
| Total __37__ | Total __78__ | Total __89__ |

| HOME 30 VISITOR 20 | HOME 17 VISITOR 42 | HOME 24 VISITOR 45 |
|---|---|---|
| Total __50__ | Total __59__ | Total __69__ |

## Page 390

### 2-Digit Addition: Regrouping

Addition is "putting together" or adding two or more numbers to find the sum. Regrouping is using **ten ones** to form **one ten**, **ten tens** to form **one 100**, **fifteen ones** to form **one ten** and **five ones** and so on.

**Directions:** Study the examples. Follow the steps to add.

**Example:**
```
  14
 + 8
```

**Step 1:** Add the ones.

| tens | ones |
|------|------|
| 1 | 4 |
| + | 8 |
|  | 12 |

**Step 2:** Regroup the tens.

| tens | ones |
|------|------|
| 1 | 4 |
| + | 8 |
|  |  |

**Step 3:** Add the tens.

| tens | ones |
|------|------|
| 1 | 4 |
| + | 8 |
| 2 | 2 |

| tens | ones |
|------|------|
| 1 | 6 |
| +3 | 7 |
| 5 | 3 |

| tens | ones |
|------|------|
| 3 | 8 |
| +5 | 3 |
| 9 | 1 |

| tens | ones |
|------|------|
| 2 | 4 |
| +4 | 7 |
| 7 | 1 |

| | | | | | | | |
|--|--|--|--|--|--|--|--|
| 28 | 32 | 54 | 19 | 44 | 25 | 29 | 79 |
| +17 | +38 | +25 | +55 | +48 | +64 | +33 | +15 |
| 45 | 70 | 79 | 74 | 92 | 89 | 62 | 94 |

## Page 391

### 2-Digit Addition: Regrouping

**Directions:** Add the total points scored in the game. Remember to add the ones, regroup, and then add the tens.

**Example:**

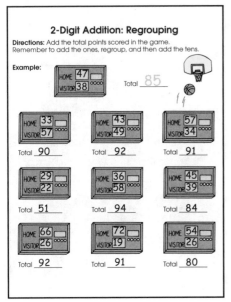

HOME 47 VISITOR 38   Total __85__

| HOME 33 VISITOR 57 | HOME 43 VISITOR 49 | HOME 57 VISITOR 34 |
|---|---|---|
| Total __90__ | Total __92__ | Total __91__ |

| HOME 29 VISITOR 22 | HOME 36 VISITOR 58 | HOME 45 VISITOR 39 |
|---|---|---|
| Total __51__ | Total __94__ | Total __84__ |

| HOME 66 VISITOR 26 | HOME 72 VISITOR 19 | HOME 54 VISITOR 26 |
|---|---|---|
| Total __92__ | Total __91__ | Total __80__ |

## Page 392

### 2-Digit Subtraction

**Directions:** Study the example. Follow the steps to subtract.

**Example:**
```
  28
 -14
```

**Step 1:** Subtract the ones.

| tens | ones |
|------|------|
| 2 | 8 |
| -1 | 4 |
|  | 4 |

**Step 2:** Subtract the tens.

| tens | ones |
|------|------|
| 2 | 8 |
| -1 | 4 |
| 1 | 4 |

| tens | ones |
|------|------|
| 2 | 4 |
| -1 | 2 |
| 1 | 2 |

| tens | ones |
|------|------|
| 3 | 8 |
| -1 | 5 |
| 2 | 3 |

| | | | | | | | |
|--|--|--|--|--|--|--|--|
| 24 | 61 | 77 | 85 | 57 | 87 | 59 | 96 |
| – 12 | –30 | – 44 | – 24 | – 23 | – 33 | – 34 | – 16 |
| 12 | 31 | 33 | 61 | 34 | 54 | 25 | 80 |

| | | | | | | | |
|--|--|--|--|--|--|--|--|
| 29 | 74 | 46 | 69 | 95 | 33 | 78 | 22 |
| – 15 | – 51 | – 32 | – 35 | – 32 | – 33 | – 26 | – 11 |
| 14 | 23 | 14 | 34 | 63 | 0 | 52 | 11 |

## Page 393

### 2-Digit Subtraction: Regrouping

Subtraction is "taking away" or subtracting one number from another to find the difference. Regrouping is using **one ten to form ten ones, one 100 to form ten tens** and so on.

**Directions:** Study the examples. Follow the steps to subtract.

**Example:**
```
  37
 -19
```

**Step 1:** Regroup.

| tens | ones |
|------|------|
| 2 | 17 |
| 3 | 7 |
| -1 | 9 |

**Step 2:** Subtract the ones.

| tens | ones |
|------|------|
| 2 | 17 |
| 3 | 7 |
| -1 | 9 |
|  | 8 |

**Step 3:** Subtract the tens.

| tens | ones |
|------|------|
| 2 | 17 |
| 3 | 7 |
| -1 | 9 |
| 1 | 8 |

| tens | ones |
|------|------|
| 1 | 12 |
| X | 2 |
| - | 9 |
|  | 3 |

| tens | ones |
|------|------|
| 2 | 14 |
| 3 | 4 |
| -1 | 6 |
| 1 | 8 |

| tens | ones |
|------|------|
| 3 | 15 |
| 4 | 5 |
| -2 | 9 |
| 1 | 6 |

| | | | | | | | |
|--|--|--|--|--|--|--|--|
| 28 | 46 | 12 | 30 | 52 | 47 | 21 | 45 |
| – 19 | – 18 | – 8 | – 12 | – 25 | – 35 | – 13 | – 25 |
| 9 | 28 | 4 | 18 | 27 | 12 | 8 | 20 |

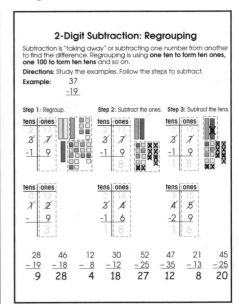

## Page 394

### 2-Digit Subtraction: Regrouping

**Directions:** Study the steps for subtracting. Solve the problems using the steps.

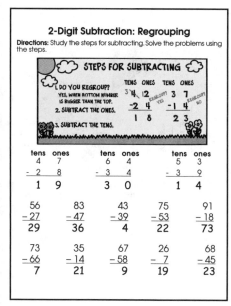

**STEPS FOR SUBTRACTING**

1. DO YOU REGROUP? YES, WHEN BOTTOM NUMBER IS BIGGER THAN THE TOP.
2. SUBTRACT THE ONES.
3. SUBTRACT THE TENS.

| tens ones | tens ones | tens ones |
|---|---|---|
| 4 7 | 6 4 | 5 3 |
| − 2 8 | − 3 4 | − 3 9 |
| 1 9 | 3 0 | 1 4 |

| 56 | 83 | 43 | 75 | 91 |
|---|---|---|---|---|
| − 27 | − 47 | − 39 | − 53 | − 18 |
| 29 | 36 | 4 | 22 | 73 |

| 73 | 35 | 67 | 26 | 68 |
|---|---|---|---|---|
| − 66 | − 14 | − 58 | − 7 | − 45 |
| 7 | 21 | 9 | 19 | 23 |

## Page 395

### Review

**Directions:** Add or subtract. Use regrouping when needed. Always do ones first and tens last.

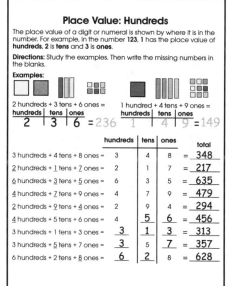

| tens ones | tens ones | tens ones | tens ones |
|---|---|---|---|
| 9 3 | 3 0 | 6 5 | 7 1 |
| − 2 5 | + 2 7 | + 1 7 | − 3 6 |
| 6 8 | 5 7 | 8 2 | 3 5 |

| 7 6 | 8 2 | 5 6 | 2 5 |
|---|---|---|---|
| − 2 8 | + 1 9 | − 2 8 | − 1 6 |
| 4 8 | 1 0 1 | 2 8 | 9 |

| 4 3 | 5 3 | 2 4 | 4 8 |
|---|---|---|---|
| − 1 4 | − 1 5 | + 5 7 | + 2 8 |
| 2 9 | 3 8 | 8 1 | 7 6 |

| 33 | 52 | 46 | 97 |
|---|---|---|---|
| + 47 | + 29 | − 37 | − 68 |
| 80 | 81 | 9 | 29 |

## Page 396

### 2-Digit Addition and Subtraction

Addition is "putting together" or adding two or more numbers to find the sum. Subtraction is "taking away" or subtracting one number from another to find the difference. Regrouping is using **one ten** to form **ten ones**, **one 100** to form **ten tens**, and so on.

**Directions:** Add or subtract using regrouping.

**Example:**

| tens ones |
|---|
| 2 15 |
| 3 5 |
| − 2 7 |
| 8 |

| 56 | 40 | 35 | 42 | 53 | 97 | 44 | 93 |
|---|---|---|---|---|---|---|---|
| − 27 | − 16 | + 27 | − 14 | + 38 | − 48 | + 27 | − 39 |
| 29 | 24 | 62 | 28 | 91 | 49 | 71 | 54 |

| 56 | 44 | 68 | 73 | 33 | 49 | 77 | 27 |
|---|---|---|---|---|---|---|---|
| − 17 | + 28 | − 49 | − 24 | + 18 | + 32 | − 68 | + 19 |
| 39 | 72 | 19 | 49 | 51 | 81 | 9 | 46 |

## Page 397

### 2-Digit Addition and Subtraction

**Directions:** Add or subtract using regrouping.

| 23 | 84 | 69 | 41 |
|---|---|---|---|
| + 48 | − 56 | + 29 | − 17 |
| 71 | 28 | 98 | 24 |

| 52 | 73 | 84 | 57 |
|---|---|---|---|
| − 28 | + 18 | − 27 | − 39 |
| 24 | 91 | 57 | 18 |

| 33 | 64 | 37 | 36 |
|---|---|---|---|
| − 15 | + 17 | + 58 | − 19 |
| 18 | 81 | 95 | 17 |

| 65 | 48 | 33 | 25 |
|---|---|---|---|
| − 28 | − 30 | + 18 | + 35 |
| 37 | 18 | 51 | 60 |

## Page 398

### Place Value: Hundreds

The place value of a digit or numeral is shown by where it is in the number. For example, in the number **123**, 1 has the place value of **hundreds**, 2 is **tens** and 3 is **ones**.

**Directions:** Study the examples. Then write the missing numbers in the blanks.

**Examples:**

2 hundreds + 3 tens + 6 ones =

| hundreds | tens | ones |
|---|---|---|
| 2 | 3 | 6 | = 236 |

1 hundred + 4 tens + 9 ones =

| hundreds | tens | ones |
|---|---|---|
| 1 | 4 | 9 | = 149 |

| | hundreds | tens | ones | total |
|---|---|---|---|---|
| 3 hundreds + 4 tens + 8 ones = | 3 | 4 | 8 | = 348 |
| 2 hundreds + 1 tens + 7 ones = | 2 | 1 | 7 | = 217 |
| 6 hundreds + 3 tens + 5 ones = | 6 | 3 | 5 | = 635 |
| 4 hundreds + 7 tens + 9 ones = | 4 | 7 | 9 | = 479 |
| 2 hundreds + 9 tens + 4 ones = | 2 | 9 | 4 | = 294 |
| 4 hundreds + 5 tens + 6 ones = | 4 | 5 | 6 | = 456 |
| 3 hundreds + 1 tens + 3 ones = | 3 | 1 | 3 | = 313 |
| 3 hundreds + 5 tens + 7 ones = | 3 | 5 | 7 | = 357 |
| 6 hundreds + 2 tens + 8 ones = | 6 | 2 | 8 | = 628 |

## Page 399

### Place Value: Hundreds

**Directions:** Write the numbers for hundreds, tens and ones. Then add.

**Example:**

1 hundred + 4 tens + 6 ones
100 + 40 + 6
146

7 hundreds + 3 tens + 5 ones
700 + 30 + 5
735

3 hundreds + 1 ten + 9 ones
300 + 10 + 9
319

5 hundreds + 8 tens + 0 ones
500 + 80 + 0
580

9 hundreds + 0 tens + 7 ones
900 + 0 + 7
907

## Page 400

### 3-Digit Addition: Regrouping

**Directions:** Study the examples. Follow the steps to add.

**Example:**

**Step 1:** Add the ones. **Step 2:** Add the tens. **Step 3:** Add the hundreds.

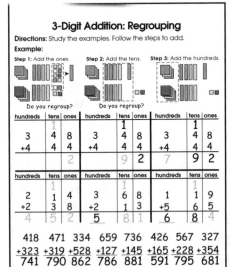

Do you regroup? Do you regroup?

| hundreds | tens | ones |
|---|---|---|
| | 1 | |
| 3 | 4 | 8 |
| +4 | 4 | 4 |
| | | 2 |

| hundreds | tens | ones |
|---|---|---|
| | 1 | |
| 3 | 4 | 8 |
| +4 | 4 | 4 |
| | 9 | 2 |

| hundreds | tens | ones |
|---|---|---|
| | 1 | |
| 3 | 4 | 8 |
| +4 | 4 | 4 |
| 7 | 9 | 2 |

| hundreds | tens | ones |
|---|---|---|
| | 1 | |
| 2 | 1 | 4 |
| +2 | 3 | 8 |
| 4 | 5 | 2 |

| hundreds | tens | ones |
|---|---|---|
| | 1 | |
| 3 | 6 | 8 |
| +2 | 1 | 3 |
| 5 | 8 | 1 |

| hundreds | tens | ones |
|---|---|---|
| | 1 | |
| 1 | 1 | 9 |
| +5 | 6 | 5 |
| 6 | 8 | 4 |

| 418 | 471 | 334 | 659 | 736 | 426 | 567 | 327 |
|---|---|---|---|---|---|---|---|
| +323 | +319 | +528 | +127 | +145 | +165 | +228 | +354 |
| 741 | 790 | 862 | 786 | 881 | 591 | 795 | 681 |

## Page 401

### 3-Digit Addition: Regrouping

**Directions:** Study the example. Follow the steps to add. Regroup when needed.

**Step 1:** Add the ones.
**Step 2:** Add the tens.
**Step 3:** Add the hundreds.

10 = 1 ten + 0 ones

| hundreds | tens | ones |
|---|---|---|
| 1 | 1 | |
| 3 | 4 | 8 |
| +4 | 5 | 4 |
| 8 | 0 | 2 |

| 348 | 172 | 575 | 623 | 369 | 733 |
|---|---|---|---|---|---|
| +214 | +418 | +329 | +268 | +533 | +229 |
| 562 | 590 | 904 | 891 | 902 | 962 |

| 411 | 423 | 639 | 624 | 272 | 393 |
|---|---|---|---|---|---|
| +299 | +169 | +177 | +368 | +469 | +418 |
| 710 | 592 | 816 | 992 | 741 | 811 |

## Page 402

### 3-Digit Subtraction: Regrouping

**Directions:** Study the example. Follow the steps to subtract.

**Step 1:** Regroup ones.
**Step 2:** Subtract ones.
**Step 3:** Subtract tens.
**Step 4:** Subtract hundreds.

**Example:**

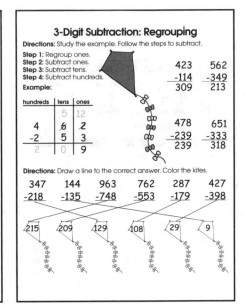

| hundreds | tens | ones |
|---|---|---|
| | 5 | 12 |
| 4 | 6 | 2 |
| -2 | 5 | 3 |
| 2 | 0 | 9 |

| 423 | 562 |
|---|---|
| -114 | -349 |
| 309 | 213 |

| 478 | 651 |
|---|---|
| -239 | -333 |
| 239 | 318 |

**Directions:** Draw a line to the correct answer. Color the kites.

| 347 | 144 | 963 | 762 | 287 | 427 |
|---|---|---|---|---|---|
| -218 | -135 | -748 | -553 | -179 | -398 |

215  209  129  108  29  9

## Page 403

### 3-Digit Subtraction: Regrouping

**Directions:** Subtract. Circle the **7's** that appear in the **tens place**.

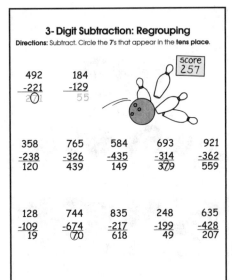

score 257

| 492 | 184 |
|---|---|
| -221 | -129 |
| 201 | 55 |

| 358 | 765 | 584 | 693 | 921 |
|---|---|---|---|---|
| -238 | -326 | -435 | -314 | -362 |
| 120 | 439 | 149 | 379 | 559 |

| 128 | 744 | 835 | 248 | 635 |
|---|---|---|---|---|
| -109 | -674 | -217 | -199 | -428 |
| 19 | 70 | 618 | 49 | 207 |

## Page 404

### Place Value: Thousands

**Directions:** Study the example. Write the missing numbers.

**Example:**

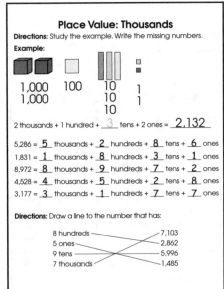

1,000  100  10  1
1,000        10  1
             10

2 thousands + 1 hundred + __3__ tens + 2 ones = __2,132__

5,286 = __5__ thousands + __2__ hundreds + __8__ tens + __6__ ones
1,831 = __1__ thousands + __8__ hundreds + __3__ tens + __1__ ones
8,972 = __8__ thousands + __9__ hundreds + __7__ tens + __2__ ones
4,528 = __4__ thousands + __5__ hundreds + __2__ tens + __8__ ones
3,177 = __3__ thousands + __1__ hundreds + __7__ tens + __7__ ones

**Directions:** Draw a line to the number that has:

8 hundreds — 7,103
5 ones — 2,862
9 tens — 5,996
7 thousands — 1,485

## Page 405

### Place Value: Thousands

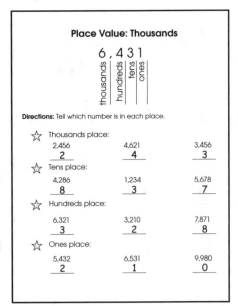

6,431
thousands hundreds tens ones

**Directions:** Tell which number is in each place.

☆ Thousands place:

| 2,456 | 4,621 | 3,456 |
|---|---|---|
| 2 | 4 | 3 |

☆ Tens place:

| 4,286 | 1,234 | 5,678 |
|---|---|---|
| 8 | 3 | 7 |

☆ Hundreds place:

| 6,321 | 3,210 | 7,871 |
|---|---|---|
| 3 | 2 | 8 |

☆ Ones place:

| 5,432 | 6,531 | 9,980 |
|---|---|---|
| 2 | 1 | 0 |

## Page 406

### Place Value: Thousands

**Directions:** Use the code to color the fan.

**If the answer has:**
9 thousands, color it pink.
6 thousands, color it green.
5 hundreds, color it orange.
8 tens, color it red.
3 ones, color it blue.

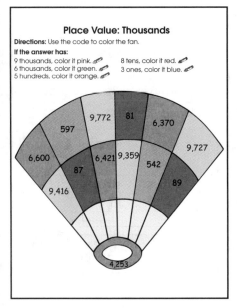

## Page 407

### Graphs

A graph is a drawing that shows information about numbers.

**Directions:** Count the apples in each row. Color the boxes to show how many apples have bites taken out of them.

**Example:**

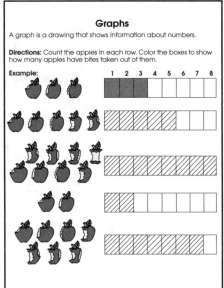

## Page 408

### Graphs

**Directions:** Count the bananas in each row. Color the boxes to show how many have been eaten by the monkeys.

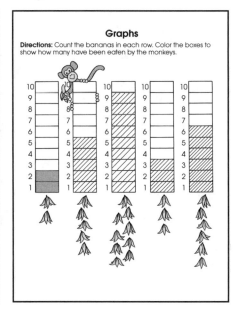

## Page 409

### Graphs

**Directions:** Count the fish. Color the bowls to make a graph that shows the number of fish.

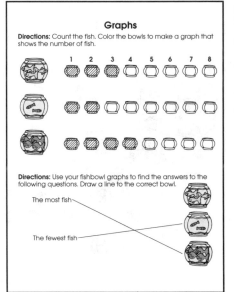

**Directions:** Use your fishbowl graphs to find the answers to the following questions. Draw a line to the correct bowl.

The most fish

The fewest fish

## Page 410

### Multiplication

Multiplication is a short way to find the sum of adding the same number a certain amount of times. For example, **4 x 7 = 28** instead of **7 + 7 + 7 + 7 = 28**.

**Directions:** Study the example. Solve the problems.

**Example:**

$3 + 3 + 3 = 9$
3 threes = 9
$3 \times 3 = 9$

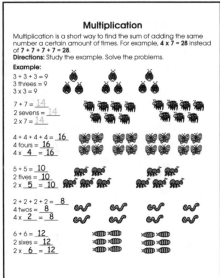

$7 + 7 = \underline{14}$
2 sevens = $\underline{14}$
$2 \times 7 = \underline{14}$

$4 + 4 + 4 + 4 = \underline{16}$
4 fours = $\underline{16}$
$4 \times \underline{4} = \underline{16}$

$5 + 5 = \underline{10}$
2 fives = $\underline{10}$
$2 \times \underline{5} = \underline{10}$

$2 + 2 + 2 + 2 = \underline{8}$
4 twos = $\underline{8}$
$4 \times \underline{2} = \underline{8}$

$6 + 6 = \underline{12}$
2 sixes = $\underline{12}$
$2 \times \underline{6} = \underline{12}$

## Page 411

### Multiplication

Multiplication is repeated addition.

**Directions:** Draw a picture for each problem. Then write the missing numbers.

**Example:**
Draw 2 groups of three apples.

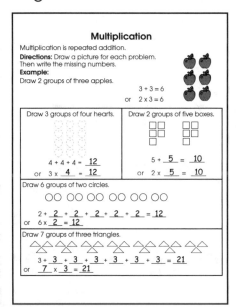

$3 + 3 = 6$
or $2 \times 3 = 6$

| Draw 3 groups of four hearts. | Draw 2 groups of five boxes. |
|---|---|
| $4 + 4 + 4 = \underline{12}$ or $3 \times \underline{4} = \underline{12}$ | $5 + \underline{5} = \underline{10}$ or $2 \times \underline{5} = \underline{10}$ |

Draw 6 groups of two circles.

$2 + \underline{2} + \underline{2} + \underline{2} + \underline{2} + \underline{2} = \underline{12}$
or $6 \times \underline{2} = \underline{12}$

Draw 7 groups of three triangles.

$3 + \underline{3} + \underline{3} + \underline{3} + \underline{3} + \underline{3} + \underline{3} = \underline{21}$
or $\underline{7} \times \underline{3} = \underline{21}$

## Page 412

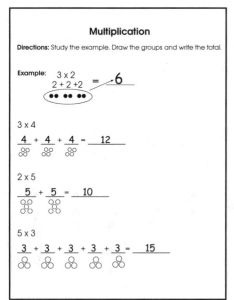

**Multiplication**

**Directions:** Study the example. Draw the groups and write the total.

**Example:**  3 x 2
2 + 2 +2  = 6

3 x 4

$\frac{4}{} + \frac{4}{} + \frac{4}{} = $ 12

2 x 5

$\frac{5}{} + \frac{5}{} = $ 10

5 x 3

$\frac{3}{} + \frac{3}{} + \frac{3}{} + \frac{3}{} + \frac{3}{} = $ 15

## Page 413

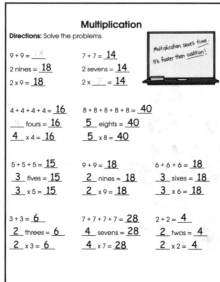

**Multiplication**

**Directions:** Solve the problems.

Multiplication saves time. It's faster than addition!

9 + 9 = 18
2 nines = 18
2 x 9 = 18

7 + 7 = 14
2 sevens = 14
2 x 7 = 14

4 + 4 + 4 + 4 = 16
4 fours = 16
4 x 4 = 16

8 + 8 + 8 + 8 + 8 = 40
5 eights = 40
5 x 8 = 40

5 + 5 + 5 = 15
3 fives = 15
3 x 5 = 15

9 + 9 = 18
2 nines = 18
2 x 9 = 18

6 + 6 + 6 = 18
3 sixes = 18
3 x 6 = 18

3 + 3 = 6
2 threes = 6
2 x 3 = 6

7 + 7 + 7 + 7 = 28
4 sevens = 28
4 x 7 = 28

2 + 2 = 4
2 twos = 4
2 x 2 = 4

## Page 414

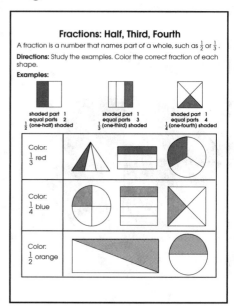

**Fractions: Half, Third, Fourth**

A fraction is a number that names part of a whole, such as $\frac{1}{2}$ or $\frac{1}{3}$.

**Directions:** Study the examples. Color the correct fraction of each shape.

**Examples:**

shaded part 1
equal parts 2
$\frac{1}{2}$ (one-half) shaded

shaded part 1
equal parts 3
$\frac{1}{3}$ (one-third) shaded

shaded part 1
equal parts 4
$\frac{1}{4}$ (one-fourth) shaded

Color: $\frac{1}{3}$ red

Color: $\frac{1}{4}$ blue

Color: $\frac{1}{2}$ orange

## Page 415

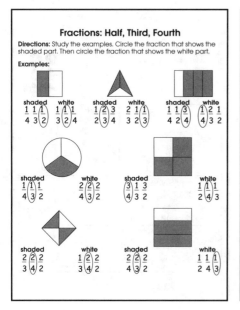

**Fractions: Half, Third, Fourth**

**Directions:** Study the examples. Circle the fraction that shows the shaded part. Then circle the fraction that shows the white part.

## Page 416

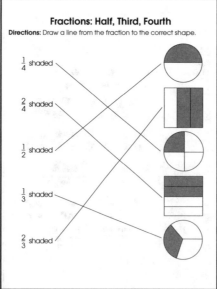

**Fractions: Half, Third, Fourth**

**Directions:** Draw a line from the fraction to the correct shape.

$\frac{1}{4}$ shaded

$\frac{2}{4}$ shaded

$\frac{1}{2}$ shaded

$\frac{1}{3}$ shaded

$\frac{2}{3}$ shaded

## Page 417

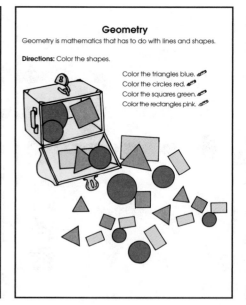

**Geometry**

Geometry is mathematics that has to do with lines and shapes.

**Directions:** Color the shapes.

Color the triangles blue.
Color the circles red.
Color the squares green.
Color the rectangles pink.

## Page 418

### Geometry

**Directions:** Draw a line from the word to the shape.

Use a red line for circles. Use a yellow line for rectangles.
Use a blue line for squares. Use a green line for triangles.

Circle    Square    Triangle    Rectangle

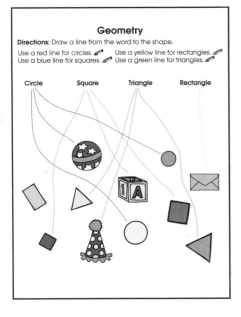

## Page 419

### Geometry

**Directions:** Cut out the tangram below. Mix up the pieces. Try to put it back together into a square.

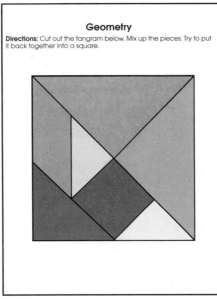

## Page 421

### Measurement: Inches

**Directions:** Cut out the ruler. Measure each object to the nearest inch.

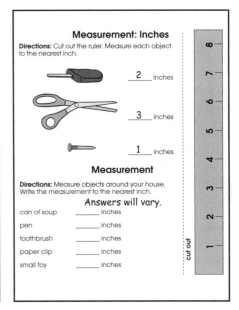

_2_ inches

_3_ inches

_1_ inches

### Measurement

**Directions:** Measure objects around your house. Write the measurement to the nearest inch.

**Answers will vary.**

can of soup _____ inches
pen _____ inches
toothbrush _____ inches
paper clip _____ inches
small toy _____ inches

## Page 423

### Measurement: Inches

An inch is a unit of length in the standard measurement system.

**Directions:** Use a ruler to measure each object to the nearest inch.

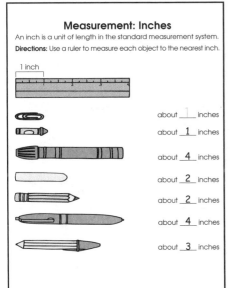

1 inch

about _1_ inches
about _1_ inches
about _4_ inches
about _2_ inches
about _2_ inches
about _4_ inches
about _3_ inches

## Page 424

### Measurement: Inches

**Directions:** Use the ruler to measure the fish to the nearest inch.

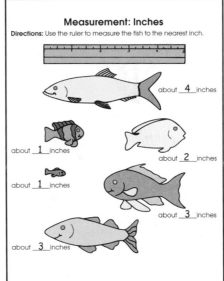

about _4_ inches

about _1_ inches

about _2_ inches

about _1_ inches

about _3_ inches

about _3_ inches

## Page 425

### Measurement: Centimeters

A centimeter is a unit of length in the metric system. There are 2.54 centimeters in an inch.

**Directions:** Use a centimeter ruler to measure the crayons to the nearest centimeter.

**Example:** The first crayon is about 7 centimeters long.

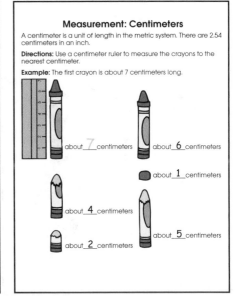

about _7_ centimeters    about _6_ centimeters

about _1_ centimeters

about _4_ centimeters

about _2_ centimeters

about _5_ centimeters

## Page 426

### Measurement: Centimeters

**Directions:** The giraffe is about 8 centimeters high. How many centimeters (cm) high are the trees? Write your answers in the blanks.

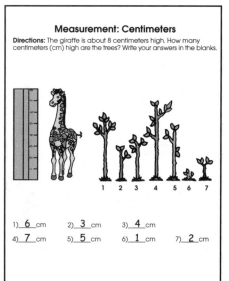

1) __6__ cm    2) __3__ cm    3) __4__ cm
4) __7__ cm    5) __5__ cm    6) __1__ cm    7) __2__ cm

## Page 427

### Time: Hour, Half-Hour

An hour is sixty minutes. The short hand of a clock tells the hour. It is written **0:00**, such as **5:00**. A half-hour is thirty minutes. When the long hand of the clock is pointing to the six, the time is on the half-hour. It is written **:30**, such as **5:30**.

**Directions:** Study the examples. Tell what time it is on each clock.

**Examples:**

9:00
The minute hand is on the 12.
The hour hand is on the 9.
It is 9 o'clock.

4:30
The minute hand is on the 6.
The hour hand is *between* the 4 and 5.
It is 4:30.

2:00    3:30    1:00    5:30    8:00

10:30    12:00    9:30    2:30    3:00

## Page 428

### Time: Hour, Half-Hour

**Directions:** Draw lines between the clocks that show the same time.

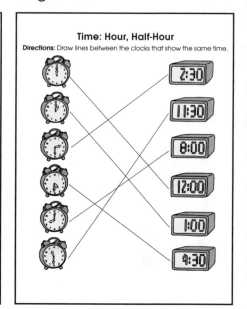

## Page 429

### Time: Counting by 5's

The minute hand of a clock takes 5 minutes to move from one number to the next. Start at the 12 and count by fives to tell how many minutes it is past the hour.

**Directions:** Study the examples. Tell what time is on each clock.

**Examples:**

9:10    8:25

7:05    3:50    2:15

6:20    5:55    5:30

11:45    12:35    2:40

## Page 430

### Time: Quarter-Hours

Time can also be shown as fractions. 30 minutes = $\frac{1}{2}$ hour.

**Directions:** Shade the fraction of each clock and tell how many minutes you have shaded.

**Example:**

$\frac{1}{2}$ hour
30 minutes

$\frac{1}{4}$ hour
__15__ minutes

$\frac{2}{4}$ hour
__30__ minutes

$\frac{3}{4}$ hour
__45__ minutes

$\frac{1}{2}$ hour
__30__ minutes

## Page 431

### Review
#### Counting

**Directions:** Write the number that is:

| next | one less | one greater |
|---|---|---|
| 68, 69, __70__ | __56__, 57 | 12, __13__ |
| 786, 787, __788__ | __649__, 650 | 843, __844__ |

#### Place Value: Tens & Ones

**Directions:** Draw a line to the correct number.

4 tens + 7 ones — 20
2 tens + 0 ones — 51
7 tens + 3 ones — 47
5 tens + 1 one — 73

#### Addition and Subtraction

**Directions:** Add or subtract.

| 15 | 14 | 7 | 8 | 10 | 14 |
|---|---|---|---|---|---|
| + 5 | - 4 | + 3 | - 6 | + 7 | - 5 |
| 20 | 10 | 10 | 2 | 17 | 9 |

## Page 432

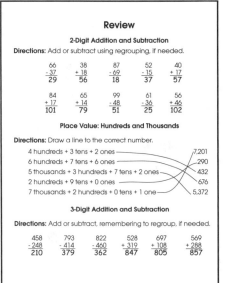

**Review**

**2-Digit Addition and Subtraction**

**Directions:** Add or subtract using regrouping, if needed.

| | | | | |
|---|---|---|---|---|
| 66 − 37 = 29 | 38 + 18 = 56 | 87 − 69 = 18 | 52 − 15 = 37 | 40 + 17 = 57 |
| 84 + 17 = 101 | 65 + 14 = 79 | 99 − 48 = 51 | 61 − 36 = 25 | 56 + 46 = 102 |

**Place Value: Hundreds and Thousands**

**Directions:** Draw a line to the correct number.

4 hundreds + 3 tens + 2 ones — 432
6 hundreds + 7 tens + 6 ones — 676
5 thousands + 3 hundreds + 7 tens + 2 ones — 5,372
2 hundreds + 9 tens + 0 ones — 290
7 thousands + 2 hundreds + 0 tens + 1 one — 7,201

**3-Digit Addition and Subtraction**

**Directions:** Add or subtract, remembering to regroup, if needed.

| | | | | |
|---|---|---|---|---|
| 458 − 248 = 210 | 793 − 414 = 379 | 822 − 460 = 362 | 528 + 319 = 847 | 697 + 108 = 805 | 569 + 288 = 857 |

## Page 433

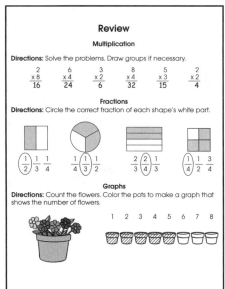

**Review**

**Multiplication**

**Directions:** Solve the problems. Draw groups if necessary.

| | | | | | |
|---|---|---|---|---|---|
| 2 × 8 = 16 | 6 × 4 = 24 | 3 × 2 = 6 | 8 × 4 = 32 | 5 × 3 = 15 | 2 × 2 = 4 |

**Fractions**

**Directions:** Circle the correct fraction of each shape's white part.

1/2 (circled)   1/3   1/4
1/4   1/3 (circled)   1/2
2/3   2/4 (circled)   1/3
1/4 (circled)   1/2   3/4

**Graphs**

**Directions:** Count the flowers. Color the pots to make a graph that shows the number of flowers.

1 2 3 4 5 6 7 8

## Page 434

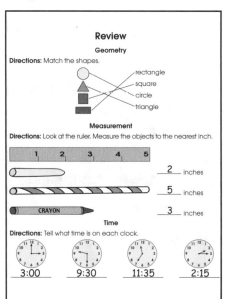

**Review**

**Geometry**

**Directions:** Match the shapes.

rectangle
square
circle
triangle

**Measurement**

**Directions:** Look at the ruler. Measure the objects to the nearest inch.

1 2 3 4 5

**2** inches
**5** inches
**3** inches

**Time**

**Directions:** Tell what time is on each clock.

3:00   9:30   11:35   2:15

## Page 435

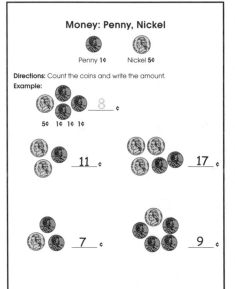

**Money: Penny, Nickel**

Penny 1¢   Nickel 5¢

**Directions:** Count the coins and write the amount.

**Example:**

_8_ ¢
5¢ 1¢ 1¢ 1¢

_11_ ¢

_17_ ¢

_7_ ¢

_9_ ¢

## Page 436

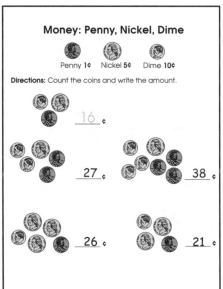

**Money: Penny, Nickel, Dime**

Penny 1¢   Nickel 5¢   Dime 10¢

**Directions:** Count the coins and write the amount.

_16_ ¢

_27_ ¢

_38_ ¢

_26_ ¢

_21_ ¢

## Page 437

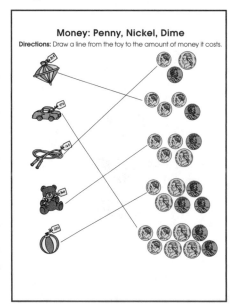

**Money: Penny, Nickel, Dime**

**Directions:** Draw a line from the toy to the amount of money it costs.

# ANSWER KEY

## Page 438

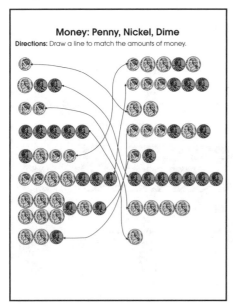

## Page 439

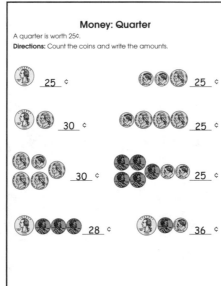

## Page 440

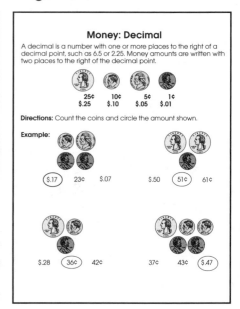

## Page 441

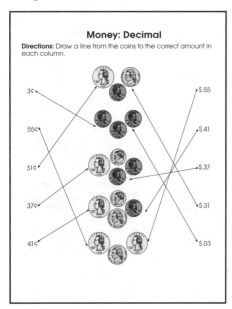

## Page 442

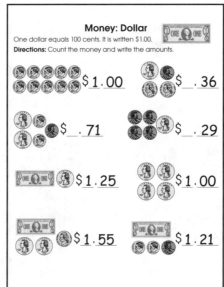

## Page 443

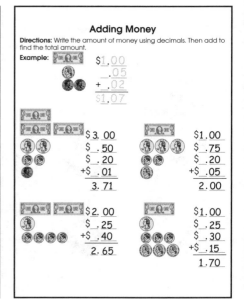

## Page 444

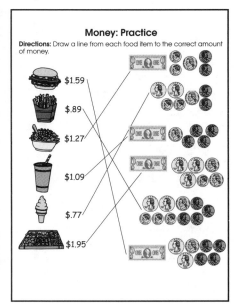

**Money: Practice**

**Directions:** Draw a line from each food item to the correct amount of money.

$1.59
$.89
$1.27
$1.09
$.77
$1.95

## Page 445

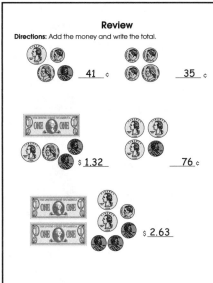

**Review**

**Directions:** Add the money and write the total.

_41_ ¢          _35_ ¢

$ _1.32_          _76_ ¢

$ _2.63_

## Page 446

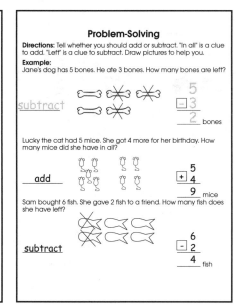

**Problem-Solving**

**Directions:** Tell whether you should add or subtract. "In all" is a clue to add. "Left" is a clue to subtract. Draw pictures to help you.

**Example:**
Jane's dog has 5 bones. He ate 3 bones. How many bones are left?

subtract

$$\begin{array}{r} 5 \\ -\ 3 \\ \hline 2 \end{array}$$ bones

Lucky the cat had 5 mice. She got 4 more for her birthday. How many mice did she have in all?

add

$$\begin{array}{r} 5 \\ +\ 4 \\ \hline 9 \end{array}$$ mice

Sam bought 6 fish. She gave 2 fish to a friend. How many fish does she have left?

subtract

$$\begin{array}{r} 6 \\ -\ 2 \\ \hline 4 \end{array}$$ fish

## Page 447

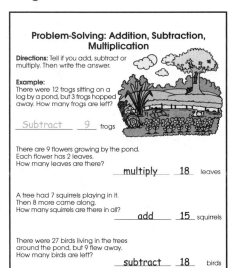

**Problem-Solving: Addition, Subtraction, Multiplication**

**Directions:** Tell if you add, subtract or multiply. Then write the answer.

**Example:**
There were 12 frogs sitting on a log by a pond, but 3 frogs hopped away. How many frogs are left?

_Subtract_  _9_ frogs

There are 9 flowers growing by the pond. Each flower has 2 leaves. How many leaves are there?

_multiply_  _18_ leaves

A tree had 7 squirrels playing in it. Then 8 more came along. How many squirrels are there in all?

_add_  _15_ squirrels

There were 27 birds living in the trees around the pond, but 9 flew away. How many birds are left?

_subtract_  _18_ birds

## Page 448

**Problem-Solving: Fractions**

A fraction is a number that names part of a whole, such as $\frac{1}{2}$ or $\frac{1}{3}$.
**Directions:** Read each problem. Use the pictures to help you solve the problem. Write the fraction that answers the question.

Simon and Jessie shared a pizza. Together they ate $\frac{3}{4}$ of the pizza. How much of the pizza is left?   $\frac{1}{4}$

Sylvia baked a cherry pie. She gave $\frac{1}{3}$ to her grandmother and $\frac{1}{3}$ to a friend. How much of the pie did she keep?   $\frac{1}{3}$

Timmy erased $\frac{1}{2}$ of the blackboard before the bell rang for recess. How much of the blackboard does he have left to erase?   $\frac{1}{2}$

**Directions:** Read the problem. Draw your own picture to help you solve the problem. Write the fraction that answers the question.

Sarah mowed $\frac{1}{4}$ of the yard before lunch. How much does she have left to mow?   $\frac{3}{4}$

## Page 449

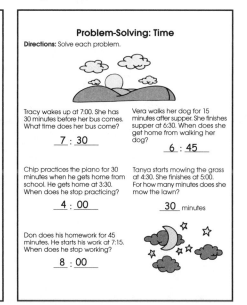

**Problem-Solving: Time**

**Directions:** Solve each problem.

Tracy wakes up at 7:00. She has 30 minutes before her bus comes. What time does her bus come?

_7_ : _30_

Vera walks her dog for 15 minutes after supper. She finishes supper at 6:30. When does she get home from walking her dog?

_6_ : _45_

Chip practices the piano for 30 minutes when he gets home from school. He gets home at 3:30. When does he stop practicing?

_4_ : _00_

Tanya starts mowing the grass at 4:30. She finishes at 5:00. For how many minutes does she mow the lawn?

_30_ minutes

Don does his homework for 45 minutes. He starts his work at 7:15. When does he stop working?

_8_ : _00_

## Page 450

### Problem-Solving: Money

**Directions:** Read each problem. Use the pictures to help you solve the problems.

Ben bought a ball. He had 11¢ left.
How much money did he have at the start?
_40_ ¢

Tara has 75¢. She buys a car.
How much money does she have left?
_30_ ¢

Leah wants to buy a doll and a ball. She has 80¢.
How much more money does she need?
_8_ ¢

Jacob has 95¢. He buys the car and the ball.
How much more money does he need to
buy a doll for his sister?
_38_ ¢

Kim paid three quarters, one dime
and three pennies for a hat.
How much did it cost?
_88_ ¢

# ALPHABETICAL (ABC) ORDER

Have your child alphabetize his/her word cards from the "Spelling Concentration" game.

Have your child list all the rainforest animals (or forest or ocean animals) that he/she can. Ask him/her to alphabetize the list on another sheet of paper. Give him/her extra help with words that begin with the same letter if needed.

Write the ABC's in a column down the left-hand side of a sheet of paper. As you read a story with your child, have him/her find and write words that begin with each letter.

Select a category. Then help your child find a word for each letter of the alphabet that fits that category. Example: Animals—anteater, bear, cow, etc.

Help your child create tongue twisters using words in ABC order. Examples: A big cat danced elegantly. Frank gave Harry icky jellybeans.

# CLASSIFYING

Have your child choose a topic and write a word list related to it. Example: Summer—hot, sun, bare feet, shorts, etc. He/she can create sentences using these words.

Help your child classify and list animals in groups: mammals, reptiles, fish, birds, amphibians, etc.

# CREATIVE WRITING

Challenge your child to use his/her spelling words to create a "word find" for you to do.

Have your child make a list of rhyming words.

Have your child practice the spelling words by using all of them to create a story.

Have your child choose a topic, then write as many words as possible that fit the category. Example: volleyball: net, ball, uniform, serve, spike, bump, set, time out, sand, court, etc.

Expose your child to words with multiple meanings and have him/her look up the words in a dictionary. Have your child practice using the words in both written and spoken words.

Encourage your child to form similes with spelling words. A simile is a comparison using "like" or "as." Examples: He is as light as a feather. She is quiet like a mouse.

Help your child create a Family Book. Have your child add photos, draw pictures and write captions for an original family scrapbook.

Teach your child to write limericks. A limerick is a five-line humorous rhymed verse. Example: There once was a cat that was fat/ Who ate on a little red mat./ She said with a smile,/ "I've been here awhile,/ So you just go on now and scat!"

Create a story jar for your child. Write several tantalizing story starters on slips of paper. Some examples might be "If I found $100 . . ." or "What was that creaking sound I heard from the attic?" When your child needs a good idea for a story, he/she can draw a slip from the jar.

## DICTIONARY SKILLS

Create a personal dictionary or a "Word Wall" poster for your child to keep track of each new word he/she learns.

Have a family "word of the week." Challenge family members to look up the word, to learn its spelling and to use it as much as possible during the week.

Make an alphabet book. Have your child cut big letters from magazines and glue each letter on a separate page. He/she can arrange the pages in ABC order. Then have your child draw pictures of objects that start with each letter.

Choose a new word each day for your child to look up in the dictionary. Discuss the word's meaning. Have your child write a sentence using the new word. He/she can keep a list of the words in a word journal.

Help your child find new words on the Internet, in newspapers, on signs, etc. Have your child look them up in the dictionary. Make a collage using the words.

## FOLLOWING DIRECTIONS

Have your child read and follow directions for constructing a model, playing a game, preparing a recipe, and so on. Ask your child to write his/her own directions for making a simple recipe or playing a simple game.

# GEOMETRY

Help your child cut out various geometric shapes and make a shape mobile to hang up.

Use construction paper to create prisms and three-dimensional objects, such as a party hat, a cube, etc.

# GRAMMAR

Have your child practice creating word families by adding "s" to the original word to make it mean more than one.

Write sentences for your child to proofread. Include both punctuation and spelling errors. Example: The bair went over the mountain?

Use your computer to write sentences for your child to correct. For example: The boys name is jim. Your child can gain valuable practice with both English skills and the computer by moving the arrow and delete keys to correct the sentence.

# GRAPHS

Graph the birthdays of the people in your family. Ask your child questions based on the graph, such as "In which month are there the most birthdays?" "The fewest number?" "In which months are there no birthdays?"

Graph the people in your family, using criteria such as "boys," "girls," "pets," etc.

# INFERENCES

Make riddle cards using clues for different fairy tale or cartoon characters. Play a guessing game with the cards. Let your child read the clues and name the character. Example: What little bear went hungry because a young girl ate his porridge? If you make these ahead of time, they can help pass the time on a long trip.

Put the pieces of a 12 to 20 piece puzzle in a bag. Let your child look at the pieces and make inferences about what the picture will be. Then put the puzzle together.

## MAKING DEDUCTIONS

Put an object in a box and write clues for it. Have your child read the clues and guess what the object may be.

## MEASUREMENT

Ask your child what other tools we use for measuring things (calendars and clocks to measure time, thermometer to measure temperature, etc.). Brainstorm a list of different measuring tools.

Show your child how to measure the circumference of cylindrical objects. For example, have your child predict the distance around a tree trunk. Pull a length of string around a tree trunk until the two ends meet. Cut the string. Then measure the length of the string in inches and centimeters. Compare the actual measurement with your child's prediction.

Present a math word problem for your child to solve. Have him/her explain and write in sequence how to solve the problem.

## MULTIPLE-MEANING WORDS

Talk with your child about multiple-meaning words when opportunities present themselves in conversation. For example: "Did you hear the phone **ring**?" and "What a beautiful diamond **ring**!" Ask your child to brainstorm other examples of multiple-meaning words.

## PARTS OF SPEECH

Play a fun "parts of speech" word game with your child. Write nouns, verbs and adjectives on index cards and have your child illustrate them. Then let your child choose a noun card, a verb card and an adjective card and put them together to form fun sentences.

Have your child select a section of the newspaper and circle as many nouns and underline as many verbs as possible. You might ask him/her to circle plural nouns in a different color.

## PATTERNS

Help your child find shape patterns as you drive or go for a walk together. Look for patterns in clothing, in billboards or on store signs.

Watch for word patterns as you read together. In the book *Too Much Noise* by Ann McGovern, your child can easily identify phrases that are repeated, and often, based on the story, predict the next phrase in the pattern.

# POINT OF VIEW

Read a chapter in a chapter book with your child. Then ask your child to draw a picture of what happened in that chapter. You could also ask your child to draw a picture of what he/she thinks might happen next.

Read fairy tales like "The Three Little Pigs," "Cinderella," "The Three Billy Goats Gruff," "Hansel and Gretel," etc. Then ask your child to retell the story from the point of view of the villain. Have him/her build a case explaining why the character did what he/she did.

# PREDICTING OUTCOMES

While reading a story, stop periodically and have your child predict what he/she thinks will happen next.

Before reading a book with your child, ask him/her questions about the story and scan the illustrations. Ask questions beginning with who, what, why, when and how. For example: "What do you think this book is about?" "What do you think the title means?" "Who is this on the cover of the book?" "What is he/she doing?" "Do you think this is a true story or a make-believe story?"

Write an incomplete sentence using descriptive words but leave off the ending. Ask your child to finish the sentence. Example: The slinky, slimy lizard crept slowly into Marco's new, shiny bookbag and ____.

# RECALLING DETAILS

Have your child choose a character from a story and write or tell about the character. Ask him/her to draw a picture of the character.

Read a fairy tale with your child. Ask him/her to tell or write the story from a different point of view. For example: Make the troll the good character in "Three Billy Goats Gruff" and the goats the bad characters.

Have your child make a story chart for a book, displaying the important events that happened at the beginning, middle and end of the story.

Your child can create a shoebox diorama displaying a scene from a favorite story, book, play, poem, and so on. A diorama is a three-dimensional scene that includes characters and objects from a story, displayed in an open box, similar to a stage. Encourage your child to be creative!

## RELATING TO THE KNOWN

Choose a topic of interest to your child, such as insects, planets, sports, etc. Then discuss what he/she knows and what he/she wants to learn about the topic. Formulate questions that will help your child learn new information based upon past knowledge. Example: How does a bee protect itself?

## RETELL

Read a book together. Then ask your child to retell the story emphasizing what happened in the beginning, middle and end.

## RHYMES

Make up silly sentences with your child to practice rhyming skills. For example, "I saw a paper star when I cleaned out the ___." You may also want to say a series of words and have your child tell you which one doesn't rhyme: coat, float, dish, goat.

## SAME AND DIFFERENT

Choose two animals, sports, toys, TV programs, etc. and ask your child to tell you how they are the same or how they are different.

Have your child compare three rooms in your home. Ask him/her to tell you how they are the same and how they are different.

## SENTENCES

Create word or sentence "dot-to-dots." Instead of numbers, write letters or words. Have your child connect the dots in the correct sequence to write a word or to correctly order a sentence.

Play a game which helps your child learn to use words in context. Write several words on index cards. Take turns drawing a card and using the word on the card in a sentence.

Print sentences or copy a story on a sheet of paper. Leave blanks for key words. Have your child read the story and supply the missing words.

Write descriptive sentences on long cardboard strips. Have your child read the sentences. Then cut the sentences into word sections and have your child put the sentences back in order.

## SEQUENCING

Invite your child to recreate a story as a comic strip. List six or more important events or scenes from a story in sequence. Then have your child write each event on a separate sheet of paper and draw an accompanying picture. Glue the pages in order on large sheets of colorful construction paper.

Write or tell a story together. Begin the story. After a few sentences, have your child continue the story. Take turns until you get to the end.

Use the comics to help your child practice sequence. Select comics that show a simple sequence, and read the comic strip with your child. Cut the comic strip apart, and challenge your child to rearrange it in the correct order. You could also draw simple pictures in a series, and have your child draw a picture to show what would happen next. Pictures from the family photo album are also fun to sequence. Your child can use the visual clues of growth to help arrange them in sequential order.

## SPELLING

Create a deck of cards with letters and letter teams. Have your child try to make words from the cards drawn.

Write each of your child's spelling words on an index card. Cut apart the cards at the syllables. Mix up the cards and have your child try to put the original words back together.

Play "Spell-o" with your child. Write each word in a box on a 5 x 5 grid. As you name a spelling word, have your child spell it back to you. He/she can then cover the square. When the card has five in a row covered, your child has "Spell-o!"

Fill a squirt bottle with water and let your child spell words by squirting water on dry pavement.

Challenge your child to think of as many words as possible with letter teams such as oy. Try other letter teams such as au, aw, ee and ow. Allow your child to check a dictionary if he/she needs to.

## SYNONYMS, ANTONYMS, HOMOPHONES

Encourage your child to create more varied and interesting sentences by substituting synonyms for words he/she uses repeatedly. As your child reads his/her writing to you, point out places where a synonym might be used, such as the use of the words "tiny" or "small" instead of "little."

Teach your child how to use a thesaurus to find synonyms (words that have almost the same meaning) of each spelling word. A thesaurus organized like a dictionary is the easiest to use.

Make a synonym memory game with your child. Write ten words on index cards. Then write synonyms for the words on additional index cards. Mix up the cards and place them facedown to play. Let your child turn over two cards at a time. If he/she matches two words which are synonyms,
he/she gets to keep the cards. If the two words do not match, he/she must return the cards to their position. Then the next player takes his/her turn. Play continues until all of the cards are gone. This game may also be played with words and their antonyms.

Act out a word (hello) from your list of antonyms and ask your child to act out the antonym (goodbye).

Create a list of antonyms or homophones with your child. Then ask your child to write a poem or limerick using the words.

Using the list of homophones, ask your child to write and illustrate sentences using a pair of homophones. Examples: I have a pair of pears. The bear had bare feet.

## TIME

Help your child create a paper plate clock. Use a paper fastener to attach the minute and hour hands. Suggest different hour and half-hour times for your child to show on the clock face.

## TRACKING

Draw a map of your home or neighborhood. Have your child draw paths from your home to other places in the area. Go for a walk or a drive, following one of the paths your child drew.

Have your child write, in order, how to escape from your home in case of an emergency. Then follow the path with your family.

# VISUALIZING

Ask your child to form a picture of a memory in his/her mind. Then ask him/her to write or draw a description of what he/she sees.

Cut out pictures of scenery from old magazines. Share the pictures with your child. Ask him/her to tell you what images come to mind as he/she views them.